LOVE ME, **TOUCH ME,** *HEAL ME*

Complete Book

THE PATH TO

*   PHYSICAL
*   EMOTIONAL
*   SEXUAL
*   SPIRITUAL

REAWAKENING

Erica Goodstone, Ph.D.

Copyright © 2009, Revised 2023   *Love Me, Touch Me, Heal Me*   DrEricaGoodstone.com

Love Me, Touch Me, Heal Me **is dedicated to**

- **Hilda Aronson, for helping me to get started**
- **Bryce Britton-Kranz, my colleague, mentor and friend, who provided support and lasting friendship that has sustained me over the years**
- **Glenn Dietzel's Awakened team, for pushing me to completion**
- **Darrell Wingerak for his ongoing computer technical support**

Publisher Data & Legal Information

Copyright © 2009 by Erica Goodstone, Ph.D. All rights reserved.
ISBN: 978-0-9824304-8-4
Published by Create Healing and Love Now Publishers
Contact the Publisher at RelationshipHealingToolboxcom

All rights reserved. No part of this eBook may be reproduced, stored in a retrieval system or transmitted in any form or by any means electronic, mechanical, photocopying, recording, or otherwise without express written permission of the author.

Every attempt has been made by the author to provide acknowledgement of the sources used for the material in this book. If there has been an omission of any source, please contact the author at
DrErica@DrEricaWellness.com

Disclaimer: No responsibility is assumed by the authors/publishers for any injury and/or damage and/or loss sustained in persons or property as a result of using this product; and/or for any liability, negligence or otherwise use or operation of any products, methods, instructions or ideas contained in the material herein.

The views and opinions expressed in this book and related materials are derived from the author's experience and research as a professor of health and physical education, yoga and meditation teacher, licensed mental health counselor, licensed professional counselor, licensed marriage and family therapist, board certified sex therapist, licensed massage and bodywork therapist, certified pain management practitioner, certified Integrative Medicine practitioner, certified Polarity Therapist, certified Rubenfeld Synergist, and involvement with numerous professional associations. She is not a licensed M.D. and does not diagnose or claim to cure any physical disease. She is also not a psychiatrist and does not claim to cure mental illness.

Any reader currently under the care or supervision of a psychiatrist, physician or other medical or behavioral health practitioner is urged to seek their professional advice before using or practicing any of the material or techniques contained herein.

Copyright © 2009, Revised 2023   *Love Me, Touch Me, Heal Me*   DrEricaGoodstone.com

ABOUT THE AUTHOR

Erica Goodstone, Ph.D., has devoted her life's work to the discovery of love, healing and the creation of intimate, satisfying, fulfilling and joyful relationships. During over two decades, through her lectures, seminars and private counseling sessions, she has worked with thousands of men and women to create love and healing in their lives.

Having studied extensively from many different sources, Dr. Goodstone is a licensed mental health counselor, professional counselor, marriage and family therapist, massage and bodywork therapist. She is a diplomate and fellow for the American Association of Integrative Medicine and a diplomate for the American Academy of Pain Management. Dr. Goodstone is also a diplomate for the American Board of Sexology, a fellow for the American Academy of Clinical Sexologists, and a certified Sex Therapist for the American Association of Sexuality Educators and Therapists.

As a former professor of health and physical education at F.I.T./State University of New York, Dr. Goodstone spent 25 years studying and teaching about the body: physical fitness, health and wellness, stress management, sports psychology, team building and human sexuality. But she did not stop there.

Dr. Goodstone also spent many years studying a wide variety of healing body therapy modalities in including massage, shiatsu, polarity therapy, craniosacral therapy, Reiki, reflexology, Chinese medical theory, Japanese healing theories. Her studies led to the combination of touch with counseling through the gentle yet profound Rubenfeld Synergy Method. In fact, she was on the original steering committee and the board of directors for the first two terms of the U.S. Association for Body Psychotherapy. This was the first organization to bring together all the different originators and practitioners of somatic body psychotherapy methods and modalities.

But Dr. Goodstone's knowledge and background does not stop there. She has also fervently and passionately craved her own inner spiritual development and outer social awareness. Her seeking led her to spend many years studying yoga, first with the Sivananda Center in New York City and at the Sivananda Ashram in Paradise Island, Bahamas, where she met Swami Vishnu Devananda and listened to Ravi Shankar play the sitar. Later she spent years working with Guru Mayi, Swami Muktananda's disciple, receiving Darshan and personl counseling as needed.

Her studies included attending many consciousness raising seminars in the 1980's, including the EST seminars led by Werner Erhard, the Living Love Workshops led by Ken Keyes, Jr., author of *The Handbook to Higher Consciousness,* and DMA seminars about the creative process and structural thinking led by Robert Fritz. She avidly studied the Rosicrucian manuals for many years, along with the Kaballah teachings of *The Builders of the Adytum* and *The Course in Miracles*. Her current focus has been upon the works of Joel Goldsmith, *The Infinite Way,* and Swami Muktananda, Siddha Yogi Guru..

Dr. Erica Goodstone has been a celebrated speaker at national and local professional and public events. Since her doctoral dissertation, which studied the effects of early mother-infant bonding upon later adult intimacy, she has continued to write extensively about creating love through the healing power of touch, intimacy, and the mind/body/spirit connection.

Dr. Goodstone's interviews and articles have appeared in *Who's Who of Medicine and Healthcare, CBS 4 TV, Blog Talk Radio Logical Soul Talk, Mademoiselle, Cosmopolitan , Marie Claire, Penthouse Forum, Journal of Sex and Marital therapy, Newsletters of the U.S. Association for Body Psychotherapy.* Dr. Goodstone has a very wide presence on the web. Her bio and blogs appear on numerous sites, e.g., Wordpress.com and Gather.com, as well as numerous ezines, most notably ezinearticles.com

Dr. Goodstone's chapter, "Sexual Reawakening" appears in the wonderfully organized book of Rubenfeld Synergy practitioners, *Healing Journeys: The Power of Rubenfeld Synergy, V. Mechner, Ed.* She has also written a section about touch therapies in the internationally acclaimed book, *The Continuum Complete International Encyclopedia of Sexuality*, R. J Noonan and R. Francoeur, Eds.

Copyright © 2009, Revised 2023   *Love Me, Touch Me, Heal Me*   DrEricaGoodstone.com

In 2012, Dr. Erica published her first novel, **_Love in the Blizzard of Life_**, a sexy romantic novel about two star crossed lovers proving that where there is love there IS a way.

Dr. Goodstone can be reached at

DrErica@DrEricaWellness.com

****

Copyright © 2009, Revised 2023   *Love Me, Touch Me, Heal Me*   DrEricaGoodstone.com

INTRODUCTION To The Complete Book

Love Me, Touch Me, Heal Me: The Path to Physical, Emotional, Sexual and Spiritual Reawakening shows us what it takes to love, touch, and heal our own self. As we heal, we develop a renewed passion for life, a deep sense of being connected to something beyond our immediate life circumstances, and an increased desire for intimate loving. **Love Me, Touch Me, Heal Me** is meant to be a coming out party, coming out of hiding, bringing our total self into the light for examination, acceptance, and readiness to share our authentic self intimately with others.

Clients, colleagues and friends have often asked me to recommend a good book about love and relationships or about emotional intimacy and sexual communication. Others have requested information about ways to heal their body through natural methods, e.g., diet, exercise, body therapy, or even spirituality. And some have wondered what the best psychological approach might be to overcome fears, anxiety, anger, depression or relationship conflicts.

Answers to the above questions will be easily obtained as you read through this series of four books. You will discover that you can find the answers to most of your problems, dilemmas, life issues and concerns through self-evaluation. As you complete the exercises, you will literally begin to heal your cellular memories, create new brain patterns and remove lifelong blocks to intimate joyful relating. You can turn to professionals for expert opinions, guidance, support and mentoring, but with this book you will begin to more fully trust your own inner knowing about what is truly best for your growth and healing.

****

FORMAT OF THIS BOOK

The *Love Me touch Me Heal Me* **Complete Book** is divided into four parts consisting of three chapters in each part as follows:

Part I   Love Me … Please

         Chapter 1   The Gift of Love
         Chapter 2   Be Who You Are
                        The Greatest Gift of All
         Chapter 3   The Delicate Dance of Love

Part II   Touch Me … Please

         Chapter 1   Your Body Believes You
         Chapter 2   It's a Sensational World
         Chapter 3   Touching Matters
                        The Profound Effects of Body Therapy

Part III   Heal Me … Please

         Chapter 1   Heal Me…Please
         Chapter 2   Let All Your Senses Speak…As You Heal
         Chapter 3   Touching Stories
                        Healing Through Body Psychotherapy

Part IV   Sexual and Spiritual Reawakening

         Chapter 1   Ordinary People
                        Ordinary Yet Extraordinary Sex
         Chapter 2   Ten Simple Steps to Sexual Reawakening
         Chapter 3   Sexual And Spiritual Reawakening
                        At Last

Copyright © 2009, Revised 2023   *Love Me, Touch Me, Heal Me*   DrEricaGoodstone.com

- Every chapter contains vital information, theories, concepts and suggestions gleaned from years of study, research, personal and professional experiences.

- Every chapter includes pertinent real-life stories, individual and partner written, verbal and contemplative exercises.

- Every chapter builds upon the previous one in the healing process.

- Every chapter is also complete unto itself.

- You may choose to read one entire book from start to finish and then begin a second book.

- You may choose to start with a specific chapter in any of the books.

- Resources, references, and keywords will appear at the end of each book.

Love Me, Touch Me, Heal Me: The Path to Physical, Emotional, Sexual and Spiritual Reawakening belongs in the personal library of anyone who truly wants to heal from the past and create loving, touching and authentically intimate relationships. This is a guidebook, a reference book, and a comforting friend along the path to reawakening. This book teaches us how to let go of preconceived ideas as we learn the true art of loving.

HOW TO USE THIS BOOK

This book is about your life, my life, and all of our lives. Read this book, follow the exercises, and watch miracles happen. *Love Me, Touch Me, Heal Me* is a life transforming healing process. For best results, you will need a few basic materials.

1. **<u>Writing Materials</u>**

   a. **A journal, preferably a beautiful, special journal, but any 4" by 6" or 8" by 10" lined or unlined, notebook will do.**

   Choosing a journal or notebook that is special to you creates an experience of sensory stimulation every time you write in it! If you choose to write all the exercises in this book on pieces of paper, that's okay. But, if the outer appearance is appealing and soothing to your eyes, if the texture satisfies your sense of touch, if there's a fragrance of fresh cut paper or soft smooth leather that comforts you, the power of the words you write will be enhanced. Your brain will connect the sensual beauty of your journal with your written words and with your life. Your mind and body will begin to believe that you are serious about creating healing, love, spiritual connection, sexual aliveness, and joy in your life.

b. **Pen, pencil, colored pencils or crayons.**

Brain research indicates that the mind absorbs information best when all the senses are involved. So get yourself a box of colored pencils, colored pens or crayons. You'll probably discover that you want some pastels, and maybe even paint and brushes before you're through. Colors and textures add additional dimensionality to your writing, increasing the possibility for your brain to record and store your hopes and dreams, uplifting words, goals, new beliefs, and appropriate affirmations. This allows your mind, at a later point in time, to easily refute your fears, frustrations and anxieties as they arise in your consciousness. Crayons and colored pencils may also stimulate your brain to create images, faces, doodles, and other self-expressions that reveal some important subconscious personal thought Processes.

2. ***A quiet place, even a corner of a room, set aside to practice the exercises.***

Energy accumulates in a space that you set aside and use specifically for one purpose. Creating a special place for your own inner work is a strong suggestion to your subconscious, (the part of your brain that allows your dreams to germinate into fruition), that you are serious about transforming your life.

3. **Recording Materials**

Choose your own recording device.

To do the exercises in this book, you can read and stop, read and stop, or you can record your own voice first. Then you will be able to go straight through the exercise without stopping. The goal is for you to comfort yourself and love yourself. Hearing your own voice is a powerful affirmation that you can create what you want and you are all you will ever truly need.

As you begin your journey along the path to love, take a moment to assess where you are right now in your life. The questions you are about to answer may seem simple but are actually quite profound. Observe your thoughts. Notice any automatic body responses you may have. You are more than your thoughts. You are more than your body. Allow your automatic responses to help you to discover who you truly are.

For all the exercises in this introduction and in the rest of this book, you have choices. You can read the exercise and then write in your journal. You can record the entire exercise with your own voice, close the book, close your eyes, and visualize freely. Or you can listen to the pre-recorded audio tapes that accompany each chapter.

****

Who Are You?

Sit in a comfortable position.

Inhale slowly, very slowly, and deeply.

Exhale slower than your usual rate.

Take three slow, deep, easy, and quiet breaths.

Close your eyes and allow your body to relax.

Take three more slow, deep, easy, and quiet breaths.

Open your eyes only to read each question.

Immediately close your eyes and allow the answer to come to you.

Accept the answers that come. Do not edit or change the response

Listen to your mind's first answer, the most correct response at this moment.

Who am I?

What are other people here for in my life?

Why am I alive now?

What do I believe about love?

Who do I enjoy touching and for what purpose?

What yearns to heal inside of me?

What does sexual reawakening mean to me?

What is the role of God, a higher power, or spirituality in my life?

TABLE OF CONTENTS

LOVE ME, TOUCH ME, HEAL ME

Introduction To The Complete Book............7

    Format of The Book
    How To Use This Book
    Who Are You?

Table of Contents……………………………...…..…........16

Part I   *LOVE ME … PLEASE*

LOVE ME … PLEASE **Introduction**……………...32

    Love Is A Gift ……………………………..…………...33
    Love Me Please Poem……………………...….………36

Chapter 1   *THE GIFT OF LOVE*……………...…..40

    Love Is All There Is …………………….……………..42
        Love And Intimacy Are Healing
        Betty's Husband Leaves
        Intimacy Is Not For The Faint Of Heart
        Separation-Individuation
        Good Enough Mothering And Fathering
        Emotions Signal Unmet Needs
        What Are Your Nurturing Needs?
        How Have You Loved?
        How Do You Love Others When You Feel Unloved?
        How Have You Loved Yourself?

I Love/I Hate……………………………………..……....57
- Beliefs
- I Believe
- Conflicting Beliefs
- Changing Beliefs
- How Do I Express My Emotions?
- What is My Loving Potential?
- Letter to My Birth Mother or Earliest Caretaker
- The Mother of My Dreams
- Letter to My Birth Father or Earliest Father Figure
- The Father of My Dreams

What Are Your Rules For Loving?..69
- This is MY Life?
- What are My Rules for Loving?
- The Eraser Game
- My New Rules for Creative Loving

Chapter 2   BE WHO YOU ARE
THE GREATEST GIFT OF ALL………..76

Who Are You?...82
- Who Am I?
- Who Are You?
- Who Is (Your Name)?
- Who Have You Been Told You Are?

How Have Others' Opinions Affected You?.......................86
- How have You Taken a Stand for Yourself?
- Playing Roles
- What Roles Have You Played?
- How Did You Become Who You Are?
- Your Family At Home
- Your Family At The Dinner Table

Your Creative Expression……………………………………….92
    Drawing, Painting and Sculpting
    Moving Your Body, Dancing and Being Athletic
    Cooking, Sewing and Cleaning
    Inventing, Building, Repairing, Doing Mathematical
        Or Electrical Work
    Speaking, Singing, Playing an Instrument, Acting,
        Being a Comic, Being a Clown
    Your Creative Expression Collage
    Sculpting Yourself -Removing That Which Is Not You

Who Are You?……………………………………………….100

Chapter 3 THE DELICATE DANCE OF LOVE……………………………………..103

My Romantic Fantasy……………………………………….108
    Why Do I Want A Love Relationship?
    What Do I Believe About Love Relationships?
    What Do I Expect To Receive From A Love
        Relationship?
    What Do I Expect To Give To A Love Relationship?

Love Is The Essence Of Life………………………………....117
    How Will I Love Today?
    Have You Given Up On Love?
    The Way Out

Don't Pass The Test Of Abuse………………………………125
    Red Flags Of Abuse
    What Is Sexual Abuse?
    Don't Rescue Anyone
    Getting Free
    Forgiveness

Being Love………………………………………….............133
    Love Changes Everything
    The Basic Decision To Love
    What Is Intimacy?
    Creating Intimacy……………………………….…….139
    Lover's Bill Of Rights
    It's The Little Things That Count

Footnotes ……………………………..............................143

PART II   TOUCH ME ... PLEASE

TOUCH ME ... PLEASE Introduction..............148

    Your Body Believes You..149
    Touch Me Please **Poem**..152

Chapter 1   YOUR BODY BELIEVES YOU.........154

    Listen To Your Body...155
        Let Your Precious Body Speak To You
        Talk To Your Body
        Love Your Body
        Touch and Soothe Your Precious Body
    Food Is The Fuel of Life..166
        Your Favorite Food
        Eating Your Favorite Food
        Inside Your Favorite Food
        Drawing Your Favorite Food
        Food As Your Best Friend
    Exercise Moves Your Life..172
        How Do You Exercise Your Body?
        Observing Your Body
        Inside Your Body
        What Do You Want To Change About Your Body?
        Your Body Image Analysis Chart
        Describe Your Body
        Your Body Outline
    Caring for Your Body...180
        Breath Is Life
        Observing Your Breathing
        Minding Your Body
        Your Emotions Are Your Best Friends
        Your Life Force
        Where Is Your Life Force?
    Loving Yourself..194
        Love And Touch Your Body

Chapter 2   IT'S A SENSATIONAL WORLD..199

Living Is Feeling………………………………………...…202
    It's A Sensational World
    Sensation Is The Language Of The Body
What Is True Intimacy?..209
    What Do You Know About Others?
    What Does Your Intuitive Sense Reveal To You?
Blocking Your Senses To Reveal More………………….…..213
    Block Your Sight
    Block Your Hearing
    Block Your Sense Of Smell
    Block Your Sense Of Taste
    Block Your Sense Of Touch
    Block All Your Senses
Go On A Sensual Holiday – Open All Your Senses…………231

Chapter 3   TOUCHING MATTERS
THE PROFOUND EFFECTS OF BODY THERAPY……………………………………..……..235

Touch Is Powerful………………………………………….…..236
    Touch in Psychotherapy
    The Profound Effects of Touch
    Touch Research Institute Studies
Body Therapy: Which One Is Right For You?........................243
    Swedish Massage/Traditional Massage Therapy
    Contemporary Western Massage And Bodywork
    Structural/Functional/Movement/integration
    Asian Bodywork
    Energetic Bodywork
    Somatic And Expressive Arts Therapies

Somatic Body Psychotherapy……………………………………254
    Touch Is Essential For Living
    The Healing Power Of Touch
    How Have You Been Touched?
    How Do You Touch?
Touch Your Body……………………………………………..259
    Massage Your Body
    Shake And Rock Your Body
    Hold Your Body
Touch Your Partner's Body…………………………………..261
    Massage Your Partner's Body
    Shake and Rock Your Partner's Body
    Hold Your Partner's Body
Footnotes……………………………………………………....264

PART III *HEAL ME ... PLEASE*

HEAL ME ... PLEASE Introduction..................265

Healing Happens In Every Moment………………….…269
Heal Me Please Poem…………………………………...272

Chapter 1   *HEAL ME ... PLEASE*.....................274

Oh My Aching Back……………………………………..274
    The People You Have Loved
    The People Who Have Loved You
    How Have You Loved Yourself?
    Your Suffering
    Forgiving Yourself And Others
    Where Is Your Passion?
The Healing Power of Love…………………………..283
    Your House Pets
    Love Your Body As Your Most Precious Pet
    How Have You Been Treating Your Body?
    A Family Affair
    How Have You Been Treating Your Body?
When Your Body Is Healthy……………………………289
    The Hospital Bed
    Life Is Precious
    Lessons From Your Illness
    How Have Your Health Practitioners Treated You?
    Your Healing History
    Your Healing Needs
    Your Health Habits Inventory
Change and Healing……………………………………297
    Your Health Investment Portfolio
    Return On Your Health Investments
    Your Commitment To Healing
What Does God Mean To You?......................................300
    Following Your Own Spiritual Path
    What Does God Have To Do With Your Healing?
    Your Connection To God
    The Joy Of Suffering

Chapter 2   LET ALL YOUR SENSES SPEAK AS YOU HEAL..........308

Touch Me Today Poem..........308

Let Your Senses Speak To You..........310
    What Are Your Five Senses Revealing?
    Reawakening Through Sensual Awareness

What Do You See?..........313
    Open Your Eyes and See
    Judge What Your Eyes See
    Set Your Sights

Do You Hear What I Hear?..........319
    Open Your Ears and Listen
    How Do You Listen To Yourself?
    How Do You Listen To Others?
    What Do You Hear When You Listen?
    What Are Your Listening And Speaking Goals?

Open Your Sense Of Smell..........324
    Breathing
    Smelling

Open Your Sense Of Taste..........327
    Taste Your World

Open Your Sense Of Touch..........328
    Touch Your World

Chapter 3   TOUCHING STORIES
HEALING THROUGH TOUCH
AND SOMATIC BODY PSYCHOTHERAPY..........333

The Story Of My Life Poem..........333

Touching Stories..........335
    George's Handshake
    Lana's Unconsummated Marriage
    The Revitalization of Steve's Life
    The Truth About John
    Carol's Vagina Speaks

    Louis's Panic Attacks
    Henry's Tears
What Is Body Psychotherapy?..350
    How Does The Body Psychotherapy Process Work?
    Body Psychotherapy Allows Us To Breathe In Life
    Body Psychotherapy Energizes Our Brain
    Body Psychotherapy Reveals And Uncovers Our Truth
    Body Psychotherapy Helps Us To Heal
    Body Psychotherapy Reopens Our Heart To Love
    Body Psychotherapy Reawakens Our Sensual, Sexual and Spiritual Aliveness
    Body Psychotherapy Reconnects Us To Our Soul
    Reminds Us To Play
A Body Psychotherapy Session……………………………….359
    Your Body's Messages
    Body Psychotherapy Clears The Path For Love, Relationships and Intimacy

PART IV   *SEXUAL AND SPIRITUAL REAWAKENING*

SEXUAL AND SPIRITUAL REAWAKENING

Introduction..369

Becoming One Poem……………………...…………....372

Chapter 1 *ORDINARY PEOPLE, ORDINARY YET EXTRAORDINARY SEX*
    Ordinary People Poem…………………………………374

Sometimes In An Ordinary Place…………………….…..376
    On The Street
    The Average Man And The Average Woman
Your Sexuality……………………………………………..379
    Sex Doesn't Live Here Anymore
    Take A Lesson From Mrs. Kalish
    What Do We Know About Sex?
    Sexual Response Is A Barometer Of How We Feel
    Opposites Attract
    Your Opposite Attractions
Sexual Relating……………………………………..……391
    What Do Men Say They Want?
    Ask Men
    What Do Women Say They Want?
    Ask Women
Marriage And Divorce On The Internet…………….…...398
    Your Online Chat
    Hot Sex On The Web
    Exploring Internet Sexuality

Good Sex..402
    Good Sex For You
    It's The Little Things That Count
    The Little Things That Count For You
Ordinary Can Be Extraordinary......................................407

Chapter 2   *TEN SIMPLE STEPS TO SEXUAL AND SPIRITUAL REAWAKENING*..........................410
    Come With Me My Love Poem...........................411

Your Unique Sexual Response Pattern.........................413
    Your Body Is Stronger Than Your Willpower
    Your Sexuality Is Not Separate From Your Life
Ten Simple Steps to Sexual And Spiritual Reawakening..417
    Factors That Have Affected Your Sexuality
Step One: Where Are You Right Now?......................418
    Your Current Lifestyle.
    Your Gender Identity And Gender Roles
    Your Health: Physical, Emotional, Sexual and Spiritual
    Your Age, Physical Appearance, and Body Image
    Your Partner Availability
Step Two: Where Did You Come From Originally?.................423
    Your Conception
    Your Mother's Pregnancy Carrying You
    Your Mother's Labor And Birthing Of You
    After Your Birth
Step Three: What Happened Along the Way?..........................426
    Your Sexual Education
    Your Earliest Sexual Relationships
    Your Adult Sexual Relationships
    The Significance Of Your Sexual History
Step Four: Your Sexual Identity And Partner Preferences..429
    Where Do You Fit On The Kinsey Heterosexual/Homosexual Continuum?

Your Sexual Identity and Partner Preferences
Step Five: Why Do You Want Sex?...433
Why Do You Want To Have Sex?
Importance of Sexuality In Your Life
Your Current Sexuality
Your Sexual Function And Dysfunction
So You Think You Have A Sexual Problem
Your Ideal Sexual Life
Step Six: What Is Your Sexual Style?..438
Your Sexual Desire Level
Your Sexual Arousal Style
Your Sexual Orgasmic Style
Your Sexual Resolution Style
Your Preferred Sources of Sexual Stimulation
Your Preferred Sexual Locations
Your Sexual Activity Preferences
Your Preferred Sexual Positions
Your Sexual Performance Style
Your Sexual Pleasuring Style
Your Sexual Communication Style
Your Sexual Commitment Style
Step Seven: What's Blocking Or Stopping You From Creating Joyful Intimate Sexual Relationships?............................447
Sex Does Not Begin In The Bedroom
How Do You Look And Feel?
Step Eight: How Can You Overcome Your Blocks And Create Joyful IntimateSexual Relationships?............................451
Sexual Healing
Your Sexual Healing
Being Celibate For A Month, Six Months, A Year Or Longer
Step Nine: Making A Commitment To Your Own Sexual And Spiritual Reawakening……………………………..……456
A Healing Journey Inward
Your Commitment To Your Own
  Sexual Reawakening
Your Commitment To Your Own
  Spiritual Reawakening

**Step Ten: Sexual And Spiritual Reawakening
At Last!**..459

Chapter 3   SEXUAL AND SPIRITUAL REAWAKENING ... AT LAST!....464
Now The Time Has Come Poem……………......464

Sexual And Spiritual Reawakening Will Transform Your Life………………………………..……….468
- Sexual Reawakening Is About Freedom
- Spiritual Reawakening Is About Freedom
- Sexual Reawakening Is About Soul Connection
- Spiritual Reawakening Is About Acceptance
- Sexual Reawakening Is About Exploring Your Own Unique Love Style

The Process of Sexual Reawakening……………………..…..473
- Discover Every Man And Every Woman In Your Partner's Eyes
- Your Ideal Man/Your Ideal Woman
- Your Sexual Experiences
- Your Partner's Sexual Style
- Your Sexual Style

Your Sexuality………………………….……….478
- What Is This Marvelous Thing Called Sex?
- Your Sexual Concerns

Your Senses And Your Sexuality……………………......484
- Your Senses And Your Sexuality
- Seeing, Your Partner And Sex
- Hearing, Your Partner And Sex
- Tasting, Your Partner And Sex
- Smelling, Your Partner And Sex
- Touching, Your Partner And Sex
- Talking, Your Partner And Sex
- Your Bodily Sensations, Your Partner And Sex
- Your Mind, Your Partner, Love And Sex
  - Mind Mapping
- Your Spiritual Reawakening
  - Mind Mapping

Copyright © 2009, Revised 2023   *Love Me, Touch Me, Heal Me*   DrEricaGoodstone.com

Letting Your Senses Speak To Your Partner..................**494**
      Allowing Your Lips To Speak
      Allowing Your Eyes To Speak
      Breathing Your Love
      Sounding Your Love
      Speaking Your Sensual Love
      Strengthening Your Internal Sexual Muscles
      Kissing, Touching, Sounds And Words
      Moving Your Body
      Letting Your Partner Guide Your Body
      Moving Together
      You Are Handsome/Beautiful, Sexy And Powerful
      Touching And Gazing Into Each Other's Eyes
      Hugging Your Partner
      Following Your Own Senses

Sexual And Spiritual Reawakening At Last!........................**507**
Footnotes..**511**
Also by Dr. Erica Goodstone...**514**

****

LOVE ME...PLEASE

Part I in the LOVE ME, TOUCH ME, HEAL ME

Complete Book

THE PATH TO

- *PHYSICAL*
- *EMOTIONAL*
- *SEXUAL*
- *SPIRITUAL*

REAWAKENING

Erica Goodstone, Ph.D.

Love Me … Please, **Part I, is dedicated to:**

- **Hilda Aronson, for helping me to get started**
- **Bryce Britton-Kranz, my colleague, mentor and friend, who provided support and lasting friendship that has sustained me over the years**
- **Glenn Dietzel's Awakened team, for pushing me to completion**

LOVE ME ... PLEASE

PART I

INTRODUCTION

Love me, please

I don't deserve it

Love me ... please

I don't know how

Love me ... please

You don't fit my pictures

Love me ... please.

Copyright © 9/20/97 Erica Goodstone, Ph.D.

Love Is A Gift

Love is a gift, given to us by our Creator. We do not have to work to become worthy of love. **We ARE love.** Our spirit is pure love. No matter what the circumstances of our birth, God intended us to be here. Otherwise, we would not exist. A wonderful poster says, "God Don't Make No Mistakes!" Believe it!

Nothing is more powerful and wonderful than love. What could be more empowering than a supportive mother's love, more endearing than a cooing baby's love, more exciting than being wrapped in the arms of a partner's passionate love, more comforting than a favorite pet's accepting love? What could be more sustaining and healing than believing in God's love and living every moment in a state of self-love?

LOVE ME … Please, **Part I**, **in the** *LOVE ME,* **TOUCH ME, HEAL ME Complete Book** leads us on a path toward loving … truly loving, from the center of our being. Love is the ultimate aphrodisiac. Love is patient, kind, unyielding, enduring and steadfast. Love overcomes all obstacles. But what most of us have called love, our human concepts and human attempts at love, with its sense of limited supply, ownership, and "what's in it for me" attitude, is filled with illusion, self-consciousness, insecurity, doubt and emotional upheaval. True love, unconditional love, a higher state of love, is limitless, boundless, and the ultimate creative power of the universe.

This book is meant for lovers, people who love, people who want to love, people who have loved, and people who want to love again. You will not find simplistic answers and easy to follow formulas for creating love. You will have to look deep into your own consciousness – your thoughts, beliefs, attitudes, memories and dreams – to find the love, the fullest love, that you can bring into your life. And you will be reminded, over and over, to bring that love back to your own self so that you can fully share your loving self with others.

****

LOVE ME ... PLEASE

"Circumcise therefore the foreskin of your heart, and be no more stiffnecked."

Deuteronomy 10:16, King James Version

Love is all there is. Love teaches. Love heals. Sometimes love hurts. You cannot will your self to love. You cannot will another to love you. Love is a feeling, a sensation, and an emotion. When you love, your emotional responses are heightened. You feel deep sorrow, intense anger, and even rage. You also feel exquisite pleasure and the emotional comfort of intimate contact. When you love, you experience the joy and wonder of being fully alive. In this book and this first chapter, you reflect upon love in your life: what you believe about love, how you have loved your self and others, how you have been loved, what you expect from love, and how you can create more love in your life.

LOVE ME ... PLEASE

Love Me ... Please

Love me…please
I am here
Right in front of you
Can you see me?
Do you know who I am?
I am just like you
Really, believe me
It's true

Don't be fooled by me
My outer appearance
Is just a show
I've covered myself
In delicate wraps
Of skin-filled matter
But I am still here
Underneath

I am…
Look deeply
In my eyes
You will find
Yourself
Really
No kidding

I'm your mirror
Polish my surface
I'll shine for you
Don't cloud my vision
You'll only block
Your own sight
Listen to me speak
You will hear
Your self talk

We belong together
Don't leave me alone
I'm hungry - feed me
I'm thirsty - let me drink
Don't turn away from me
Where else is there
For you to go?
We're here together

Now?
Why?
Let's find out
Let's share ourselves
Expand our views
Teach each other
What we need
To know

Let's love each other
For being here
That's all
Just for being
For existing
We're here
Together
Now

Copyright © 2009, Revised 2023   *Love Me, Touch Me, Heal Me*   DrEricaGoodstone.com

Don't you get it?
The cosmic joke
Ha, ha!
And we keep trying
To run away
From what?
From whom?
From love?

Loving being
Let me rest
In the power
Of your presence
Love me
Now
And always
Please!

Copyright © 9/20/97 Erica Goodstone, Ph.D.

THE GIFT OF LOVE

LOVE ME ... PLEASE

CHAPTER 1

THE GIFT OF LOVE

The Gift Of Love

I have given you
The gift of love
My love
In my way
What have you done
With my love?

Have you welcomed me
Into your heart?
Have you heard
My silent song?
Do you want
To play and know me?

Or- - -

Would you rather
Remain stuck
In your illusion
Of who
You think
I am?

*Would you rather
Be right
And close your heart
Than forgive me
For being less
Than you expect?*

*How can I help you
Overcome your fear
Of loving me so deeply
That you will be
Swallowed up by me
And disappear?*

*What would it take
For you and I
To open our hearts
And keep them open
Through all the anguish
Of becoming real?*

*Let's take that first step
Now
See with our eyes
Hear with our ears
And Listen
With our hearts.*

Copyright © Erica Goodstone, Ph.D. 4/10/99

Love Is All There Is

Love is a gift, given to us by our Creator. We do not have to work hard to become worthy of love. We are love. Our spirit is pure love. No matter what the circumstances of our birth, God intended us to be here. Otherwise, we would not exist. But you and I do exist. A wonderful poster I have seen says, **"God Don't Make No Mistakes!"** Believe it!

Each of us was granted life for a reason. There is wisdom in our cells. Our mother's egg connected with our father's approaching sperm. This was not an accident! Our birth was a gift of the Divine. Our birth was a gift of love to humanity, to this planet and beyond.

Who we are is our gift of love. Each of us has an equally important right to be here, to love and be loved. Love is all there is. When we reach the end of our life, as our death is approaching and we review our life, we will probably not think about the money we have earned, the careers we have created, or our favorite automobile. What we will recall, regret, or grieve about is the way we have loved and whether or not we have enjoyed living. As we feel our life slipping away, how we have loved and lived is all that really matters.

When I was 20, in my senior year of college, my father, Morris had a stroke, became progressively more ill, and passed on. All I wanted to do was run away, to escape from feeling the sadness, confusion, fear and loss. Twenty-eight years later, when my mother was dying, I stayed by her side, day and night, throughout her last few days. All I felt was the enduring quality of love and the loss of this precious human life, my mother, Muriel.

We don't need to wait for devastating loss or impending death to feel the love that has always been inside of us. **This is the reawakening.** Regardless of the loss or pain we have endured, in every moment of our life, we can choose to close our heart or open our heart to love.

Love And Intimacy Are Healing

Dean Ornish, M.D. (*Love and Survival,* 1997*)*) says that without love, connection, and intimacy, we are more likely to suffer and become ill. Without love, we do not thrive. Without love, we seem to just go through the motions of daily life, devoid of pleasure and excitement.

Although love creates the most profound feelings of peace and joy, most of us have not learned how to truly love our self or another. Relationships become a place to suffer. Having suffered once too often, many of us have actually given up on love.

Betty's Husband Leaves

"It's too painful to let anybody get close. I would be devastated if they left. I just can't risk it anymore." These are the words of Betty, a client who was divorced from the man of her dreams and who now appears to have given up on love.

When Betty was a young child, her father moved out of the house, visiting only on birthdays and holidays, when he would arrive loaded down with gifts in beautiful boxes. Betty has been spending the rest of her life searching for the love she never received from her father. She has always expected the man in her life to provide boxes of beautiful gifts just for her, all the time, every moment.

Her husband, Alan, could not compete with the bigger than life image she had of her hapless father. Betty demanded constant, and sometimes impossible, proof that Alan loved her. No matter how much he gave, it was never enough. Finally, Alan gave up and left. Just as her mother had lived without a man since her husband deserted her thirty years earlier, Betty was prepared to spend the rest of her life alone.

Just as we naturally learn a language in the first few years of life, so too, we learn how to love in our earliest years. Synapses and pathways in the brain (as well as intricate chemical reactions that release neuropeptides to receptor cites throughout the body), develop at birth or perhaps even earlier, while we are still growing in our mother's womb. Sensual stimulation, including eye contact, sounds, touch, and mirroring of who we are, in our earliest years, helps these pathways to develop and the neuropeptides to spread. Not receiving that early attention and recognition, our pathways may remain underdeveloped and our chemical responses dulled. We may spend the rest of our life seeking, but not quite getting enough, acceptance and approval from others. Being on the receiving end of too much stimulation, we may develop lifelong states of anxiety, fear, or continually stressful guardedness and a fear of being overwhelmed by what appears to be too much emotional or physical closeness.

Intimacy Is Not For The Faint Of Heart

David Schnarch, Ph.D, (*Passionate Marriage*, **1997***)* describes the way many married couples dance between feeling alienated and emotionally distant and feeling pressured and smothered. He devotes an entire chapter to the warning concept "Intimacy is Not for the Faint of Heart." According to Schnarch, intimacy in long-term marriage may require validating our self rather than expecting to receive the mirroring, acceptance and validation from a partner. How we have been loved has a profound effect upon our ability to validate our self and share our love with others.

My doctoral dissertation, based upon the theories developed by psychologist and researcher, Dr. Margaret Mahler, studied the overpowering and conflicting emotions of separation anxiety, intense ambivalence, and anxiety about marriage, residual emotions from our earliest bonding experiences, that can easily interfere with our ability to sustain satisfying love relationships.

Separation – Individuation

Dr. Margaret Mahler (*The Psychological Birth of the Human Infant, 1975)***)** observed infants' behavioral and emotional responses, during their first three years of life, to their mother's bonding behavior. She concluded that all children go through a *separation-individuation* process that is strongly influenced by the type of mothering the child receives.

According to Mahler, the infant's first month of life is non-relational. The infant mostly sleeps, awakening only to satisfy hunger, elimination, or other physiological needs. From the second to 18th month, the *symbiosis* stage, an infant is vaguely aware of mother as a source of getting basic needs met, but there is no sense of boundary between infant and mother.

The *separation-individuation* phase, from around the fifth month to 3 years of age, begins with experimentation. Recognizing mother as a separate being, a child discovers his or her own body parts and develops a body image. Early behaviors include pulling mother's hair, ears or nose, putting food into mother's mouth, or the infant straining his or her body away from mother to have a better look at her. From about 7 to 8 months, the infant compares mother to other people. Responding to unfamiliar people with *stranger anxiety*, the child clings to mother and gradually begins to leave mother's side to explore the world. Not ready to go out into the world alone, the child returns often to mother for comfort and *emotional refueling.* With proper mirroring and acceptance from mother, a child begins to individuate, gradually separating, creating boundaries and distance, while still remaining close to mother.

From about 18-24 months and beyond, the **Rapprochement Crisis** is said to occur. During this phase, recognizing both parents as separate individuals, a child realizes he or she must cope alone as a small and helpless person. With parents' continual acceptance, love, and encouragement to explore the world, a child learns that separating from a loved one is not the same as losing that person's love. A child who is stifled, held back, or pushed out on his or her own too soon without the emotional support of either parent, will probably grow up with **intense ambivalence** about intimacy. As an adult, he or she may either fear the **separation anxiety** that would result from being abandoned or the **merger anxiety** that would result from being stifled and overwhelmed by another in the process of becoming close. During this rapprochement phase, a child develops, or fails to develop, empathy for others.

The final phase, *Individuality and Object Constancy,* is crucial for the creation of mature, satisfying, and egalitarian, love relationships in adult life. This is the ability to accept both the good and bad qualities in oneself, mother, father, and others. Without a clear sense of individuality or an inability to retain a constant sense of the other person, we will alternate between closeness and distance, creating emotional ups and downs with our most intimate partners.

Good Enough Mothering and Fathering

If we have had *good enough mothering*, a term coined by noted psychologist Winnicott, as well as **good enough fathering,** we may be able to overcome our dependency needs, differentiate from our intimate partners, and validate our own self. If we have not received good enough loving as a child, we will probably spend the rest of our life searching for the love and acceptance we never had. Because we have not learned to trust, we will probably tend to push others away, keeping them at a safe distance, afraid to show how much we need them. It is hard for even the most caring and patient partner to continually support someone who distrusts and feels unloved.

Even if we have had very poor mothering and fathering, painful, neglectful or downright abusive beginnings, we **do have the ability to overcome our past**, create new pathways in our brain, differentiate as adults, and create intimacy in our life. Intense therapeutic work and powerfully intimate love relationships can assist us to overcome early childhood deficiencies, but nothing can totally erase what has happened, or not happened, in our life. The memories remain. We have to allow our self to feel and express all of our emotions, even the most painful, to reach a point of being able to accept the truth about what is.

Emotions Signal Unmet Needs

Our emotions are signals to us that we have unmet needs. Often we seek to satisfy certain needs while totally ignoring others. For example, one of our needs may be to nurture others. In even the most abusive relationship, we may be able to satisfy that need. But we may be ignoring two equally important needs, the need to nurture our self and the need to be nurtured by another. It is essential to understand our own needs and whether our emotions are a response to our current situation or to an unresolved situation from the distant past.

We often project onto those we love the power to permanently satisfy or deny our unfulfilled childhood needs. During our bouts of lovesickness and despair or unrealistic demands and expectations, we do not realize that this other person is just another human being. We forget that this person was also once a child and may also be harboring some unresolved and unmet childhood needs.

Many of us, men and women alike, give our self away in an attempt to please another. Some of us, on the other hand, put our efforts into influencing, convincing, manipulating, and controlling others to do things the way we decide they must be done. Either of these approaches has disastrous effects upon relationships, especially long term.

All we can have, if we suppress our own emotions or coerce others into suppressing theirs, is some approximation, some illusion, of our own controlled version of love.

What Are Your Nurturing Needs?

Sit quietly. Close your eyes. Breathe deeply and slowly as you allow your body to relax.

Now, reflect upon your most significant relationships, past and present. Do you tend to nurture and validate yourself? Do you tend to nurture and validate others? Open to a new page in your journal and answer the following questions:

In my relationships, in what way do I tend to:

* *ignore my own needs to please others?*

* *make unfair demands on others to please myself?*

* *give more than my share so the other person will need me and not leave?*

* *attempt to keep others off-balance and disempowered, by controlling them with words, money, or unpredictable behaviors?*

* *allow others to control, unbalance and disempower me?*

* *refuse to give to others what they desire, ask for, or say they need?*

* *allow others to deny me what I desire, ask for, or say I need?*

* *usually express my own feelings and ask for what I want?*

* *allow others to express their own feelings and ask for what they want?*

Reflect upon your responses to the previous questions. Decide now:

- *Is this the way I want to be with others?*

- *Is there something more I can do to nurture and validate myself?*

- *Is there a way I can communicate my needs more effectively to others?*

- *Can I can allow others to express their needs without suppressing my own?*

Learning how to love can be difficult. We have to give up the narcissistic belief that we are entitled to immediate gratification of our own needs at the expense of others. We have to let go of our desire to control people and situations. Love involves more than giving and receiving. **When we love, we allow others to exist.** We allow others to be themselves, to strive for their own goals, even if their goals sometimes directly interfere with our own needs and desires.

Research at the Institute of Heartmath indicates that our heart has an intricate electrochemical circuitry that connects directly with our brain. When we feel upsetting emotions, our heart rhythms become uneven and send jumbled information. We are unable to think clearly. Feeling love, we can literally activate coherent heart rhythms and send coherent messages to our brain, leading to emotional well-being and mental clarity.

When we love, there is a rippling effect. Each person who receives our love has more love energy to share with others. Imagine what a world this would be if everyone loved freely, instead of reserving it for only a precious few valued loved ones.

Most of us misunderstand love. We believe that love means loving others regardless of the effect upon our self. Or, we believe we must love our self at the expense of others. Love often requires strength, discipline, and making appropriate choices. Sometimes we must place our own needs on hold while we serve another. At other times we must care for our self first, as in the airplane instructions to put on your own oxygen mask first before helping others.

How Have You Loved?

Looking back at your life, what might you discover about the way you have loved and how you have received love from others? You do not have to wait until you have only a few months, days or moments left to live. You can examine and review your life right here, right now, with the remainder of your life stretching out in front of you.

As you answer the following questions, pay attention to your thoughts, emotions, and bodily sensations. Open your journal to a new page or keep a sheet of paper and pen ready. Sit quietly in a comfortable position. Take a few easy, slow, deep breaths. Relax.

Think about all the people you have loved - family, friends and romantic partners. Select one significant person you have loved. Remember, you can repeat this exercise over and over, focusing on a different person each time, if you choose. Now, answer the following questions about your relationship with one significant person.

How have I shown my love?

How have this person shown love to me?

How have I received their love?

How have they received my love?

How could I have loved them better?

How could they have loved me better?

How could I have loved myself better?

It is often easy to love another when they respond to us in the way we believe is appropriate. But what happens when another person's response is not at all what we feel we deserve, desire or expect? What if someone we love ignores, demeans, invalidates, or outright rejects us?

Not being loved by a particular person does not, by any means, indicate that we are unlovable. Another person's particular needs and desires may not be fulfilled by receiving the gift of our love. All we can do is offer our love and appreciate whatever comes back to us. **We simply cannot please everyone.** In another situation with another person whose needs match our own more closely, we may be accepted and loved exactly the way we are.

Some of us have found that when we loved in the past, the person we loved did not reciprocate by loving us back in the same way with the same intensity. Feelings of abandonment, loss and devastation may have caused us to suppress our emotions and try to protect our self from ever hurting that much again. We begin to behave in unpredictable ways. The result of suppressing our emotions is often misunderstanding, distancing, and hurt feelings. When people disappoint or disagree with us, we may unexpectedly explode in a burst of rage or break down in tears. With self-awareness, self-acceptance, and understanding of the human condition, we can overcome even the most painful loss, rejection or abuse.

How Do You Love Others When You Feel Unloved?

Close your eyes. Sit quietly. Breathe deeply and allow your body to relax. Remember a time when you loved someone who did not behave lovingly toward you.

Ask yourself the following questions:

What did this person say or do?

How did I respond to this person's words or actions?

How might I have responded if I felt loved no matter what this person said or did?

Was my response and behavior loving toward this person?

Was my response and behavior loving toward my self?

Now, go back to that situation and imagine what would have happened if you had felt totally secure, if you knew with total certainty that you are a worthwhile, lovable person, that your self-worth does not depend in any way upon this person's responses toward you.

Repeat this exercise as often as you like, recalling incidents with different people you have loved.

It is truly impossible to love another person if we do not love our self. Yes, we can feel the stirring of emotions. We can feel lust, desire, even longing. But love is much more complex and inclusive. Love also involves acceptance, forgiveness, and freedom. When we truly love, from the depth of our being, we allow the other person freedom to be who they are, even if we wish they were different.

How Have You Loved Yourself?

Sit quietly. Close your eyes. Breathe deeply and easily. Allow your body to relax.

Ask yourself the following questions:

In what ways do I show love and appreciation toward myself?

Is there anything I find impossible to love about myself?

What would have to change for me to be able to love myself fully?

Through loving and being loved, we know we exist. The opposite of love is not hate. The opposite of love is indifference. Painful as it is to be mistreated or even abused, it may be even more damaging and life threatening to be ignored. Being disregarded tells us we don't count and we do not affect the world around us. Studies have shown that infants who do not receive attention, stimulation, love, and touch, become increasingly despondent, depressed, withdrawn, and eventually die. Even if basic needs for food, water, clothing, and shelter are provided, they do not thrive. As adults, we continue to need to feel loved and to share our love with others. Loving and caring for another person (a child, an adult, even a pet) can be more healing than feeling loved by someone else.

I Love, I Hate

If we do not know what we love or hate, what we want, enjoy, desire, or fear, we cannot know love and we cannot truly love another.

Divide a piece of paper into 3 vertical columns. Put the following words at the top of each column: **I Love / I Hate / I Feel Neutral.** Write at least (20) twenty words or phrases in each column. Notice in which column you have written the most and which column the least words or phrases. As you begin to discover what you truly love, hate, and feel indifferent about, you can return to this page to add and delete words and phrases.

Beliefs

Many of us behave and respond the way we think will be accepted by others, rather than expressing what we truly want and feel in the moment. We may develop self-protecting beliefs that keep us safe and distant from others and perpetuate our inability to recognize and accept love, even when it is right in front of us.

Here are some common beliefs that prevent us from getting close to others.

"If I tell people how I feel, they will humiliate me or abandon me."

"If I tell the truth about someone abusing me, I am hurting someone else."

"I must do everything perfectly in order to be liked and accepted by others.

"If I don't have control in any situation, others will try to hurt me."

"I must be young and fit and beautiful to be desired and loved."

"If I let someone get close and they leave me, I will be devastated and could die."

"If I the person I love rejects me or leaves me, I will never find love again."

"If people disapprove of me, it means something is wrong with me."

"It is safer for me to stay with people and activities that are familiar."

"A good man, lover, husband, father, son, brother should …."

"A good woman, lover, wife, mother, daughter, sister should …."

"Sexual desire cannot last even in the best of relationships."

Unfortunately, there may be some truth in some of these statements. We have all had the experience of telling someone how we felt only to be misunderstood, rejected, humiliated or abandoned afterward. Yes, there are some people who will only like us if we do things perfectly, exactly the way they expect. Sometimes if we let others have control they may attempt to hurt us. At times we are temporarily devastated by the loss of another person's love. Yes, some people will not love and desire us if we don't fit their physical ideal. And sexual desire often does not last in long-term relationships. In some situations, with some people, some of the time, we will not be loved the way we want no matter what we say or do. But that does not mean we are unlovable and it does indicate we will never find a person to reciprocate our loving feelings. Our experiences in the world help to create our beliefs. What we believe helps to shape our world.

I Believe

Sit quietly and take a slow deep breath. Allow your body to relax. Open to a new page in your journal. Write each of the following statements at the top of a separate page. Contemplate the first statement for a moment, then close your eyes briefly. Open your eyes and immediately write what you believe about that statement. Repeat this process until you have written your initial beliefs about each statement.

- *I believe ... about love and relationships*
- *I believe ... about touching and being touched*
- *I believe ... about sensuality and sexuality*
- *I believe... about healing*
- *I believe ... about spirituality, a higher power, and God*

Reread your entire list of beliefs and then answer the following three questions:

How have my beliefs affected the way I feel about myself?

How have my beliefs affected what I dream about and strive to accomplish?

How have events, experiences, and specific people influenced my beliefs?

For the next few days, notice in what ways your life seems to conform to your beliefs. As you complete the exercises in this book, you may be surprised to see that your beliefs gradually change, that they are not as firm and true as you originally thought. Reread your list of beliefs at least once every week. Cross out, revise, and add to your list of beliefs as your life circumstances and your depth of understanding shifts. As you reread your list, you may want to add additional categories, listing your beliefs about such important aspects of life as creativity, money, aging, illness, parents, and children.

Conflicting Beliefs

As you review your list of beliefs, you may be surprised to discover that you hold two or more conflicting beliefs about the same aspect of your life. Harbouring conflicting beliefs can easily interfere with getting what you truly want to have in your life.

For example, if you are a woman who wants a relationship, you may believe, *"A woman must look attractive and sexy to be loved by a man."*

As a woman you may also believe, *"Men use, abuse and leave women who look attractive and sexy."*

A third belief of yours, as a woman, might be, *"I must be strong and never let a man use, abuse and leave me."*

If you are a man who wants a relationship, you may believe, *"A man must always be in control and never reveal his insecurities to be loved by a woman."*

As a man you may also believe, *"Women use, abuse and leave men who are not in control and reveal their insecurities."*

A third belief of yours, as a man, might be, *"I must be strong and never let a woman use, abuse and leave me"*

Given those three beliefs, how might you, as a woman, behave with men?

Given those three beliefs, how might you, as a man, behave with women?

Changing Beliefs

Believing is receiving. Change our beliefs and miracles happen. But how do we change beliefs that developed so long ago and seem so real and true to us?

By feeling our feelings, expressing our emotions, and recreating the story of our life. We cannot change our beliefs with our mind. Beliefs change through bodily experience. Through our bodies, we feel sensations and express our emotions.

Love is an emotion. Hate is an emotion. Anguish is an emotion. Humans are capable of a wide range of emotions, but most of us have not been allowed to freely express many of our basic emotions. When we do regularly feel and express our true emotions, we may lose something we really want, we may hurt for the moment, but we will also be able to heal more rapidly. Watch children play. They get hurt. They scream and cry and sulk and pout and whine. Suddenly they get distracted. Once again they are playing and giggling as if nothing has happened. Let's become like children in our emotional expression.

How Do I Express My Emotions?

Sit quietly. Close your eyes. Breathe deeply and slowly. Allow your body to relax. Open to a new page in your journal. Contemplate each of the following questions, one at a time, and write your immediate response to each one. After reading each question, briefly close your eyes, contemplate your response, open your eyes, and immediately write your ansswers.   Do not stop to think or censor your responses.

While growing up, what emotions was I allowed to feel and express?

> *With whom?*

> *In what situations?*

While growing up, what emotions was I taught to hide, suppress, or deny?

> *With whom?*

> *In what situations?*

How did others respond to me when I showed unacceptable emotions?

As an adult and in recent years, what emotions have I allowed myself to feel and express?

> *With whom?*

> *In what situations?*

How have I responded when another person expressed emotions I have not allowed myself to feel or express?

How have others responded to me when I expressed emotions that were previously unacceptable for me to feel and express?

Many of us are afraid we will be punished and rejected if we express our true feelings.   Or we fear that uncontrollable and overpowering emotions will come flooding out and we will have an emotional breakdown. We may even be afraid, if we express what we truly feel, our world as we know it will collapse and we will no longer exist.

Research reveals that keeping our emotions locked inside, not expressing our true feelings, can and does make us sick. Such diseases as cancer, arthritis, asthma, high blood pressure, skin rashes, and heart disease can be exacerbated by holding feelings inside. Traditional Chinese medicine associates blocked or weakened organ meridians, such as heart, lungs and large intestine, with specific emotions. Of course, emotions are not the only cause of illness. A healthy life requires balanced living: adequate nutrition, exercise, sleep, rest, stress management, social and spiritual connection. In a later chapter, we will revisit our body in greater detail, but for now, let's take a look at the ways we have loved, nurtured, or ignored our emotional needs.

Each of us has a unique gift to share with the world. We were born into this body at this time for a reason. We may not know the reason, but we do have a purpose for being here. If we cover up our feelings and deny our natural way of being, how can we discover our life's purpose?

We have the power to change our life, to create more of what we want and less of what we don't want. We can begin by telling our self the full truth about where we are in this process, right here, right now. We can review and evaluate the experiences of our upbringing and early childhood. We can discover what we believe was nurturing, non-nurturing, abusive or neglectful. Developing the capacity to create intimate and loving relationships with others requires that we understand and accept our own ability to give and receive love.

What Is My Loving Potential?

Close your eyes. Breathe deeply and quietly. Allow your body to relax. Reflect upon the following question:

How loving am I with the people in my life?

Open to a new page in your journal. Make a list of your current closest friends, lovers, family members, colleagues or anyone with whom you've been spending time lately.

For each person, answer the following questions.

Why am I choosing to be with this person?

What pleases or displeases me about him or her?

What does he or she offer or provide for me?

What do I offer or provide for him or her?

How do I show, hide or disguise my love and other feelings?

Only when we have faced the dark side of our own soul, can we relinquish our demand for approval, acceptance and love from others. At that point, we may be ready to forgive our human mothers and fathers and all those who have hurt, ignored, or disappointed us, for their human frailties, for having given us less than our optimal doses of love, acceptance, and even discipline and boundaries.

Letter to My Birth Mother or Earliest Caretaker

Write a letter to your birth mother or your earliest caretaker, whoever was most significant to you, the one who sometimes, frequently, or rarely, showed you love and affection, the one who sometimes neglected, disregarded, or hurt you. Express your feelings of disappointment, sadness, rejection, loss, yes, even bitterness, anger and rage. Bang a pillow and scream into it if you must. If you also have some wonderful feelings, then thank your mother for whatever you do appreciate. Hug the pillow if you please.

The Mother of My Dreams

After you have completed this letter, close your eyes and imagine being taken in, nurtured, loved and cared for by the mother of your dreams. Imagine being filled up with a sense that you truly count, you are special, good, and you deserve to be loved and to receive all the good things that life has to offer. Remain connected to this place inside where you feel full and you know you are loved, cared for, and pleased with your life. Coming from that internal place of self-acceptance and self-love, express your true disappointment with and then appreciation, even the smallest amount, for your birth mother or primary caretaker, for who she was, how she raised you, and how you were treated by her.

Letter to My Birth Father or Earliest Father Figure

Write a letter to your birth father or earliest father figure, the one who sometimes, frequently or rarely, showed you love and affection, the one who sometimes neglected, disregarded, or hurt you. Express your feelings of disappointment, sadness, rejection, loss, yes, even bitterness, anger and rage. Bang a pillow and scream into it if you must. If you also have some wonderful feelings, then thank your father for what you do appreciate. Hug the pillow if you please.

The Father of My Dreams

After you have completed this letter, close your eyes and imagine being taken in, protected, loved and cared for by the father of your dreams. Imagine being filled up with a sense that you truly count, you are special, strong, good, and you deserve to be protected and loved and to receive all the good things that life has to offer. Remain connected to this place inside where you feel full and you know you are loved, cared for, and pleased with your life. Coming from that internal place of self-acceptance and self-love, now express your true disappointment with and then your appreciation, even the smallest amount, for your birth father or primary father figure for who he was, how he raised you, and how you were treated by him.

What Are Your Rules For Loving?

Reread your list of beliefs. Select those 5-10 loving beliefs that seem to rule your life.

On a new page, write: **My Rules For Loving.** Your life is unfolding in accordance with your rules for loving. Change your rules and you change your life.

Many years ago, there was a wonderful TV program, *This Is Your Life*. Each week, a celebrity would be invited for a full life review. Relatives, friends and lovers that had not been seen for many years miraculously appeared. Private fears, insecurities, and childhood problems were revealed and even laughed about. Finally, the invited relatives and friends gathered around to acknowledge and exchange hugs and kisses with the celebrity. At the end of the show, the book was closed. That celebrity's current life story was complete.

This Is My Life

Join me on a journey back into your distant past. Have your journal ready and opened to a new page. Together we will uncover some early thoughts and experiences, those that helped to form your current beliefs and rules for living.

Sit quietly for a few moments. Breathe slowly, softly and easily.

Allow your mind to wander back along the years to your earliest memories of life. Recall the words and feelings expressed by your mother, father or other early caretakers about love, touch, healing, spirituality, God, sensuality and sexuality.

Allow your mind to recollect how your beliefs and rules for living were created and developed.

What Are Your Rules for Loving?

Open your eyes and write about your own rules for loving.

Write whatever thoughts fill your mind. Write in short phrases, outline form, sentences, or brief paragraphs. Just write and write and write until your mind begins to quiet down, the thoughts slowly dissipate, and you know you are finished for now.

The Eraser Game

Read what you have written about your rules for loving.

Now, reread your long list of Beliefs.

Reread your short list of My Rules for Loving.

Take a red pen and draw a thin line through any beliefs or rules that will not assist you at this point in your life to attain your goals and live your dreams.

Copyright © 2009, Revised 2023   *Love Me, Touch Me, Heal Me*   DrEricaGoodstone.com

This is your life. How do you choose to live it? What rules do you really want to follow? What beliefs and rules will lead you to the promised land, to fulfillment of your dreams and your life's purpose.

My New Rules for Creative Loving

On a new page, rewrite your list of rules for loving, retaining only those items that were not crossed out. Add any additional rules for loving that you know will support your goals and dreams, what you want to create in your life. These are your new, expanded, uplifting **rules for creative living.** For example:

> "When I speak my truth, others listen."
>
> "Love and respect are part of my life."
>
> "It is fun and exciting to try something new, to learn something I don't already know."
>
> "It is okay for me to make mistakes. I can study, take lessons, practice and improve and become much more skillful than I am now."

Keep an ongoing, expanding list of these uplifting, broadening, expansive, loving, and flexible beliefs and rules for living. Read spiritual and positive books. Add to this list review the list at least once every week, and cross out any rules beliefs that no longer serve you.

It is not the events in our life that count. It is the way we interpret events and how we choose to live afterwards. Nelson Mandella, a political prisoner in Africa for many years, emerged from his prison ordeal to become the Prime Minister of South Africa! Victor Frankl and Elie Weisel, having suffered unimaginable abuse and indignity for years in concentration camps. Nelson Mandela spent many years incarcerated in Africa due to racial prejudice and political chastisement. These are people who did not bask in their "poor me suffering mentality." Instead, they dedicated the rest of their lives to recording their experiences and teaching others to value their own internal lives, no matter what is happening externally.

Each of us has the potential to be or become almost anything we can imagine. The most important ingredient is belief in what's possible, not what appears to be possible, but what **is** possible. Every great event began with a few brave individuals who were not afraid to speak their truth and make a difference. You and I can make a difference too.

Very few of us have been totally loved and accepted for who we are. Most of us learned that we must do something, become something, or be something, in order to be loved. Even if you were raised by the most exceptionally loving and secure parents, at times you have probably felt hurt, disappointed, frustrated, or even temporarily abandoned. These experiences, painful as they may have been at the time, caused you to feel your feelings, to have compassion for your self and others and to be open to love. Part of being a healthy human being is the ability to feel and express your emotions. Feeling your most painful emotions enables you to also feel your most pleasing emotions. When you allow your self to feel and express all of your emotions, you develop a true sense of integrity, an inner knowing of who you are. The next step is to acknowledge, accept and appreciate your self for being who you are.

BE WHO YOU ARE

THE GREATEST GIFT

OF ALL

LOVE ME ... PLEASE

CHAPTER 2

BE WHO YOU ARE ...

THE GREATEST GIFT OF ALL

Be Who You Are

Man child of the world
Enfold me
Wrap me in your fatherly arms
Protect my fragile spirit
From the dangers
Of my untamed mind

Child woman of the earth
Hold me
Caress me with your motherly touch
Arouse my tired senses
From my fear
Of life and love

Precious child of God
Your firelight
Enriches me
Ignite the smoldering embers
Of my inner fire
So bright

Shine your love light
On my heart
Watch my firework display
Let me dream about
The power
Of your embrace

Copyright © 8/24/99 Erica Goodstone, Ph.D.

THIS CHAPTER IS ABOUT YOU

- **Who you are**
- **Who you have been told you are**
- **Who you believe you are.**

Nobody in the world can tell you who you are. You have your own DNA, your own fingerprints, your own beliefs, and your own sense of self. The purpose of this chapter is to guide you to uncover and discover more and more about who you are.

When someone asks you, "Who are you"?, what is your immediate response?

- *Do you define yourself by your family roles (wife, husband, girlfriend, boyfriend, mother, father, daughter, or son)?*

- *Do you define yourself by your abilities, skills, hobbies, or favorite leisure activities (golfer, chess player, musician, stamp collector, dancer, nature lover, theatre goer)?*

- *Do you define yourself by your work, profession, or non-profession (teacher, lawyer, secretary, truck driver, actress, unemployed, housewife, physically challenged, welfare recipient)?*

- *Do you define yourself by your personality or life experiences, either positive or negative (honest, reliable, intellectual, difficult, easy-going, hot-tempered, recovering alcoholic, adult child of sexual abuse)?*

- *Do you define yourself by focusing on your physical appearance (facial features, body shape, height, weight, age, attractiveness)?*

- *Do you define yourself by your most common emotions (angry, sad, lonely, happy, sensual, frustrated, self-doubting)?*

- *Do you define and describe yourself in any other unique way?*

Would you have described yourself the same way: Ten years ago? Five years ago? Two months ago? Last week? Yesterday? Earlier today? Think about what life events have changed your self-image in the past? Imagine how your self image might change now if:

- your financial situation drastically changed, if you fell in love with someone new, or lost your current partner.

- you completed a new training program or degree, got a new job, gave birth, adopted a child, or became a stepparent, a foster parent or a grandparent.

- you injured a body part, gained or lost a lot of weight, or contracted a life-threatening disease.

- you found yourself in a relationship where the only choice seemed to be to either abandon yourself or abandon another.

Your opinion of yourself, who you think you are, shifts according to your life experiences and the people with whom you spend your time.

You Are Unique And Special

No Matter What You Think About Yourself!

Each of us is unique and special. There never was an **Erica Goodstone** before. There never will be an **Erica Goodstone** again. And there never was a **YOU** before. There never will be a **YOU** again. Even if someone shares the same name or if you have an identical twin, nobody has your exact appearance, mannerisms, background, experience, or knowledge. Nobody has your exact fingerprints or your DNA.

You are a unique and special human being. How can anyone else in this entire world tell you how you should think, feel or behave? How does anyone else know what caused you to think, feel or be the way you are? Our body, mind, and all of our senses, are bombarded every single moment of every single day with continuous internal and external stimulation. Each of us responds in our own unique way.

Nobody else can determine how we should be. So, why do we spend so much of our personal resources (time, money, emotions, energy) trying to please others, suppressing our own unique traits, even attempting to become something or someone else? Why do we attempt to hide or deny who we are, change our appearance, behavior, even our beliefs, to please or displease others?

Each of us has a unique gift to share with the world. We were born into this body, with this genetic constitution, in this gender, with these racial features, in this family, in this part of the world. I believe that each of us has a purpose for being here, exactly where we are. In my experience over the years with many clients, if we cover up our feelings and deny our natural way of being, we tend to lose our zest for life, become bitter, resentful, angry, or even chronically depressed. Let's take a look at where we are right now, in a non-judgmental, private, personal way.

As you go through these exercises, you may feel uncomfortable and even emotionally upset. But please be reassured now. At the end of this chapter, we will do some special exercises to help you reshape your past, yourself and get you ready for the future you.

Who Are You?

Let's Take A Deeper Look.

Sit facing a mirror. Breathe deeply, slowly and softly. Observe your face and body carefully. Ask the following questions as you gaze deeply into your own eyes.

Allow the answers to come to you spontaneously. Speak your answers out loud, directly to the face you see in the mirror. Write your responses in your journal or on a plain piece of paper. Do not pause to think about your responses.

The exercise you are about to do will be repeated three times. This is a quick method for gathering information about your self from a very deep source within. You will be asking the same questions:

- In the 1st person (Who Am I?)
- In the 2nd person (Who Are You?)
- In the 3rd person (Who is [Your Name]?).

For the third part of this exercise, if possible, have a fairly recent photograph of yourself available; a driver's license or work I.D. is okay. Respond immediately with the first answers that occur to you.

Who Am I?

Looking directly into your own eyes in the mirror. Ask yourself and answer in the first person:

Who am I?_____

I am a woman/man who_____

What do I like about me?_____

What do I dislike about me?_____

What do I want to change about me?_____

Who would I like to be?_____

Who am I?_____

Who Are You?

Looking directly into your own eyes in the mirror. Ask yourself and answer in the second person, as if you were talking to a close friend:

Who are you?_____

You are a woman/man who_____

What do I like about you?_____

What do I dislike about you?_____

What do I want to change about you? _____

Who would you like to be? _____

Who are you? _____

Who Is [Your Name]?

Sign your full name legibly in your journal or on a piece of paper. If you have a recent photograph of yourself, alternate between looking directly into your own eyes in the photograph and looking at your own signature. If you do not have a photograph, keep your eyes focused on your written signature as you ask yourself and answer the following questions in the third person:

(For example, *Who is Erica? Erica is ....*)

Who is [your name] _____

[Your name] is a woman/man who _____

What does [your name] like about herself/himself? _____

What does [your name] dislike about herself/himself? _____

What does [your name] want to change about herself/himself? _____

Who would [your name] like to be? _____

Who is [your name]? _____

Copyright © 2009, Revised 2023   *Love Me, Touch Me, Heal Me*   DrEricaGoodstone.com

Who Have You Been Told You Are?

Sit quietly and close you eyes. Take a few easy, slow, deep breaths. Write your responses to this exercise in your journal.

List the names of people who have expressed opinions about you, positive and negative, accurate and inaccurate, honest and dishonest.

What words have they used to describe you, your appearance, your personality, your emotions, and your behavior?

Continue listing names and their opinions of you until you find you are becoming repetitive and have exhausted most descriptions and opinions that others have expressed about you.

No man or woman is an island. We are energetic, sentient, feeling human beings. We affect and are affected by others. No matter how strong, powerful, independent, cool or indifferent we may appear to be, we are all affected, to a greater extent than many of us care to admit, by the attitudes, opinions and behaviors of others toward us. When we are treated with loving kindness and respect, we usually feel good about our self. When we are disregarded, abused, humiliated, or mistreated, we often feel bad about our self.

How Have Others' Opinions Affected You?

Take a careful look at the way other people's opinions have affected you. Ask yourself the following questions. Write the answers in your journal.

What makes me feel good about myself?

What makes me feel bad about myself?

What makes me believe in myself?

What makes me doubt myself?

What makes me feel most proud?

What makes me feel most ashamed?

You are not the opinions that others have of you. You are more than the way you have been treated. You are even more than your own opinion of yourself. Whoever you have become is a result of a lifetime of experiences plus your own unique way of perceiving life.

By now you have probably discovered that you do not need to judge your own value by the responses, actions or reactions of others. Others always see you through their own filters. No matter who you are or what you do or say, they will probably only see you according to their own projections. You may remind them of someone else, you may say something they like or something else they misinterpret, you may need something they can or cannot give, or they may want something they believe you can or cannot give.

Reading this book and doing the exercises can and will change your life. For most of us, revealing our internal truth is terrifying. However, sharing our deepest thoughts and feelings can be life saving. Studies show that women with breast cancer live longer when they regularly attend a group sharing session. Sharing with others, being listened to, and being heard, without judgement, can lessen our fear. Just knowing we are no longer totally alone, no longer forced to face our problems in the dark, allows us to begin the long, slow journey toward healing.

How Have You Taken a Stand For Yourself?

Sit comfortably. Take a few slow deep breaths and relax. Scan through your life.

- *Remember a time when you gave yourself away, did what another person wanted, without expressing your own needs.*
- *Remember a time when you did not tell the truth and face some difficulty directly.*
- *Remember a time when you persuaded another person to give them self away, to do what you wanted, without expressing their own needs.*

- *Remember a time when you expressed your own needs and took a stand for yourself.*

Playing Roles

I grew up believing that smart women know how to handle men. I knew I wasn't being "smart" with men, but my education had not been complete. I never did learn what smart women knew. I never learned what a smart woman does, what she says, how she behaves, or how she "gets" from her man what it is she wants.

So--- I lived relationships in a role. I behaved the way I thought a smart woman would behave or I did just the opposite to test out the smart woman theory. I placated, pleased, and gave myself away, or I demanded, expected, and complained. No matter how I tried to figure out the way to handle a man, the smart woman way, nothing worked.

What Roles Have You Played?

What roles have you played in your life?

What roles are you currently playing in your life?

Why do you play these roles?

What would happen if you stopped playing these roles?

*What stops you from being **who you are**?*

Playing a role, even if you have figured out the best way to play it, as I never managed to do, is living an incomplete life. Keeping your true self in hiding perpetuates a state of insecurity and often self-loathing. Being yourself -- blemishes, flaws, insecurities, obsessions, peculiarities and all -- allows you to let down your guard, relax and become intimate with others. Hiding in any way prevents the full experience of intimacy. It may prevent you from feeling devastating emotional setbacks but it will also block your passion.

How Did You Become Who You Are?

List the significant events and people in your life that you believe had the greatest effect upon you (positive or negative), the ones who influenced the way you feel about yourself. Summarize the way you feel about yourself in a short descriptive, exaggerated phrase, e.g., Poor Abandoned Rich Girl, The Town Loser, The Stud, The Prom Queen.

In a moment, you will be asked to draw. Have several pieces of plain white paper and plain or colored pencils ready. Drawing, painting and other forms of creative expression can help us to discover deeper meanings about our life than words can ever explain. The shapes, colors, textures and symbols often reveal our unconscious feelings about life and about who we are. It doesn't matter if you draw stick figures or elegant portraits, your message will be clear. Trust in the wisdom of your body and mind to allow your hands to do the drawing. Whatever you draw offers valuable information about who you are. The people in the drawings do not have to appear realistic. They are merely representing the message you received and internalized.

Your Family At Home

Draw a picture of your apartment or home when you were a very young child. If it was more than one level, find a way to show that, even with just a straight line. Locate each person in your family in the part of the house you most remember them being. For example: brother in the tool room, father in the garage, mother in the kitchen or bedroom, you sitting with your brother watching TV in the living room.

Your Family At the Dinner Table

Draw a picture of your family at dinner.

Write at the top of the picture, "**Dinner With [My Family]**"

For example, "Dinner With The Goodstone Family"

Answer the following questions:

Did you all sit around a table together?

Where did each person sit?

Who cooked?

Who cleaned up after?

What was the general theme? For example, *don't make waves; love and acceptance; criticizing, arguing, insulting; intellectual conversation; solving the world's problems; gossiping; food; money; beauty.*

Now, give the picture a title that represents the mood of your family at the dinner table. For example, "The News of The World," "How to Save a Buck."

Your Creative Expression

These exercises are designed to help you remember what it was like for you as a child when you were drawing, painting or sculpting; moving your body, being athletic, or dancing; cooking, sewing or cleaning; inventing, building, repairing, solving mathematical problems or connecting electrical wires; speaking, singing, acting, being a comedian or a clown.

Drawing, Painting and Sculpting

Sit quietly. Breathe deeply and allow yourself to relax. Remember a time, when you were very young, when you were drawing, painting or sculpting.

What responses do you remember receiving from others?

What do you remember being told about the way you draw, paint or sculpt?

Who told you this?

Were you encouraged and guided or discouraged and criticized?

What effect did those words and reactions have upon your ability, confidence, and freedom to draw, paint, sculpt, and express yourself?

Imagine yourself drawing, freely expressing your creative genius. Imagine yourself painting with different mediums (watercolor, oils, pastels). Imagine yourself sculpting a work of art with clay or plaster or chipping away at a piece of marble. Imagine yourself to be a creative genius at work, on the level of the masters (Monet, Picasso, Rembrandt, Michelangelo). In your mind, see the people who guided, taught, encouraged and applauded you and your work. In your mind, see the *people* who criticized, judged, interfered with, blocked, repressed or stopped your creative genius from expression.

Moving Your Body, Dancing and Being Athletic

Remember a time, when you were very young and you were moving, dancing, or participating in an athletic activity. You may have received different responses to the way you moved, danced or about your athletic ability.

What responses do you remember receiving from others?

What do you remember being told about the way you move, dance, or your athletic ability?

What do you remember being told about the way men or women should move, dance, or do athletic activities?

What do you remember being told about your athletic ability, flexibility, strength, coordination, endurance?

Who told you this?

Were you encouraged and guided or discouraged and criticized?

What effect did those words and reactions have upon your ability, confidence, and freedom to move, dance, participate and succeed in sports, and express yourself?

Imagine yourself moving and dancing.

Imagine yourself to be a creative genius at work, on the level of the masters (Rudolph Nureyev, Martha Graham, Magic Johnson, Roger Federer).

Draw yourself freely expressing your creative genius.

Imagine yourself being athletic in a solo activity (running, swimming, bicycling).

Again, imagine yourself to be a superior athlete, at a highly competitive level.

Imagine yourself being athletic in a team sport or activity (basketball, volleyball, football, soccer, cheerleading).

In your mind, see the people who guided, taught, encouraged and applauded you and your work.

In your mind, see the people who criticized, judged, interfered with, blocked, repressed or stopped your creative genius from expression.

Now, imagine playing music and dancing around the room. Imagine yourself playing basketball, volleyball, tennis, golf, or whatever sport you may have strong feelings about. If you feel competent or afraid, allow the feelings to emerge.

Remember, **your feelings are not who you are**!

Cooking, Sewing and Cleaning

Remember a time, when you were very young when you were cooking, sewing or cleaning.

What responses do you remember receiving from others?

What do you remember being told about the way you cook, sew or clean?

What do you remember being told about the way men or women cook, sew, or clean?

Who told you this?

Were you encouraged and guided or discouraged and criticized?

What effect did those words and reactions have upon your ability, confidence, and freedom to cook, sew, clean, and express yourself?

Imagine yourself cooking and sewing. Imagine yourself to be a creative genius at work, on the level of a master chef or master tailor. Imagine yourself freely expressing your creative genius.

In your mind, see the people who guided, taught, encouraged and applauded you and your work.

In your mind see the people who criticized, judged, interfered with, blocked, repressed or stopped your creative genius from expression.

Now, imagine cooking a delicious gourmet meal. Now, imagine taking a needle and thread and sewing of competently using a sewing machine.. Now, imagine cleaning your apartment or house. Allow this exercise to bring you deeper into your own feelings. If you feel competent, incapable or afraid, allow the feelings to emerge. Remember, **your feelings are not who you are!**

Inventing, Building, Repairing, Doing Mathematical or Electrical Work

Remember a time, when you were very young when you were inventing, building, repairing, or solving mathematical problems or connecting electrical wires.

What responses do you remember receiving from others?

What do you remember being told about the way you invent, build, repair, or work with electrical wires?

What do you remember being told about the way men or women invent, build, repair, or work with electrical wires?

Who told you this?

Were you encouraged and guided or discouraged and criticized?

What effect did those words and reactions have upon your ability, confidence, and freedom to invent, build, repair, work with electrical wires, and express yourself?

Imagine yourself inventing, building, repairing, solving mathematical problems or connecting electrical wires. Imagine yourself to be a creative genius at work, on the level of a master inventor, builder, mathematician or electrician.

In your mind, see the people who guided, taught, encouraged and applauded you and your work.

In your mind, see the people who criticized, judged, interfered with, blocked, repressed or stopped your creative genius from expression.

Speaking, Singing, Playing an Instrument, Acting, Being a Comic, Being a Clown

Remember a time when you were very young when you were speaking, singing, playing a musical instrument, acting, being a comedian or a clown.

What responses do you remember receiving from others?

What do you remember being told about the way you speak, sing, play an instrument, act, tell jokes, or behave like a clown?

What do you remember being told about your ability to speak, sing, play a musical instrument, act, be a comedian or a clown?

What do you remember being told about your right to speak, sing, play a musical Instrument, act, be a comedian or a clown?

What do you remember being told about the way men or women speak, sing, play a musical instrument, act, be a comedian or a clown?

Were you encouraged and guided or discouraged and criticized?

What effect did those words and reactions have upon your ability, confidence, and freedom to speak, sing, play a musical instrument, act, be a comedian or a clown?

Imagine yourself speaking, singing, playing a musical instrument, acting, being a comedian or a clown. Imagine yourself to be a creative genius at work, on the level of a masterful and famous speaker, singer, musician, actor, comedian or clown. Draw yourself freely expressing your creative genius.

See the people who guided, taught, encouraged and applauded you and your work. See the people who criticized, judged, interfered with, blocked, repressed or stopped your creative genius from expression.

Now, imagine giving a lecture to a large audience. Now, imagine singing a song out loud. Now, imagine playing a musical instrument like a virtuoso. Now imagine being a star, acting in your favorite drama, romance, mystery or comedy. Now imagine yourself being an hilarious comedian. Now, imagine yourself being a famous clown. If you feel competent or afraid, allow the feelings to emerge. Remember, **your feelings are not who you are!**

Your Creative Expression Collage

You are about to create a collage that represents your creativity and self-expression. Before you begin this exercise, have the following materials ready.

- Different types of magazines (financial, sports, entertainment, hobbies)
- Scotch tape or paste
- Scissors
- Pen, pencil or magic marker
- Large piece of white paper, preferably heavy like cardboard, or several pieces of white paper that you can scotch tape together to make a larger sheet

Now that you've gotten a good sense of who you are, how you feel, how your creative expression has been allowed to develop or how it was discouraged and suppressed, you are ready to begin removing what doesn't really feel like who you are.

Sculpting Yourself
Removing That Which Is Not You

Write each of the questions in this exercise at the top of a separate page in your journal or on a piece of paper. *Who Am I,?, Who Are You,? Who Is [Your Name]?*

Sit facing yourself in the mirror. Gaze into your own eyes. Breathe slowly, deeply and softly. Ask yourself the same three questions that you asked at the very beginning of this chapter. Write your answers now in your journal.

Who am I?

Who are you?

Who is [Your name]?

Re-read your three lists.

Cross out any statements that do not belong to you, that do not truly express who you are.

Add any additional statements that reflect who you now think you are.

Who Are You?

Sit facing yourself in the mirror.

Take a few slow, deep, soft breaths.

Gaze into your own eyes in the mirror.

Read aloud the three new lists of statements (*Who am I? Who are you? Who is [your name]?*).

Congratulations!

In finishing *LOVE ME … Please,* **Part I in the** *LOVE ME, TOUCH ME, HEAL ME* **Complete Book,** you have done some of the most intense and difficult work on yourself that you have probably ever done. You are now becoming more deeply acquainted with who you really are. Before you can connect intimately and truly love another person, it is essential that you know, acknowledge and accept who you are. When you truly allow your authentic self to shine through and you actually are able to appreciate yourself for being who you are, you are finally ready to begin the ***Delicate Dance of Love***.

THE DELICATE DANCE OF LOVE

LOVE ME ... PLEASE

CHAPTER 3

THE DELICATE DANCE OF LOVE

The Delicate Dance of Love

In my dreams
I see you
Valient angel
Of the vast blue sky
You sit upon a floating cloud
Waiting for me

In my prayers
I call to you
Courageous voyager
Through uncharted paths
Lead me to my dream
I'll follow

Now you're here
In front of me
Imagined lover
Come to life
Let's walk the path of love
Together

Come with me
To a quiet place
And rest awhile
Our journey has just begun
Take my hand and hold me
In your heart

Let's build a bridge
Stairway to heaven
Let's take those long steps
One by one
See the blossoms all around us
Feel their fragrance in our hearts

Love's sweet journey
Moves us onward
Hearts in sync with nature's flow
Do not fear
Our hearts are open
Do not fear our love is pure

Dancing gently
Toward each other
Moving freely as we meet
Long embrace in cold of winter
Cooling breeze
In summer's heat

First you lead
Through storm and passion
Walking forward toward the light
The path of love continues onward
Hearts on fire
Leading home

Copyright © 8/19/99 Erica Goodstone, Ph.D.

The Delicate Dance of Love

Two people meet. Tingly sensations delight their bodies. Their eyes sparkle at the sight of this wondrous face and body. Each one feels the vibrant pull of ecstatic energy. Their skin moistens with excitement and anticipation. Their ears perk up as each one savors the sound of the other's voice and heartbeat. Their hearts are soft and open. As their lungs expand, their sinuses widen and their throats enlarge. Their noses sense the other's being and retain the sweet smell of imminent pleasure. Their groins ache with desire for love. They breathe like sweet ambrosia the sight and sound and smell of their object of desire.

A line of unseen energy pours between them, holding them still, entranced. Opening their mouths and almost tasting each other's lips, they begin to speak -- tender, gentle, receptive words of admiration, appreciation and unconditional recognition of each other's worth. Even if their words appear harsh, as may be their style, the underlying meaning is clear to both.

And they begin the dance of love….

He fixes his tie (that may not be there) as she pushes back her long flowing hair (that may be closely cropped). The energy in the ethers between them intensifies and spreads beyond. Easing into each other's space, slowly, effortlessly, a force of nature seems to pull them, magnetically, along an electric wire about to explode.

Finally ... they touch, a fleeting touch at the very outer surface of the hairline of their skin. Waves of shock spread throughout their electrified bodies. Hearts aflame, mouths moistening, they have met - - and touched - - at the contact zone of love.

Passionate Hollywood movies and popular romantic novels reveal to us the power of physical attraction and intimate contact. Man meets woman. Man meets man. Woman meets woman. Woman meets woman. Electricity fills the air. This is the beginning of love at the contact zone, a term coined by Laura Perls, wife of the originator of Gestalt Therapy, Fritz Perls. The contact zone is a place of ultimate intimacy, a place where our body, mind and spirit join with another. At the contact zone, there is bare honesty in the moment, without need to pretend, to hide, or to escape. This is a sacred place and time, where our body cells listen, respond and openly receive love. This level of intimacy can occur in any relationship -- with close friends, business associates, acquaintances, family members, as well as and with our most intimate lovers.

Love begins at this point of pure contact, but it does not end here. Loving and learning to love is an ongoing creation. It requires mindfulness, attention, commitment, practice, caring and creativity. The most loving thing we can do for others is to honor them by speaking our truth, gently yet firmly, in the moment, the right moment, as if the hands of our heart could caress their soul as we speak.

None of us is an island unto our self. We affect and are affected by others all the time. This world and the entire universe is based upon relationship, one electron to another, one planet to another, one cell to another, one person to another. No matter how cool, indifferent, isolated or independent any one of us appears to be, we have all been affected by others and we all have our unique affect upon others.

Through our skin and all of our senses, we make contact with the world, we know and become known by others. Our eyes see and we are seen. Our ears listen and our voices are heard. We taste and smell our environment and our scent is experienced by others. Our energy and life force, our thoughts and our body posturing, our subconscious beliefs and attitudes, are seen or felt and responded to by others.

Some of us are currently unable to tolerate the pleasurable sensations of intimate contact. From negative life experiences, we may have become so numbed to sensation that the intensity must be high, even painful, for our mind to allow our body to feel. But all is not lost. Healing is possible in every moment, if we truly desire to create intimate relationships in our life.

If we have received caring and tender love, if our senses have been allowed to feel, explore and connect without interference, then we may easily and often reach that place of pure contact with others. At that intimate place, we understand each other without words. Our body comes alive with passionate desire and sensual pleasure.

In the following exercise, you have an opportunity to allow your mind to create the ideal romantic fantasy that you imagine would bring forth your own sexual and romantic passion. Your mind is powerful. Allow your self to dream, to fantasize, and to imagine the way it could be, if only….

My Romantic Fantasy

You are about to become the director, producer, and leading actor in your own romantic fantasy. Create a cast of characters. Put in as many details as you choose. Place yourself as the leading man or leading woman in your own romantic story. Exaggerate! Think big and beautiful, rich and famous. Celebrate *you* in your own romantic vision. Imagine yourself having and being more than you ever dreamed possible. Not just for the moment; for a lifetime, your lifetime, this lifetime, now. Ask yourself the following questions:

Who is romantically involved with me?

How do I look, feel, behave, and express myself?

What do I experience, receive, or become?

Where do I live, travel, and play?

When do the events happen: daytime, evening, season, and year?

Why have I chosen these people in this romantic fantasy?

How does my romantic vision compare to my current romantic life?

Imagination is the most powerful tool we will ever have in our lives. Nobody can take our imagination away from us -- except -- if **we** allow our own dreams to be denied, suppressed or invalidated. Nothing has ever been achieved without starting in somebody's mind as an idea, a thought, an image or a concept. Imagination has led to every major scientific breakthrough, musical and artistic masterpiece, architectural monument, and even Olympic or World Cup athletic competition.

The lives and physical brains of acknowledged creative geniuses, such as one of the leading scientist of the 20th century, Albert Einstein, have often been examined in the futile attempt to discover a unique physiological reason for such unusual creative ability. Brain researchers have found no physical manifestation of creative genius within the brain, no one location, no unique size or shape or density of brain tissue.

What researchers have discovered about creativity is that it often appears to come as a moment of revelation, a sudden insight, a dream, an image or a symbol. The original idea, the necessary steps to be taken, or the final solution to an ongoing problem have usually not been found by working hard at trying to figure out a solution. It seems to be that we must take the necessary steps to learn what we can learn through our brains and logical abilities. But if we rely solely upon our brains and what appears to be logical in the present moment, we will be unable to create. **Logic and control do not lead to creative solutions.**

We cannot control our imagination but we can allow it to flourish. We can use our imagination to create, first in our mind and eventually in physical reality, the type of love relationships we truly want, not the ones we think we must settle for because of some preconceived idea of who we think we are and what we think is possible.

If we give up our dreams before we allow them to manifest in reality, we lose out on an opportunity to discover our own creative powers. Before attempting to imagine and dream about what we want to manifest, it is important for us to examine our current thoughts. And we need to know what we want. Once we have done the logical thinking and we know what we want, we can sit back, relax, and enjoy the show. We can imagine having it all -- exactly the way we want it to be.

Why Do I Want A Relationship?

Why do you want to have a love relationship?

How do you feel when you are alone and not involved in a love relationship?

What do you hope to experience, to feel, or to have by being romantically involved with another person?

How is a love relationship better than being alone, better than friendship or family?

Is there any other way for you to achieve the same feelings or goals?

No matter how much activity and how many people we use to fill the hours and minutes in our daily life, none of us can escape the ultimate truth. We are, each of us, inescapably alone. We are also, all of us, inescapably connected to each other and to everything around us.

We are born alone. Nobody can be born for us. Even identical twins are born separately. We die alone. Nobody can die for us. Even if others are dying at the exact same moment, each of us will experience our own death.

Since we are ultimately alone, why do we need each other? Why not learn to face our own aloneness now? The answer is simple. We need contact with our environment and with each other to know we are alive, to stay alive, to stimulate our senses, to touch, to heal, and to love and be loved. We require contact with others to know our own self.

People naturally make contact with infants, smiling at them, cooing and googling with contorted faces and sounds, often imitating and mirroring the baby's expressions. Without such contact, infants do not thrive. Foundlings raised in The Crêche, an orphanage in Lebanon in the 1950's, received only minimal sensual stimulation, touch, and human contact. Their intelligence did not develop past an IQ of about 80. However, once Lebanon's laws changed and adoption became legal, infants who were adopted into families before two years of age, were able to re-establish average levels of intelligence. Too little stimulation proved to be equally, or even more, detrimental to emotional and physical development as intense stimulation or actual physical and sexual abuse can be.

Intimacy with another, from infancy onward, allows us to expand all of our senses. We discover sounds, sights, words, images, feelings, and tastes that stimulate us. True intimacy requires sensitivity and kindness. It is not blatant honesty and continual verbal communication. It is not continual, intrusive physical contact. Intimacy allows us a combination of closeness, privacy, and personal space, to think our own thoughts, feel our own feelings, re-establish our own body rhythms, and connect with our own self.

When we are intimate, we are aware of how we affect others and how they affect us. If we are afraid to touch or be touched and our partner grabs us too soon, we may give in, we may even feel pleasure -- for awhile. But sooner or later, as we "come to our senses," reconnect with our own inner self, we will probably pull away to find a safe retreat. Sometimes our body responds and we become physically intimate with another, ignoring the effect upon our emotions. Once the bodily sensations have dissipated, we may be left with confused and painful emotions about having been so physically intimate. This can happen when we become involved sexually with a person we hardly know, when someone that we do know coerces, manipulates, or threatens us into sexual involvement, and even at times within a long term committed love relationship.

With a partner who cares about our feelings, one who allows us the time and space to open up at our own pace, we may gradually begin to reach out to touch and be touched. Together we can tentatively explore more and more sensual and intimate touching.

Problem is often the person who allows us to take our time, to open up slowly, is also a person who is fearful about becoming intimate. If we are not careful, we may retreat from each other and lose the moment, the possibility of a deeper physical and emotional connection.

Ultimately, a close relationship allows us to become more intimate with our own self. Just as nobody else can be born or die for us, each of us must eventually face our own self and do our own inner work. No relationship or loving romantic partner can save us from having to face our own self. They may delay the process, but in the end, we cannot escape the inevitable.

Before we can become intimate with another person, we need to know what we want, what we believe, what we think about our self, about others, and about relationships. Once we are clear about our own thoughts and our true desires, only then can we begin to create what we truly want.

What Do I Believe About Love Relationships?

Sit quietly. Breathe deeply and slowly. Open to a new page in your journal. Make a list of what you believe about relationships. Here are some samples, but you can add many of your own ideas and concepts and beliefs.

Relationships are difficult because....

Men/women always ....

Men/women should ....

If I show how I feel ...

I'm too good, too difficult, too set in my ways, too ....

List all those beliefs that you are aware of now and add to the list over time.

What Do I Expect To Receive From A Love Relationship?

How do you expect your partner to behave with you, with others?

What actions do you expect your partner to take for you?

What gifts and material comforts do you expect your partner to provide for you: emotional, physical, mental, social, financial, and spiritual?

What do you feel and how do you respond when you did not receive what you expect in a relationship?

What determines whether you stay or break off the relationship?

What Do I Expect To Give To A Love Relationship?

How do you expect yourself to behave with your partner, with others?

What actions do you expect to take for your partner?

What gifts and material comforts do you expect to provide for your partner: emotional, physical, mental, social, financial, and spiritual?

What do you expect your partner would feel and respond if you did not give what he or she expects to receive in a relationship?

What determines whether your partner will stay or break off the relationship?

In the early stages of a relationship, many of us give beyond the call of duty. Some of us will appear to be self-less and unconditionally loving, giving and caring. Sometimes both of us are giving more than our share, but in different areas. One of us may pay the bills while the other gives up freedom of choice and independence. Women often give sex in order to receive love. Men often give gifts of love in order to receive sex.

Sex and love are not up for barter in an intimate relationship. The whole point of being intimate is to reveal ourself to others and in that process become intimately connected to our own self. When we are intimate, there is no place for deception and manipulation. Intimacy is a shared, beautiful, heart-warming, expansive connection between two people who care about each other. Why give the most precious jewels we have, the doorway to our soul, for anything less than intimate connection with someone who loves, accepts, and encourages us to be who we are?

Love Is the Essence of Life

Love is the essence of life. Love inspires us and instills us with confidence. Love provides us with honor and strength, ambition and hope, and the promise of fulfilling our dreams. Love is the answer to any question. Love is also the question.

We love another person for what they represent to us -- wealth, sophistication, beauty, intelligence, comfort or recognition. We love another person who seems to embody a quality we think we are lacking and would like to attain. We love someone for a quality we believe we both have in common. We love someone who lacks an important trait as long as we believe, often erroneously, that we can teach, train, discipline or change that quality because of our love.

We feel love for someone who listens and seems to understand us. Sometimes, we feel love when we are rejected, ignored, misunderstood, frustrated and demeaned. At times, we love someone who does all the "right" things for us. At other times, we love a person who seems to do everything "wrong."

No matter what we do, **all of us need love.** We are born to love. All of our actions can be seen as an expression of love, a rejection of love, a cry for love, or even a screaming for love:

- *Why can't you love me?*

- *Why do you have to love me?*

- *How mean can I be, how much can I hurt, reject, and abandon you, yet still know you will love me and not abandon me?*

- *How good an actor do I have to be to win your love?*

It doesn't matter what you do, what you say, or what you feel at any given moment. In the end, all you are is pure love, forever searching to be loved and accepted.

Following the path of love is rarely easy. It is strewn with obstacles and problems. Some of us are easy to love. We look inviting, act friendly, entertain, joke, and touch with gentle abandon. Some of us are distant and aloof, shy and clumsy, arrogant and difficult. Perhaps we keep people at a distance and wonder why we feel alone.

It is usually easy to love someone who pleases us and behaves in a way that we find appropriate. The true test is whether we can maintain our equilibrium and continue loving when the other **does not** offer us what we think we want, need, or desire. The question to ask ourself is: *Can I continue loving when love keeps testing my fortitude, pushing my limits of endurance, dipping the scales of my self-esteem?* Only **you** can decide if you have given your very best love to another. Only you can love. Nobody else can do it for you!

In the following exercise, we are beginning the path toward unconditional love. It starts with the simple yet powerful intention to love. We notice how we are loving or not loving in every moment of our day. And we review our day by recalling how we have loved.

How Will I Love Today?

Beginning this week

- Practice waking up each morning with the question, *How will I love today?*

- Then, in each moment and every activity throughout the day, ask yourself, *Is this love? Is this the most loving I can be --* **to myself** *and to others?*

- As the evening draws to a close, review your day by asking, *How have I loved today? Could I have loved more?*

- Always remember to add: *How have I loved* **myself** *today? Could I have loved myself more?*

Does the thought of waking up intending to love, spending the day engrossed in love, and going to sleep still pondering love, seem impossible? It's only impossible if you believe it is. Why not try it and see what happens?

Loving does not begin out there. The more our focus is outside our own self, expecting to receive love from others, the more we see lots and lots of evidence that most people are unworthy of our limited, narrowly focused small amount of love.

Learn to focus inside, inside your self, inside your own private thoughts and feelings. Notice the way your mind judges your self and others. Notice when your heart refuses to open. It takes great courage to love another as we get to know them better. It takes even greater courage to love our own self as we come face to face with our own shadow: our own fears, insecurities, weaknesses, inadequacies, failings, and flaws.

Love begins as truth. Truthfully, we look inside our own mind. We gradually release and discard old messages, old feelings, old beliefs, and old conditioning. Truth washes away all deceit, all pretense, and eventually all expectation and emotional pain.

What remains, when all else dissolves, is love. Love is behind all emotion. Love is behind all desire. Love is behind all thought. Lack of love is behind all pain. If we delve deep enough inside and continue long enough, we will always reach love.

Why not reach inside now? Discover the love inside just waiting to be expressed.

Have You Given Up On Love?

Have you given up on love? After years of struggling with difficult and painful relationships, many of us feel like giving up. We may come to the conclusion that sex and passion are a hassle and life is calmer, easier and better without the entanglement of attempting to get close to someone else. If we are confused or have given up, we may have some very good reasons.

Most of us are not taught how to love. Many of us do not know how to give love. We may also have difficulty accepting love. And most of us do not know how to sustain love. We may believe that love comes to those who are entitled to it, those who are young, beautiful, clever, rich, successful, with special abilities, or just born lucky. We may believe we have not yet met the right person. We may believe we were raised in a hopelessly dysfunctional family and because of that we have an inexcusable, reprehensible, and unchangeable personality flaw.

No matter what we believe, somebody out there is waiting to love us. All we need to do is let go of our preconceived ideas and open our heart to love. If we have even the smallest desire to be close to another person, it is vital for us to examine our own patterns: what we think, what we say, and how we respond to others. Emotional, physical, spiritual and sexual reawakening is about discovering the hidden potential in our life and in our relationships, eliminating whatever interferes with our capacity for intimate connection.

Touch, love and intimacy are basic human needs, as necessary as the food we eat and the air we breathe. These should be natural and easy components of our intimate relationships. But for many of us, touch is something to be avoided, love is scary, and intimacy is impossible. Sometimes we are involved with a partner who is fearful of intimate touching. Sometimes, we are the one with touch aversion. Sometimes we have a partner who oversteps our boundaries, ignores our requests for intimate touching, or is unable to let us freely be our self in their presence.

Sometimes, we are with a partner who is verbally demeaning or physically abusive. With a partner whose ability to love is stifled, blocked or mixed with abandonment, hatred and abuse, we are unable to thrive. We begin to close down our natural intuitive and creative abilities. We learn to doubt our own feelings, live with anger, frustration and even rage, and ignore what we want most in our life.

Eventually, we may rebel and begin to develop a sense of strength, resolve and determination to take care of ourself. When we are seriously ready to leave, this difficult partner's sweet, loving, tender side may reappear. Whatever our partner has been witholding, he or she may lavish upon us with flamboyant exaggeration. Suddenly we receive those flowers, that anniversary gift, a home cooked meal, or a night of tender sex that we have been requesting for a long time. But once we are back in the relationship, the patterns that created our desire to leave will probably return.

If you currently feel stuck in an emotionally painful relationship that you are unable to leave, you are not alone. The emotional web of intimate relating is often complex. Many of us feel guilty, ashamed, and even humiliated when we find we are confused and unable to make a firm decision. There is no shame in being confused about love. Whatever you avoid confronting will probably continue to plague you. There is nothing in your life you cannot face. Begin to face your life now. Deal with the fears and problems now. Your future life is created by the thoughts and beliefs you develop and the steps you take now.

The Way Out

If you've been struggling with an emotionally difficult relationship, perhaps for years and years, don't despair. **There is a way out!** Begin by taking an objective look at your current relationship situation.

- *Are your needs, desires and dreams being satisfied?*
- *Are you expecting too much or too little from your partner?*
- *Is your partner showing a willingness to meet you halfway?*
- *What could you do together to improve the situation?*

- *Is your sexual relationship the glue that is holding together an otherwise impossible situation?*
- *Is your lack of pleasurable sex together destroying an otherwise good relationship?*

Remember the following four statements about your relationship:

- **I cannot willfully change my partner to be the way I expect.**
- **I cannot control my partner's attitudes, behaviors or responses.**
- **I CAN offer my love without demanding an expected response.**
- **And most of all, I can always LOVE MYSELF.**

LOVE YOURSELF, LOVE YOURSELF, LOVE YOURSELF!

Now, love your partner in a way that allows you to continue loving yourself. Allow the relationship to take its natural course. Reread the above section as often as you like.

DON'T PASS THE ABUSE TEST

This is one test you want to fail, you need to fail. Don't be a winner at the expense of your heart, your self-esteem, and your well-being. Don't be a winner at the expense of your partner's heart, your partner's self-esteem, and your partner's well-being. For each of the following situations, ask yourself:

- *Is this an abusive pattern or was one of us momentarily self-absorbed and accidentally disregarding the other's needs?*
- *How do each of us typically respond?*
- *Do I see any similar patterns in my other intimate, social, or professional relationships currently or in the past?*

RED FLAGS OF ABUSE

- You or your partner regularly arrives very late for appointments with a lame excuse.
- You or your partner cancels plans at the last minute, or forgets and doesn't show up.
- You or your partner's requests and feelings are often ignored.
- You or your partner spends more time with others than alone together.

Copyright © 2009, Revised 2023   *Love Me, Touch Me, Heal Me*   DrEricaGoodstone.com

- You or your partner expresses their own views and interrupts when the other speaks.

- You or your partner flirts with others and labels the other "insecure" or "crazy" if they get upset.

- You or your partner calls when to get some need met -- money, a sympathetic ear -- but has little time to call when the other person expressed a need.

- You or your partner seeks the other's professional expertise -- legal, accounting, counseling, fitness training -- for free.

- You or your partner seems sensitive and caring, but criticizes or attacks when the other is most vulnerable.

These and other similar behaviors are red flags of abuse. Abusive attitudes and behaviors do not magically disappear. If you are currently involved in an abusive relationship, be reassured. You are not alone. You have lots of company. Many of us have been there. In fact, many of us are there right now. Sometimes the abuse goes back and forth. Sometimes it is only one-sided. The red flag is the way you feel whether you remain in a calm and loving state together or if you are both riding an emotional roller coaster.

What Is Sexual Abuse?

You may be one of the lucky people who have never had to deal with physical or sexual abuse. Statistics indicate, however, that as many as one in four women and one in seven men have been sexually abused at some time in their lives. And that is only the number of reported cases.

Sexual abuse comes in many forms. Blatant physical sexual assault is fairly easy to identity and even confront. There's a more subtle form of abuse, often difficult to recognize and label as abuse. One type is physical stimulation that is too intense for the individual's system, such as inappropriate touch and persistent tickling. Visual stimulation can be equally overwhelming, especially for a prepubescent child. For example, a boy is asked to hook up his mother's brassiere, a young girl shares a bath with her naked father, a fully clothed nanny touches a naked child in a sensual way, or a pre-adolescent boy follows his mother into the ladies' locker room, where adult women are coming out of the shower naked.

A form of sexual abuse that is rarely talked about is a subtle form of sensual and emotional manipulation. This is often behavior that is emotionally beneficial to an adult or parent without regard for the potential effect upon the child. A woman who is frustrated in her marriage and makes derogatory comments about men, may affect her son's ability to accept himself as a man. A girl whose father really wanted a son may literally become the "man" her father always wanted. A girl may become "daddy's girl," a substitute for the wife her daddy is not intimate with. A boy may play the role of husband to a sexually or emotionally unfulfilled mother.

Abuse can also happen verbally. Teasing, suppressing, denying and invalidating another person's appearance, thoughts and emotions can lead to lifelong emotional insecurity that affects the potential for intimate relating. Older brothers and sisters can sometimes traumatize their younger siblings without the parents awareness or protection.

Have you been sexually abused in a subtle or not so subtle way? Go back in time, and attempt to recall the physical, emotional, visual and verbal messages you received.

- *What examples did your relatives and teachers present to you?*
- *Did people in authority allow you to express yourself or be yourself?*

The first step to uncovering and then undoing childhood abuse, no matter how small and insignificant or devastating and overwhelming, is to take an honest look at what actually happened, what you experienced, what you believe about yourself and others as a result, and the long-term effects in your current life.

If you feel that some of your early experiences are now interfering with your current relationships, why not seek professional help? Our feelings and memories are stored within our body cells. Body oriented and somatic psychotherapy can help us to uncover suppressed emotions and understand what interferes with our ability to enjoy pleasurable and intimate love in our close relationships. Seek help from a qualified therapist in your own community. Contact the U.S. Association for Body Psychotherapy, the American Counseling Association, the American Psychological Association, a local mental health clinic or rape crisis center, a local domestic violence hotline, or another reputable national organization. Most organizations have web sites that offer a referral service and list detailed qualifications of affiliated therapists. Check the appendix of this book for more detailed information.

Don't Rescue Anyone

Many of us are not in an abusive relationship, but have fallen into a different kind of relationship trap. Are you a helper and savior who has fallen in love with a lost soul, someone who needs your help, who might not make it without you? The power to rescue another human being is a great aphrodisiac. Many of us have tried. Very few of us succeed. The prognosis is quite poor.

Needy people who claim they cannot function without our help usually would benefit from professional counseling. Even if in our profession we are a therapist, in our own personal love life, it is doubtful that we can cure or save another adult: a child perhaps, an adult, no.

By the time a man or woman is past their teens, their personality and character traits are well formed. Work habits, attitudes toward life, and approach toward achieving success are, for the most part, already determined. Will they succeed or won't they? Take a look at their track record. Observe their present condition. Talk to their friends and relatives. Pay attention to the words they say and the actions they take. Are they grounded in reality or creating unrealistic castles in the sky, someday in the future?

- *What's going on right now?*

- *Is this person planning for the future or expecting you to be the rock, the savior, and the escape valve?*

- *Does this person take personal responsibility or blame others for most problems?*

- *Does this person threaten self mutilation, suicide, or the intent to harm someone else, maybe you?*

Nobody can protect another adult around the clock. Do not keep these problems a secret. Inform someone close to you. Seek professional help and personal protection.

Not quite ready to give up on a difficult relationship? Still believe your partner has potential that has not yet been realized? Then give yourself a time period. Check back in six months. Check again in one year. Give yourself regular checkpoints. Take another look at yourself and your partner. It may be time to give up a losing battle.

Love doesn't have to be difficult or painful. Love can be a healing, joyful and blissful partnership.

Getting Free

Sit quietly for awhile. Allow your mind to focus on your most significant relationship, past or present. If you like, you may repeat this exercise for different relationships. In your journal make two lists:

What I Have Given to the Relationship -- What I Have Received From the Relationship

When you have completed both lists, ask yourself the following questions:

- *How do I feel about myself in this relationship?*
- *How do I feel about my partner?*
- *What would have to happen for me to leave?*
- *What would have to happen for me to stay?*

Do you feel nurtured, pampered, special, honored, and respected? Then stay and languish in the pleasure. However, if you feel unhappy, frustrated, neglected, and insecure, it may be time to make some changes. Talk to someone who understands and can help. Attend codependency anonymous meetings. Sign up for a local lecture or course about relationships. See a professional psychotherapist, body oriented or somatic psychotherapist. Seek spiritual counseling from a local minister, rabbi or priest.

If you decide to stay, your relationship will not flourish if you are holding on to painful memories and explosive feelings. Body therapies can help your body to release the tensions that hold your emotions locked inside. Body psychotherapy can help you to uncover the deeper meanings in your own life.

Once you have truly acknowledged, experienced and released the painful emotions that have kept you stuck, you may finally be ready to forgive. Without forgiveness, we remain a victim of our feelings and maintain the sense of being less than whole. Forgiveness frees us to openly enjoy our life again.

We cannot **pretend** to forgive. If you are not ready to forgive, that's okay. Just admit the truth. Hold on to your anger, rage or sadness for as long as you need. When you are finally ready, six months or two years from now, you can return to this page and begin the forgiveness process. You will not regret it. In fact, after years of suffering, forgiveness can give you some closure and a sense of relief. After you have forgiven others, and most importantly, forgiven your self, you may finally be ready to create intimacy in your relationships.

Forgiveness

Can you honestly forgive your partner for the ways he or she has hurt or disappointed you?

List the ways your partner has hurt, disappointed, discounted or betrayed you?

Explain some possible reasons why this happened?

Describe what it will take for you to forgive your partner and for your partner to forgive him or her self.

Can you honestly forgive your self for the ways you have hurt or disappointed your partner?

List the ways you have hurt, disappoint, discounted or betrayed your partner?

Explain some possible reasons why this happened?

Describe what it will take for your partner to forgive you and for you to forgive your self.

Being Love

"Being love," a term coined by humanistic psychologist Abraham Maslow, is more important than merely showing and expressing love. Being love is being who you are. Being love is allowing the other to see you in all your shades of color, from beautiful tender pink to insecure, jealous green, to dark gray and even nasty black. Being love is also looking clearly at the other person, observing all their shades of emotion, feeling and expression.

What would it be like for you to experience **BEING LOVE** for one day, for one hour? Imagine freely saying what you feel, without needing to be right, good, bad, appropriate, or accepted?

Imagine your partner "being" love. Imagine seeing the full range of beauty and darkness inside your lover's mind and heart. Each of us holds within us thoughts and feelings, like barely perceptible but always threatening to destroy the moment, clouds. What would happen if, just for a few brief moments, we allowed our love, our being, to pour forth unhampered?

We often try to control another person by suppressing and inhibiting their natural way of being. Imagine allowing each other to "be love", free from the every day restrictions that keep us tied to half-truths and superficial images. Imagine allowing another the freedom to be fully him or her self, knowing they may say and do things that you would prefer not to hear or experience, knowing they may disappoint or even dishonor you. Imagine remaining internally confident, knowing who you are, no matter what the other person says or does. Imagine two people "being" love together in an intimate and sexual relationship. Imagine the physical, emotional and spiritual passion that could come forth. Sex would never be the same again. Would there be a need for any other?

Love Changes Everything

Love has a mind all its own. When hit by the "bug", the "victim" may appear to have suddenly gone insane. A woman with very high standards of etiquette may find herself paying for her man's dinners and even loaning him money. A man who has been a "stud" for years may find himself crooning over a woman who barely allows him to touch her. A sophisticated, successful married man may become involved with a stripper or call girl from a lower class and a different race.

How do you know if you're in love? One clue is that your logical, reasonable mind tells you to do one thing and your heart leads you on another path. Your mind tells you: "Danger. This relationship is not safe because ...." But, whenever Mr. or Miss Danger calls, your former resolve melts and you go running to be with this person.

Is it worth pursuing love at all costs? For many people it is. Sometimes the path ahead is laden with pain and eventual loss. But taking the safer route, avoiding passion to select a logical, compatible partner, is not always the best choice. For some of us this may eventually lead to a sense of isolation, loneliness, even despair. At some point, we may betray our compatible partner to be with someone else who does inspire passion, and, of course, is not "safe".

If you are in a quandary, loving someone "not appropriate" but wanting someone "safe" to spend your life with, there **is** a solution. Speak to a professional about your confusion, someone who can provide counseling and give you a broader perspective. But talk therapy alone may not be the solution. The confusion, turmoil and indecision may result from memories, feelings and emotions that remain locked inside your body. **Touch therapy and body psychotherapy** may assist you to unlock the mystery of your own mind. Only when you have examined your own thought processes and connected with your own innermost feelings, can you begin to choose how you want to live your life and with whom.

The Basic Decision To Love

For most intimate relationships, there is one basic decision, **Do I want to be with this person or would I rather leave to find someone else?** Ask yourself the following questions. Answer as truthfully as you possibly can.

- Would I prefer to leave but I'm afraid of losing the security, money, or friendship of this person?

- Do I really want to stay but I'm afraid of admitting something -- I don't plan to finish graduate school, write that novel, make a million dollars, or have a baby?

- Am I afraid of revealing some deep, dark personal secret?

- Would I rather run away than take the chance of revealing myself and becoming close to someone who seems to care?

If your true desire is to leave, to run for your life, to find your own center, then find support to face the truth, plan your exit -- and -- **walk out the door!**

Do you want to stay? Do you really love this person? Do you feel passion and truly believe your life is better together than apart? Have you eliminated the red flags of abuse? Are you no longer seeking to rescue or be rescued by anyone? Then, begin to examine your motives, attitudes, expectations, and behaviors. Search for the underlying goodness of your partner. Find out how you can make your relationship work. Then don't worry what anybody else thinks or tells you is right or wrong. Do what you feel in your own heart is true for you. Do whatever it takes for both of your to feel the joy that is possible in a truly loving relationship.

What Is Intimacy?

Intimacy is being willing to tell your truth, moment to moment. Intimacy is also being willing to listen and to hear your intimate companions' truth, moment to moment, even when you are hearing things you would rather not know.

What does it take to create long-lasting, satisfying love? Long-time married couples would probably answer: "Hard work!" Newlyweds might say: "Passionate sex!" Others might add, "Money, financial security, a good home, vacations...."

How do we create long-lasting intimacy in our life within our current relationships? We begin by facing our self, admitting what we truly feel, want, desire and need. Depending upon our personality and lifestyle, we may choose talk therapy, body psychotherapy or self-help peer groups. It is never too late to learn to love and accept our self. It is never too late to love and accept others. Why not begin now? Learning to love takes time. How much longer do you want to wait for love?

Creating Intimacy

This exercise is designed for couples. If you are alone, sit facing yourself in the mirror, as if the person you see is your partner. Set aside a definite block of time, at least one hour per week, for one month.

Begin each session by placing your chairs face to face and closing your eyes. Breathe quietly, slowly, deeply and rhythmically. Open your eyes and gaze softly into your partner's eyes. Observe the subtle colors and movements. Smile openly. Gradually, allow your breathing to synchronize with your partner's breaths. Take turns asking each other the following questions. When it is your turn to respond, please answer as truthfully and kindly as you can.

- *Is there anything bothering you about me, our relationship, or your own personal life right now?*
- *Is there anything you would like me to change right now?*
- *What are you willing to change right now?*
- *What are you willing to accept or overlook right now?*
- *Is there anything you want to tell me or discuss with me right now?*

After the first person has responded to all the questions, the one who asked the questions should say, **"Thank you for sharing your truth with me."**

When both have responded to all the questions, smile, kiss and give each other a warm, tender, loving hug that lasts at least one minute.

Now, sit facing each other, continually gazing into each other's eyes.

For two minutes, take turns saying back and forth,

> "Every moment we are together, I am discovering who you are."

Then, one person keep repeating the following words, for two minutes, gently and lovingly touching different body parts on your partner each time.

Insert your name or your partner's name where appropriate.

> "<u>Carol</u>, you're a beautiful, sexy, powerful woman."
>
> Or "<u>Sam</u>, you're a handsome, sexy, powerful man."

Each time, the listener responds by touching the partner gently and saying,

> "Yes, I'm a beautiful, sexy, powerful woman"
>
> Or "Yes, I'm a handsome, sexy, powerful man."

Finally, hold hands and gaze into each other's eyes.

> The first person says, **"In my heart, I am sharing my love with you."**
>
> The second person responds, **"In my heart, I am receiving your love."**
>
> The second person says, **"In my heart, I am sharing my love with you."**

Copyright © 2009, Revised 2023   *Love Me, Touch Me, Heal Me*   DrEricaGoodstone.com

The first person responds, **"In my heart, I am receiving your love."** Remember to breathe together as you gaze into each other's eyes.

Finish with a long kiss, an even longer hug, perhaps offering each other some massage and telling each other sweet nothings that you have both been longing to hear.

If these exercises don't stimulate or rekindle your love, perhaps it is time to say goodbye or maybe it is not too late for couples' therapist or marriage counselor to help. If not, if you are married and contemplating divorce, seeing a divorce mediator or divorce lawyer may be the next step. The choice is yours. How do you want to live your life:

- In anger, despair, confusion, and loneliness?
- In love, emotional closeness, pleasure and joy?

Lover's Bill Of Rights

Create your own Lover's Bill of Rights.

- *What do you believe are your rights as a lover?*
- *How do you want and expect your lover to behave?*
- *What do you believe are your lover's rights?*
- *How do you believe your lover wants and expects you to behave?*

It's The Little Things That Count

What do you focus on in selecting an intimate partner or lifetime mate? Many of us seek a partner who we believe will make our life easy, provide for us, pay our bills, and offer us gifts. For some of us, an exciting sexual relationship or an attractive partner we are proud to be seen with, is enough. For others a satisfying relationship is with a partner who builds and repairs things, a partner who cooks and cleans, someone who listens to our problems, plays with us when we're happy, or someone who hugs us when we are sad.

For most of us, some combination of all of the above, plus more, is what it takes to create and remain in a relationship. A popular song in the 1950's summed it up in the title: **Little Things Mean a Lot.** Each of us has those "little things" that may mean more to us than money, power, good looks, or sex. Choose a partner who naturally and easily does those little things. Sometimes a reluctant partner can learn, but more often, those little things become a sticking point as we spend extended periods of time with our partner.

Tell the truth to yourself. Do you have the patience to teach and persuade your partner to provide those little things for you? Or are you the no nonsense, quick fix type, who would rather switch than fight? Know yourself and decide. The choice is yours. Choose carefully. Your choice may remain with you for a lifetime!

It is an awesome responsibility to love another. Just as an infant depends on its caretaker for love, feeding and mirroring, when we fall in love as an adult, we become like an infant. In loving another, we allow our self to be emotionally affected. Our partner's words, actions, even thoughts, have the power to hurt us or uplift us, to make us angry, confused, sad or elated. Most of us do not even fathom the power we have to affect those we love. Isn't it time **you** learned to use your power wisely, with compassion and kindness for yourself and for others?

FOOTNOTES

Chapter 1

1. Ornish, Dean, M.D. (1997). *Love and Survival: The Scientific Basis for the Healing Power of Intimacy.* New York: HarperCollins Publishers.
2. Schnarch, Ph.D. (1997). *Passionate Marriage: Sex, Love and Intimacy in Emotionally Committed Relationships.* New York: W.W. Norton & Company, Inc.
3. Mahler, Margaret S., M.D., Pine, Fred, Bergman, Anni. (1975). *The Psychological Birth of the Human Infant: Symbiosis and Individuation.* New York. Basic Books, Inc.

Chapter 3

1. Wayne, Dennis (1973). *Children of the Creche.* New York. Appleton-Century-Crofts.

CONGRATULATIONS!

By finishing *LOVE ME…PLEASE*, **Part I** in the *LOVE ME, TOUCH ME, HEAL ME* **Complete Book,** you have completed some powerful, life-transforming exercises. You have self-reflected and contemplated what you have and what you want in your life. And – you have revealed to yourself how you want to love and be loved. In this book you have gained an intimate knowledge of your own self – the ways you think, feel, behave, respond and influence the thoughts, behaviors and responses of others.

TOUCH ME ... PLEASE

Part II in the *LOVE ME, TOUCH ME, HEAL ME*

Complete Book

THE PATH TO

* **PHYSICAL**
* **EMOTIONAL**
* **SEXUAL**
* **SPIRITUAL**

REAWAKENING

Dr. Erica Goodstone

Touch Me … Please, **Part II, is dedicated to:**

- My teacher and mentor, Ilana Rubenfeld, whose gentle yet powerful training which combined talk with touch, The Rubenfeld Synergy Method, set the course for my life's work.
- Dr. Seena Russell, for mentoring me in both Rubenfeld Synergy and spiritual centeredness
- Waturo Oshashi, who taught me the meaning and depth of shiatsu meridians, energy, physical and emotional anatomy and healing
- Dr. John Upledger, for teaching me that only 5 ounces of touch can be more powerful and curative than any amount of deep and painful pressure
- Dr. John Beaulieu, for mentoring and guiding me in the use of sound, vibration, color, observation, Eriksonian hypnosis, and Dr. Randolph Stone's comprehensively holistic Polarity Therapy Method
- Dr. Tiffany Field, for creating a massive amount of research revealing and corroborating the healing potential of massage and body therapies
- Dr. Candace Pert, for her ground breaking research about the way neurotransmitters spread throughout the body, in her book, *Molecules of Emotion*

TOUCH ME ... PLEASE

INTRODUCTION

Touch me … please

I want to know you

Touch me … please

I don't know how

Touch me … please

We'll know each other

Touch me … please.

Your Body Believes You

Your body listens to every thought you have and every word you speak. And your body believes you. Your body speaks to you in body messages: sensations, pleasant and unpleasant, injuries, discomforts, aches and pains, and illnesses.

Other people recognize and respond to your body messages. You cannot hide who you are because every minute movement, expression and nuance is perceptible to anyone who sees you, regardless of whether they consciously know what they are seeing.

Whether you realize it or not, your five physical senses and your sixth intuitive sense are continually being stimulated by everyone and everything in your environment and beyond. You are literally touching and being touched by everyone and everything. The choice is actually very simple – to touch and be touched with conscious intention or unconsciously, with mindless lack of awareness.

Touch Me … Please, the second book in the ***Love Me, Touch Me*, *Heal Me*** Series, leads us on a path toward conscious, intentional touching … truly touching the heart and soul and spirit of everyone and everything, with all of our senses. Touch is the ultimate tool of intimacy, a no nonsense way of becoming close to another being. Touch is gentle, powerful, healing, all-knowing, deep, and reaches beyond any time, space or human concepts of boundaries. Touch allows us to overcome all obstacles and heal from whatever ails us. But the way most of us touch others and allow others to touch us, is often limited by our mental condition and personal beliefs. Touch is generous, magnanimous and offered freely to all who are receptive and in need. Touch is not for personal benefit, personal satisfaction, or personal gain. Touch is for interpersonal sharing, communication, intimate connection, love and healing.

Part Two is meant for people who touch, people who want to touch, people who want to be touched and people who want to touch again. You will have to explore your own bodily sensations, needs, cravings, desires and pleasures. You will also need to examine your personal thoughts, beliefs, attitudes, memories and dreams – to find the healing and loving touch, the most profoundly sensational touch, touch that you can bring into all aspects of your life. And you will be reminded, over and over, to bring that touch back to your own self so that you can fully share your healing and loving touch with your own self and with others.

****

TOUCH ME ... PLEASE

*"The very strength that protects the heart from injury
is the strength that prevents the heart from enlarging
to its intended greatness within."*

The Treasured Writings of Kahlil Gibran, Castle Books, P. 236

Touch connects us to the world. Touch teaches. Touch heals. Sometimes touch hurts. Touch is powerfully intimate. Through touching and being touched, we feel. When we are touched with love, respect and gentle caring, our heart becomes open and receptive to love.

Through loving touch, we feel accepted, acknowledged, understood and loved. In Part II we look at our body and our senses, especially our sense of touch. We examine what we believe about touch, how we have touched and been touched, how we expect to be touched, and how we can create loving touch in our life. Here we are introduced to the various body therapies available that can help us to release whatever blocks us from the enjoyment of love, pleasure and health in our life.

TOUCH ME ... PLEASE

Touch Me ... Please

Touch me ...please
Reach inside
My mind
Turn the knob
To open the safe
Learn
The secret combination
To unleash
My inner truth

I will share myself
With you
Be patient
Be kind
Wait awhile
Discover
The subtle ways
I hide from you

We can be together
Right now
Giving love
Being love
Joyous
Happy
Let us
Open the door
To each other's hearts

Copyright © 2009, Revised 2023   *Love Me, Touch Me, Heal Me*   DrEricaGoodstone.com

Touch me
Feel my heart beat
See soft colors
Surrounding me
Love me
Love you
We are one
Our energies connect
We feel
We're alive
We're free

Touch me ... please

Copyright © 8/21/97 Erica Goodstone, Ph.D.

TOUCH ME ... PLEASE

CHAPTER 1

YOUR BODY BELIEVES YOU

Your Body Believes You

Your body believes you

Tell it what you want it to hear

Your body speaks the truth

Listen to its wisdom

Your body is your temple

Honor it

Sanctify it

Love it

You and your body are one

Treat it as your beloved companion

It is yours for life.

Copyright © Erica Goodstone, Ph.D. 01/29/00

Listen to Your Body

Your body listens to every thought you have, every word you speak. And your body believes you. Your body speaks to you in body messages: sensations, pleasant and unpleasant, injuries, discomforts, aches and pains, and illnesses.

Pay attention! Listen to the subtle messages your body offers you, moment to moment. Ignore these body messages (a knot in your stomach, a stubbed toe, an ache in your neck or shoulders) and the signals may intensify (full blown indigestion, a broken toe, whiplash, shoulder injury).

Your body sends us messages all the time. Physical symptoms are often a warning from your subconscious, reminding you to pay attention to your body or to some person, situation or life event.

- "Watch it! My heart is hurting from that person's remarks."
- "Look at that! I really can't stomach my work."
- "I have no support. My back is up against the wall."

Disease is not an external thing that happens to you. Disease is not a noun: "I **have** a cold, I **have** a cancer." Disease is a verb, an action, a happening, an allowing of something foreign to grow and develop, sometimes even with your own consent.

- "I am tensing my head, neck, back and allowing pain signals to intensify."
- "I am constricting my blood vessels, my nerves, my breathing."
- "I am straining my heart, my liver, my kidneys, my intestines."
- "I am supporting the growth of cancer cells in my body."

Research with patients who display dissociative identity disorder, formerly called multiple personality disorder, have verified the power of our mind in our own illness. One personality could have all the symptoms of a disease, such as diabetes or skin rashes, while once another personality emerged, the doctors found absolutely no signs of that same illness, through blood tests and medical workups, in the very same person's body. Disease is a messenger from your body/mind system. It is your body's attempt to heal itself by correcting imbalances and restoring harmony. A cold eliminates excess mucus. Almost like tears, it is your body's way of crying when life gets us down. A tumor or cyst is the body's attempt to encapsulate cells gone haywire.

When decoding the meaning behind a physical symptom in your body, always search for the physical causes first. Sometimes the cause is hereditary, genetic. Sometimes an injury is just that, an injury, or an infectious disease is just that, an infectious disease. After examining and exhausting the possible physical causes, then begin to look for possible emotional causes, beliefs and meanings in your own life. Examine your words, your verbal communication with and about your body.

Your body speaks your mind.

- Is something in your life eating away at you?
- Is something lying heavy in your gut?
- Are you unable to digest the meaning of an experience?

Use your words, your speech as a guide to your own unconscious. Pay attention to the words you use to describe you life and the sensations and symptoms in your body. Your underlying beliefs will become clear. And you may be amazed. Your words may match a symptom exactly. A highly regarded teacher of this unique Korean mind-body-spiritual method called Chun-Do-Sun-Bup, appeared one day using crutches. When I asked her how she had broken her leg, she replied: "I kept on saying, I lost my footing in America." Those were not just idle words. Her body actually responded to the way she was feeling.

Every thought and every emotion we have alters our immune system. Dr. Candace Pert, in her groundbreaking book, *Molecules of Emotion,* revealed that neurotransmitters travel fast throughout our body, into all of our body cells, not just in our brains, and are affected by our thoughts and emotions. It's not just the stressors in our life but how we interpret them and feel about them that creates our illnesses. Dr. Steven Locke of Harvard University Medical School found that natural killer cell activity is diminished, not by severe changes or stressors in healthy human volunteers, but by people's interpretations of the stress and whether they have a sense of being able to control or deal with it.

Your body speaks its mind. Illness often results from negative and ineffective communication between you and your body. Healing often happens when we develop effective conversation, a healing conversation. What are some of the conversations you have had with your own body recently, or on a regular basis?

- "He's making me sick." – stomachache
- "I can't stand it anymore." - leg or back problems
- "I wish I'd kept my big mouth shut" or "Nobody listens to me." - loss of voice
- "I can't listen to people's problems anymore" - hearing loss
- "I have to get out of here." - knee problems
- "I've lost my footing, my grounding" - broken foot or toe
- "Too many conflicting thoughts" - migraine headache
- "I can't take the steps I need to take in my life" - multiple schlerosis
- "That makes my blood boil." high blood pressure

Let Your Precious Body Speak To You

Sit quietly, in a comfortable position.

Place both of your feet securely on the ground.

Close your eyes and take an easy, slow, soft, deep breath.

Allow your mind to focus on your body.

Listen for those body signals that are loud and clear.

What do you notice first?

What part of your body is calling for your attention right now?

If more than one body part wants attention, **choose one part now.**

You may repeat this exercise again for other parts.

If this body part had a mind and a voice, what would it tell you about your life, your relationships, or your self?

Is something or someone causing you to feel pain, anger, frustration or some other upsetting emotion?

Sit quietly and breathe deeply.

> **If the answer is "No."**
>
> Appreciate any good feelings you may have.
>
> Appreciate your body as your temple, your home.

If the answer is "Yes."

Ask yourself the following questions.

Allow the answers to come to you.

Just listen to the answers you receive without judging or censoring.

What has happened that you have allowed this person or situation to disturb you?

Is there something you've been trying that you've been unable to do?

What do you need to learn, change, practice, experience or study?

Imagine your body is your precious newborn baby.

Would you continually ignore your baby's cries for attention, food, or comfort?

Would you let your baby scream until he or she totally shut down?

Would you make your baby keep moving without any rest?

Would you deliberately deprive your baby of food and nourishment?

Listen to the message your body is sending you right now.

Stay quiet.

Reassure your body that you are indeed paying attention.

Imagine gently rocking and hugging your whole body.

Talk to Your Body

Talk to your body, either aloud or silently in your mind.

Ask your body what it wants and needs right now.

Talk to the parts that are injured, ill or hurting.

Discover what you can do to soothe yourself.

Talk to the parts that are old or no longer attractive.

Send them your unconditional love and acceptance.

Talk to your organs or body parts that are missing.

Send them your love, thank them for having served you in the past, and say goodbye to them now.

Talk to the tumors, cysts, cancers and other growths that have been removed.

Forgive them for any pain or problems they caused, thank them for what they have taught you, send them love, and say goodbye.

Talk to any unwanted cell growth on your body now.

Ask why the cells are growing and what lesson they might provide for you.

If you have had any miscarriages or abortions, talk to those unborn fetuses now.

Ask for their forgiveness, or say whatever you need to say, send them your love and say goodbye.

Copyright © 2009, Revised 2023   *Love Me, Touch Me, Heal Me*   DrEricaGoodstone.com

If your body has been abused, physically or sexually, by someone else, give your body the love, compassion, understanding and acceptance it has been craving.

If you have abused your body or have allowed it to be abused, physically or sexually, forgive yourself and give your body the caring love that it so desperately needs.

Is there anything else you want to tell your body now?

Promise to be kind to your body in thoughts and words and actions.

Love Your Body

Love your body just the way it is!

Forgive your body for any changes, flaws, blemishes, weight changes, or other problems.

Love your body for its ability to adapt as it ages.

Love your body's size and shape.

Love the color and texture of your skin, hair and nails.

Love your fat, your scars, your freckles, your brown spots, your white spots, your purple scars and any other blatant damages.

Love all your organs, especially the troublesome ones.

Love all your organs or body parts that have been removed.

Love your wrinkles and frown lines that give your face expression.

Love your aches and pains for reminding you to pay attention.

Love your thinning hair, your bald spots, your saggy skin, pot belly, and cellulite.

Love your blemishes, burns, infections, and even rashes.

These are all reminders that you are alive, that your immune system is still working.

Once you have passed on, your body will no longer feel pain, there will be no more wrinkles, blemishes and other growths. There will no longer be a body.

Love your body

Love your body

Love your body

It is the only one you have

Your body is the temple for your soul

Love it

Honor it

Appreciate it

Be amazed by its intricate detail and magnificent coordination

Allow your body to heal

IN A MOMENT YOU WILL BE ASKED TO TOUCH YOUR BODY.

This simple gesture can have a profound and lasting effect. For some of you this may be a new, and even scary, experience. Honor yourself. Don't push. If anything you're asked to do doesn't feel right or safe for you, **STOP THE EXERCISE IMMEDIATELY!** Put a sticker on this page, reminding yourself to return to this exercise at some future time.

Touch and Soothe Your Precious Body

Imagine your body is your precious newborn baby.

Send the following loving thoughts to your body.

"I love you. I will soothe and take care of you from now on."

Allow one hand to gently touch and soothe your body, part by part.

Now let your other hand gently glide all over your body.

Notice which body parts you touch, don't touch or tentatively touch.

Notice any differences in sensation, feelings and thoughts when your body is touched by your right hand or your left hand.

Gently rub and soothe and rock your body, thinking how much you love it.

Notice how your body feels right now.

Your body reveals to you the mystery of life. Your body warns you of impending danger through fear, pain and automatic fight or flight responses. Your body impels you to connect with other humans through our thoughts, hearts and hands. Most of us search endlessly for pleasurable sensations, love and physical contact. Some of us have learned to fear pleasure, deny love, and avoid human contact. Within every cell, our body retains memories of all the sensations, thoughts and emotions we have experienced in this lifetime and perhaps even before.

At times we treat our body as if it is not part of us. For a moment of pleasure or purposely to dull our conflicted and stressed out mind, we may eat, drink, inhale or inject substances that over-stimulate, suppress, or clog up our bodily systems. We often push our self to keep going when our body is begging for rest. We ignore our aching muscles and continue working or playing sports until injury strikes. Most of us would never consider putting the wrong type of gasoline in our automobile or an inferior brand of detergent in our washing machine. Why then, do we so often neglect to give our own body the food, rest and love that we know will enhance our health?

Health is no longer a mystery. We now know a lot about attaining and maintaining good health. Containing all of our organs, our body represents us to the world. How we love and nurture our body determines who we ultimately become.

Food Is The Fuel of Life

Food is the fuel of life. Without adequate nutrients, our mind is unfocused, we become fidgety, irritable, and tired. Without good enough nutrition, we are not able to function at an optimal level. It's that simple. It is well-documented that we need carbohydrates for quick energy, fat for more sustained energy, protein to build and repair tissues, vitamins, minerals, trace elements and water to maintain a healthy immune system.

Knowing the essential value of food, why do we often choose to not nourish our body? Why do we crave unhealthy foods and over-indulge in foods that may otherwise be good for us? Why are so many of us addicted to drugs, cigarettes, alcohol, caffeine or sugar? We know the dangers of continuing our habits: depleting our vitamins and minerals, decreasing our breathing capacity, interfering with our brain functioning, and lowering our immune system. What is it that prevents many of us from choosing an optimal balance of healthy foods to sustain our body?

Your Favorite Food

Open to a new page in your journal and write the words at the top: My Favorite Foods.

List your 10 favorite foods.

What is it about these foods that you like (color, taste, texture, fragrance, memories evoked, or the way you feel during or after eating)?

What emotions do you feel before, while eating, and after eating your favorite foods?

List your 10 least favorite foods.

What is it about these foods that you dislike (color, taste, texture, fragrance, memories evoked, or the way you feel during or after eating)?

What emotions do you feel before, while eating, and after eating your least favorite foods?

Eating Your Favorite Food

Imagine one of your favorite foods.

Visualize the color, texture, appearance, shape, and fragrance.

Imagine taking a bite. Savor the taste as it passes your lips and tongue and travels down your esophagus toward your stomach.

Notice how your body feels as you soak in the fragrance and taste and feel the texture of this delicious food.

Inside Your Favorite Food

Imagine this favorite food is growing larger right before your eyes.

Take a fantasy trip right into the center of this favorite food.

Imagine this food surrounding all of your cells.

Feel the sensation of your body being enveloped by this food.

Describe your thoughts, feelings and sensations?

For example, "You soothe me when I feel anxious."

"You comfort me when I'm upset."

"You're with me when I feel lonely."

Imagine stepping outside of this food into a warm, clean shower.

Allow your body to feel clean and tingly all over.

Drawing Your Favorite Food

On a clean sheet of paper or in your journal, draw a picture of your favorite food.

Now draw yourself near this food, eating or playing with it, resisting it, ignoring it, squashing it or climbing inside of it.

Describe your thoughts, sensations, and reactions to this food now.

Food as Your Best Friend

Imagine that this food is your best friend, your lover, or a very close relative.

Have a conversation.

Talk to this food about your attraction to it and the benefits of your friendship.

Find out if there are any problems between you. Have a real intimate discussion.

For example, "You're always here when I need a friend." "You help me forget or ignore my problems when I'm upset."

This food may be jealous and keep you away from other food that is good for you.

Talk to this food about your fears.

"Sometimes I'm afraid you control me."

"You have the power to fill me up and prevent me from eating other foods that I need to maintain my health."

Copyright © 2009, Revised 2023   *Love Me, Touch Me, Heal Me*   DrEricaGoodstone.com

"If I eat too much of you, I may gain weight, become lethargic, lose my appetite for other foods."

What have you discovered about your relationship to food?

What have you learned about your relationship to your favorite foods and your least favorite foods?

Food has a profound effect upon your life. Some of us live for our next meal, preparing, talking, even dreaming about the taste and sensual pleasure of eating. Years ago, I spent Christmas week with a boyfriend and his family. From a traditional ethnic background, his family sat around the table talking about food for hours and hours. His overweight mother complained about her difficulty keeping a diet. She spent most of her days shopping, cooking, tasting, talking about, and serving food. How could she possibly lose weight without changing her lifestyle and affecting the comfort of her family?

On the other hand, there are others of us who are overly disciplined about our eating. We carefully select only the most essential foods. Limiting our portions, we eat bland and raw foods, vegetable juices, fiber drinks, whole grains, abundant fruits and vegetables, and very limited desserts, sugar, oils or salt. Being cautious about our eating, we make sure to eat slowly, chew our food carefully, stop eating before we are completely full, plan our meal schedules and prepare foods to take with us during the day. We may be physically healthy. We may live longer lives than the more sensual eaters. But, perhaps, we are denying ourselves one of the truly great pleasures of life, **Food**.

Recent studies have found that people who ate dessert once or twice a week were actually healthier than those who never ate dessert. In a stress management class, I asked my students to list their favorite foods. Nobody listed broccoli, bean sprouts, or tofu. The students' favorite foods were chocolate cake, ice cream, pizza, cheese, spaghetti, and mashed potatoes. Their favorite foods were emotionally soothing and pleasing to the taste buds.

Denying yourself the pleasure of food may symbolize the way you live your life. If you deny yourself food, you may also tend to limit your emotional involvement, deny your deepest emotions, and ignore your body's messages.

For some of us, some of the time, food is our only friend, our solace in times of need. Food can look good, smell good, taste good, calm our emotions, and comfort us. For others, food can be our way of hurting our self, damaging our body, proving how tough we are, or gaining control over something. In extreme cases, such as anorexia nervosa and bulemia, our relationship to food can take over our life, interfere with intimacy, and threaten our very existence. For others, chemical substances such as alcohol, recreational drugs, and prescription drugs can become our favorite food, interfering with the health of our mind, body and spirit.

Copyright © 2009, Revised 2023   *Love Me, Touch Me, Heal Me*   DrEricaGoodstone.com

Exercise Moves Your Life

Some of us fill our body with the most powerful and healing nutrients. At the same time, we may either avoid exercise or overtax our muscles through excessive exercise, improper body alignment, or not enough stretching to keep us limber. Some of us are afraid to exercise, afraid of the pain, discomfort, and normal sweating. Some of us exercise moderately, eat a healthy, balanced diet, yet we may still manage to injure our body through repetitive patterns of overuse.

As far back as I can remember, I was always athletic, climbing trees and hiking in the woods, skating, skiing, dancing, and playing team sports. Although physical activity was pleasurable, even exciting to me, I thought being athletic and physically fit meant pain, perpetual pain. I had a tendency to overdo a good thing, not knowing when to stop.

How Do You Exercise Your Body?

What are your favorite physical activities?

Do you enjoy working out and exercising your body?

What influenced you to enjoy or not enjoy exercising your body?

How do you usually feel when you exercise regularly?

How do you usually feel when you don't exercise regularly?

Our body not only belongs to us, it **is** us. Without our body, we would no longer exist as the person we know our self to be. Some of us attempt to live separately from our own body, as if that were possible. We continually ignore our body's messages. We refuse to accept our God-given shape, health, fitness or advancing age.

Observing Your Body

Get ready to look at your body.

Remember to use soft and gentle eyes.

Your goal is to observe and evaluate - not to judge and criticize.

Stand in front of a full length mirror.

You can choose to observe yourself fully dressed, partially clothed or totally undressed.

Have a conversation with yourself looking back at you in the mirror.

Describe what you see.

Talk as if you were telling your own little child how he or she looks.

Speak to the person in the mirror as gently and kindly as you can.

What do you find is attractive, appealing, sexy, youthful, charming...?

What do you find is unattractive, fat, skinny, soft, hard, unappealing...."

Tell the person in the mirror what you like best and least about your body.

Imagine your body parts responding to your words.

What do you body parts want to tell you?

Notice how you feel as you observe and talk about your own body.

Listen to your body's subtle and not so subtle responses.

Inside Your Body

Imagine for a moment your consciousness could travel into the center of your body.

How do you feel inside your body?

Do you feel restricted, compressed, shocked, over-stimulated, exhausted, or depressed?

Do you feel happy, free, joyful, elated, or ecstatic?

Now, imagine travelling inside your own body.

Explore your organs (liver, kidneys, bladder, pancreas, spleen, heart, lungs, small intestine, large intestine, urinary tract, reproductive organs [uterus, testes], external sexual organs [penis, vagina], anal canal). Explore your nervous system (brain, spinal cord, cerebrospinal fluid, membranes, spinal nerves emanating toward your organs, nerve plexuses).

Explore the muscles, tendons, ligaments and bones throughout your body, from your head, scalp, face, neck, shoulders, arms, hands, fingers and upper torso to your lower body, legs, feet and toes.

Explore the liquids (blood, lymph, water, and cerebrospinal fluid) flowing through your arteries, veins and interstitial spaces.

In what places do you get stuck and find you cannot move?

In what places do you move easily and effortlessly?

In what places do you move too easily, without enough boundary or separation?

Which parts do you pay most attention to?

Which parts do you ignore?

Which parts are you afraid of, ashamed of, proud of, neutral about, or angry at?

What would it take for you to become intimate with every part of your own body?

What Do You Want To Change About Your Body?

Tell yourself in the mirror what you would like to change about your body.

Copyright © 2009, Revised 2023   *Love Me, Touch Me, Heal Me*   DrEricaGoodstone.com

Don't worry right now about how you will accomplish this change.

Don't think about whether or not you believe the change is possible.

Just tell the truth about what you would like to change.

Talk to yourself about current activites that affect your weight, fitness, health and body image.

What are you currently doing that you wish to continue?

What activities, habits would you like to stop doing?

What activities, habits would you like to add to your life?

Body Image Analysis Chart

In your journal, create the following chart and put a check mark in the appropriate column for each body part.

	Love It	Not Happy But Can't Change	Want To Change
Attractiveness			
Face			
Hair			
Eyes			
Mouth			

Chin

Ears

Neck

Shoulders

Arms

Chest

Back

Waist

Abdomen

Hips

Buttocks

Thighs

Calves

Ankles

Feet

Toes

Posture

Other

Copyright © 2009, Revised 2023   *Love Me, Touch Me, Heal Me*   DrEricaGoodstone.com

Describe Your Body

In your journal, answer the following questions about your body.

What do I like about my body?

What are the most attractive parts of my body?

What are the least attractive parts of my body?

What body parts am I most proud of?

What body parts am I ashamed of?

What are my strongest body parts?

What are my weakest body parts?

What is the most vulnerable, most easily injured, part of my body?

What body parts have been injured, broken, operated upon?

Where do I habitually carry tensions in my body?

In what areas of my body am I most flexible?

In what areas of my body am I least flexible?

What habitual thoughts and actions enhance my body image?

What habitual thoughts and actions destroy my body image?

What would I like to change about my body?

What do I believe I would have to do to make that change happen?

What could I do now to become more satisfied with my body image?

Your Body Outline

Draw a large outline of your body. If possible, lie down on a life size sheet of paper and have a friend or partner draw your an actual outline of your body.

With colored pencils or crayons, express the emotions of each body part.

Write the words or an image that each body part would say or express if it had a voice.

Now, in your journal, answer the following questions about your body.

How do you habitually hold and carry your body?

What purpose does each part of your body have for you in your life?

Do your tense back muscles help you keep up a good front while your back is up against the wall?

Do your shoulders allow you to carry on by holding onto problems?

Do you dig your toes into the ground to hold your position?

What thoughts, emotions, sensations do you regularly feel?

What thoughts, emotions, sensations do you avoid feeling?

When was the last time you:

- *laughed a hysterical belly laugh?*
- *threw a temper tantrum, screamed and jumped up and down?*
- *punched a person or banged a pillow in raging anger?*

Copyright © 2009, Revised 2023   *Love Me, Touch Me, Heal Me*   DrEricaGoodstone.com

- *giggled in mischievous delight?*
- *cried at a sad movie?*
- *told someone your deepest fears, your secret longings, your private pleasures?*
- *allowed yourself to follow your own dream?*

Your body is your teacher. Pay attention to its messages. Explore the hidden meanings. Take a peak inside yourself. Discover what you truly feel and who you really are.

Caring For Your Body

Our body is a finely tuned machine. The parts can work throughout our entire life. However, in the same way that a machine requires proper care, oiling, checkups, part replacements, and to not be overused or abused, our body also requires adequate care throughout our life.

Each of our body systems needs to be maintained. Although no one bodily system is more important than any other, our breathing apparatus and how we use it can create or solve many of our health problems. Proper breathing allows our blood to circulate freely bringing nutrients to all of our cells. Breathing allows our central nervous system to signal our muscles to move and our pituitary gland to regulate our hormones. Breathing allows our autonomic nervous system to stimulate our vital organs to circulate blood, take in oxygen and eliminate stale air, digest, store, receive nutrients from our food, and eliminate toxins and waste products. Breathing allows our body to become sexually aroused, to build to a crescendo of passion, and to have a release of sexual energy that spreads peace, calm and relaxation throughout our bodily cells. Breathing allows us to feel our loving and tender emotions, synchronize our bodily rhythms, and connect intimately with our partner.

Many of us have long ago forgotten how to breathe. Just watch a baby breathe the "happy baby breath," a term coined by leading breath work expert, Gay Hendricks. A baby's head moves back and its belly rises up as it arches into a full abdominal breath and releases into a relaxed wide open back. Normal, healthy babies do not restrict their breathing. Abused, traumatized and neglected babies reflexively contract, constrict and become despondent. Restricted breathing is one of the major deterrents to a flexible body, peaceful mind, and loving, pleasurable sexuality.

Breath Is Life

Life begins when we take our first breath and ends when we breathe for the last time. We can live for weeks without food or sleep and days without water. Unless we are advanced yogis who can retain their breath for 1/2 hour or longer, if we are deprived of oxygen for only a few minutes, we will die. Deep and rhythmical breathing nourishes our body cells, assisting fluids and basic nutrients to be absorbed into our tissues and organs. When we restrict our breathing, our cells do not fully receive nourishment. Our body becomes inflexible, our muscles tense, our posturing armored, and we find our self agitated, easily frightened, even panicked.

If your breathing is full and you spot danger, your heart rate quickens and your breathing becomes more shallow. You inhale and exhale in a shorter range. When the danger passes, your breathing soon returns to normal. If your breathing is already restricted, the slightest perceived danger can prompt a panic reaction. Panic (intense anxiety and shortness of breath) often results when shallow, restricted breathing is restricted a bit more. Your brain may interpret the restricted breathing as severe danger, even dying. As human beings we are equipped to breathe deeply when we want to relax, to conserve our breathing when we are under attack or in a state of danger, to retain our breath for a length of time, to breathe through each of our nostrils instead of mainly through our mouth, and to regulate and vary our breathing as the situation requires. Flexibility and variability in our breathing mirrors the flexibility and variability in our life. Changing the way we breathe affects our thoughts and our emotions. Changing the way we breathe transforms our life.

Observing Your Breathing

Observe yourself breathing.

Begin by sitting comfortably in a chair with your feet placed firmly on the ground.

Listen for the sounds of your inhale and exhale.

Describe the quality of your breath (deep and full, short and shallow).

Are you actually holding your breath, resisting breathing?

Which is longer and fuller, your inhale or your exhale?

Are you breathing through your mouth, your nose, one or both nostrils?

Is your breathing quiet or forceful, smooth or choppy, loud or soft?

Is there any pain, tension or discomfort as you breathe?

What parts of your body move as you sit and breathe?

Which parts of your body are touching or not touching the chair as you breathe?

Now find a comfortable place to lie flat on your back, preferably on a cushion, mat, a couch or a bed.

Listen for the sounds of your inhale and exhale.

Describe the quality of your breath (deep and full, short and shallow).

How is your breathing the same or different now that you are lying on your back?

What parts of your body move as you lie flat on your back and breathe?

Is there any pain, tension or discomfort as you breathe?

Which parts of your body are touching or not touching the floor or mat as you breathe?

Now come to a comfortable standing position with your feet facing forward, about shoulder width apart, your knees ever so slightly bent.

Feel the soles of your feet spreading out, every part contacting the ground.

Bring your awareness to your each of your toes, the inside arch, the balls of your feet, your heels, and your ankles.

Listen for the sounds of your inhale and exhale.

Describe the quality of your breath (deep and full, short and shallow).

How is your breathing the same or different now that you are standing?

What parts of your body move as you stand and breathe?

Is there any pain, tension or discomfort as you breathe?

Which parts of your feet are touching the floor where you are standing?

Now begin to move your body.

Notice how your breathing shifts and changes as you move.

Bend, reach, stretch, twist and turn.

Walk, run, hop, skip, and jump.

Put on some music and let your body dance.

In your journal, describe what happens to your breathing as you move your body in different ways.

Most of us are unaware of our habitual breathing patterns. Many of us allow our shoulders to slump forward, constricting and compressing our ribs, chest and lung capacity. In this position, we can hardly take in enough air, inhaling and exhaling quickly but not deeply, in order to survive. Some of us have been taught to "stand up straight." So, we proudly lift and expand our chest, constricting our back muscles and ribs. In this position, we may be able to inhale deeply, but we cannot fully exhale. We can literally become stuck in our own breath. Some of us breathe up into our clavicles and chest, our abdomens tightening in the process. This type of breathing can keep us in a perpetual state of readiness to fight, to run, and to spot any danger in our environment. Some of us are perpetual deep abdominal breathers, so relaxed that we fail to garner up the required energy for a hard day's work.

The way we breathe has a powerful effect upon the way we live our life. Constricted breathing reflects fear and insecurity in our thoughts and emotions. Full, deep, regulated breathing reflects control, confidence and joy in our everyday life.

We can control our thoughts and feelings by changing the way we breathe. We can also control our breathing, by changing our thoughts.

Minding Your Body

Our mind controls our body and affects all the events of our life. It is not what actually happens to us that ultimately counts, but how we perceive what happens and how we recall it later. Our body is continually bombarded with incoming stimulation. All sensory input is recorded in our cells. Our mind selectively interprets, judges, and evaluates the encoded data. We cannot possibly remember and focus on all incoming sensations. But, long after the stimulation has been withdrawn and our conscious mind has forgotten the experience, our body retains the memory.

If the circuits in our brain are functioning properly, we will automatically perceive incoming stimulation accurately. We will recognize pain, pleasure, and other stimuli, and respond appropriately. For some of us, however, as we grew up, pleasurable and painful sensations were at times intermingled with abandonment, rejection, sexual abuse, and even, love. Our mind may have become confused. It's as if our circuits have crossed and our brain signals are scrambled. We may have lost our ability to interpret incoming stimulation accurately. We may actually perceive pleasure as pain, love as abuse, or touch as rejection. Losing the brain connection to our body, we may actually behave as if our body is separate from our mind and thoughts.

If the stimulation we received was intense or overwhelming to us, we may have learned to block our ability to interpret or even feel certain sensations. Our body may feel numb in response to pain or pleasure. Wilhelm Reich, colleague of Freud and forerunner of body psychotherapy, coined the term "body armoring" to describe this phenomenon. Resulting from specific stimuli, life events, and our personal responses and interpretations, most of us develop a habitual way of holding our body. Depending upon where in our body we have developed armoring, different emotions and thought processes may be blocked from our conscious awareness.

Armoring yourself does not prevent stimulation from reaching your senses. It merely blocks your mind's ability to recognize and respond appropriately. Armoring allows you to maintain the semblance of a healthy, organized existence. However, one intense life event, touching or being touched, sexual arousal, falling in love, abusing or being abused, feeling rejected, returning home from war, or even giving birth to a child, can temporarily shatter your armoring. Emotions you didn't even know you had can come crashing to the surface, literally causing you to have an emotional breakdown.

Many of us will do almost anything to avoid facing our hidden feelings and the possibility of breaking down. Chemical and sexual addictions are the most obvious. But some of the most positive and constructive activities: career building, exercise, shopping, travelling, even reading, can also be used to numb our mind and prevent us from facing our feelings.

No amount of stimulation and activity can help us to avoid our deepest feelings for our entire life - for decades perhaps, but not forever. Lying in a hospital bed with less than three weeks to live, my mother finally faced the feelings she had avoided and dreaded all of her life. When she could no longer escape into activity, she finally confronted her self, her fears, and her life. She cried every day. Terrified of dying, she was afraid to feel the fear and pain she had never allowed herself to embrace in her 76 years of living. It wasn't until her final day on earth that she came to terms with her own life. Reaching a point of acceptance, she finally said, "I feel encouraged."

You and I do not have to wait until we have only a few weeks left to live. We have the opportunity to assess and review our life, right now, and at regular intervals, while we are fully alive and fully active. We can begin by observing our thoughts, discriminating between what is true for us and what is merely repetition of other people's beliefs.

How do we ultimately discover our own truth? The answer is very simple. Our emotions do not lie. Without premeditated effort, when we feel wronged, we get angry. When we feel hurt or rejected, we become sad. When we feel excited and stimulated, we feel happy. Sometimes our thoughts tell us not to listen to our emotions. Perhaps we have learned that it is not okay to smile and feel pleasure; it is better to be serious. Perhaps we have learned not to express anger; it is better to remain calm, cool, and accepting. Perhaps we have learned not to allow our self to feel sad; it is better to put on a happy, contented expression or to keep a stiff upper lip as we quietly endure the inevitable suffering. Listen to your emotions. They will provide answers that cannot be obtained from any other source.

Your Emotions Are Your Best Friends

Your emotions are your best friends. They arrive at just the right moment. Pay attention. Your emotions are messengers from your higher self. Listen and they may remind you about something you have been ignoring, avoiding, or refusing to see in your life. Pleasant emotions may tell you that you are okay right now, you are on the right path. Painful or debilitating emotions may force you to halt your current activity, disconnect from friends, acquaintances, and lovers, or prepare to leave your current job.

Neurobiologists have isolated some of the brain functions responsible for imprinting a traumatic event in the subconscious while blocking that event from the conscious mind. Studies show that intense emotions interfere with our ability to process information and behave appropriately.

Quantum physicists describe our emotions as energy particles. If not released through expression, these particles can become trapped in our body, in the spaces between the atoms. Sexual and physical abuse, trauma, and intense emotions may cause us to naturally constrict our breathing and tense our muscles. When the excitation becomes overwhelming, our brain may not be able to process the information accurately. The trauma may remain embedded in our physical body, while the emotions become dull and blocked. When our brain circuits are overloaded, we may experience temporary amnesia, inability to remember our experiences. As adults, we may recall, in detail, the events of a traumatic episode, an emotional upset, or even physical abuse, but we may find our self unable to feel any emotions about the memory. Erroneously, we may believe that we were not emotionally affected. In reality, intense emotions may be lying dormant in our subconscious, waiting for the proper moment to explode outward.

It takes a certain amount of life energy to encapsulate our emotions and keep them hidden from our conscious mind. Our body is a hologram. Every part affects every other part. When any part is constricted, other muscles, organs and our entire nervous system must work overtime to maintain the homeostasis of our living and functioning body.

Your Life Force

You have a body and a mind. Your breathing keeps you alive. Food sustains you. Exercise energizes and strengthens you. Your mind controls you. But there is something more, some unseen force that enables you to thrive and flourish or to struggle and suffer. This life force, energy or spirit, has been recognized by most cultures. The Yogis call it "kundalini," Sigmund Freud called it "life instinct," Wilhelm Reich labeled it "orgone energy." A rose by any other name still smells the same. Whatever it is called, it is one and the same energy, and all of us have it. In many of us, this powerful force lies dormant, waiting to be awakened. For others, it has been awakened, yet we continually attempt to control, suppress or ignore it. And for the lucky few, this life force energy is harnessed, savored, and used to create whatever is most desired in life: love, professional recognition, financial comfort, family, emotional well-being, and sexual intimacy.

Where Is Your Life Force?

Sit quietly and close your eyes. Breathe slowly, deeply and effortlessly.

Locate your life force.

Scan through your body.

Where do you most strongly feel your life force, the energy that sustains you and propels you into action?

Now, consciously move your life force.

Allow your life force to travel downward towards your feet and toes.

Become aware of your feet and your entire body connecting with the grounding earth.

Feel the earth's magnetic power spreading through the muscles, tissues and reflexes in the soles of your feet.

Allow your life force to begin to move upwards through your legs, pelvic area, torso, and into your arms and shoulders.

Raise your arms above your head, allowing your life force to move upwards toward your hands and fingers.

Now, allow your life force to radiate outward from the top of your head and the tips of your fingers toward the energy of the sun, the moon, the planets, the stars, and the entire universe.

Now, gathering strength from celestial energy, allow your life force to re-enter your body from above, through the top of your head and the tips of your fingers. Pull your life force down into your neck and shoulders, torso and center of your body.

Now, allow your life force to emanate outward from the center of your body, your hara, your belly, the container for most of your vital organs.

Feel the strength and power of your own life force to enter and return from the world outside.

Now raise your life force up to your heart as your feel your heart beat with your own life force.

Now, allow your life force to emanate outward from your heart. Feel the joy and wonder and ecstasy of connecting your heart to all the energies around you - people, plants, animals, and non-living, manmade forms of all sorts.

Bring your life force back into your body. Allow the energy to spread through all your cells. Feel your cells opening, smiling, even laughing at the joy and wonder of you.

Retain your life force inside your body. Feel your own power and connection to the source, to life, and to everything that is.

We are more than our physical body. Every cell contains our spirit. Our body is the container for our soul. Why not allow our soul to love and touch us now? We will never *need* anyone else again. Of course, we may prefer to share our life, our body and our sensual pleasures with another person, but we will not *need* them to make us feel good. Let's love our self now. Honor our self. We will then know with total certainty that we are loved, that we can be touched and held any time we choose, that we can heal from whatever ails us, and that we are not alone.

Loving Yourself

Stand or sit in front of a mirror.

Tell yourself the words you are longing to hear from someone who loves you.

Say to yourself,

"I love you, my precious angel, sweet darling dearest jewel."

"I love you, powerful leader, intelligent dreamer, exquisite lover."

Tell yourself all those poetic, dramatic, loving, romantic words and phrases from your favorite Hollywood movies.

Tell yourself the loving, respectful, joyful words you may believe are only meant for others who are more beautiful, more creative, more wealthy, more connected, more clever, more cultured, more powerful, or more deserving than you.

Repeat to yourself those loving words that someone told you, long ago.

Tell yourself all those words you've never heard before.

Gaze into your own eyes in the mirror.

Take five or ten long, slow, deep, rhythmical breaths.

Breathe in the feeling and power of these tender, loving words meant only for you.

Love and Touch Your Body

Continue to breathe slowly and deeply at a steady pace.

Gaze into your own eyes in the mirror.

Begin to touch and caress your body, part by part, all over your body surface.

If your touch becomes sensual or even sexual, allow that to happen naturally.

Keep repeating loving words to your own image in the mirror.

"I love you my dearest darling, precious angel."

"You are the salt of the earth, the god or goddess of the heavens, the entrance to the river of love."

"You are beautiful and radiant."

"Your soul shines brightly."

Copyright © 2009, Revised 2023   *Love Me, Touch Me, Heal Me*   DrEricaGoodstone.com

"You are the dream of every man and the heart's desire of every woman."

"You are the flame of my life."

"You are the one true love I have been searching for, waiting for all my life."

"You are with me now and I will never leave you."

If you find it difficult to create your own romantic words, read aloud the words above or words from your favorite poems, novels, plays or movies.

Buy a book of love poems. Pablo Neruda's, Kahlil Gibran's, and Rumi's love poems are exquisite.

Read the poems aloud as you gaze into the wondrous, beautiful eyes in this mirror of your own life.

Tell the person in the mirror how much in love you are and that you will remain in love forever.

Always be there for yourself

Love yourself.

Honor yourself.

Breathe your body.

Touch your body.

Clear your mind.

Awaken your spirit.

Listen to your heart.

Your body believes you

Tell it what you want it to hear

Always be there for yourself

And you will wake up singing

The sweetest and most powerful

Poignant melody of life

Your life

Right here

Right now

Copyright © 2009, Revised 2023   *Love Me, Touch Me, Heal Me*   DrEricaGoodstone.com

IT'S A SENSATIONAL WORLD

TOUCH ME ... PLEASE

CHAPTER 2

IT'S A SENSATIONAL WORLD

It's A Sensational World

My tongue has tasted
Better days
My throat collapsed
From closed up ways
Half opened eyes
Refuse to see
This beautiful world
Especially me

I hear the sounds
Of laughter calling
On the ground
My knees are crawling
Shoulders ache
My neck is tight
My poor back spasms
I shake with fright

*All because
My body tells me
Everything
I need to know
Full sensation
Living, breathing
Listen to me
Let me go*

*Lift my shoulders
To the heavens
Open up
My hungry throat
Let me speak
From deep within me
Hear the wisdom
Of my soul*

*My mind pretends
To have the answers
My mind believes
It has to know
Let my mind
Release its thinking
Let my thoughts
Begin to slow*

*Life surrounds me
Joy and sorrow
Filling up
My soulful heart
Crying, laughing
Sad, now angry
Raw emotions
Stop and start*

Touch my heart
With joy and wonder
Let me know
I'll be okay
I will feel
All life's sensations
Knowing
I'm alive today.

Copyright © 8/20/99 Erica Goodstone, Ph.D

Living Is Feeling

It's a sensational world! Living is feeling. We feel the beauty and wonder of this world with all of our senses. Being fully alive is feeling pleasure and feeling pain, allowing our self to explore the heights of joy and also delve into the depths of darkness, the parts of our self and others that we wish did not exist. Often it is precisely these deep dark painful feelings and emotions that catapult our creative urges to fruition. If we seek to dampen and dull our painful feelings, we are in danger of also limiting our joie de vivre, our creative spirit, our compassion, our sensitivity, and our passionate enjoyment of life.

Imagine animals in the wild or our beloved pets in our homes, taking drugs to suppress their fears, to boost their energy, or to allow their bodies to relax. Cats and dogs, fish and birds, horses, rabbits, elephants, and all animals do not need drugs to accept themselves. They do not avoid feeling their emotions. Tigers and fawns, lions and kangaroos, insects and mice, and all animals utilize their feelings, both positive and negative, for their very survival. They use their hostile and aggressive feelings to obtain food, fight off attackers, and to protect their territory and the weaker members of their species. They use their fearful emotions to guide them to seek safety for themselves and their young ones. Their positive feelings lead them to play in their natural environment while their bodies secrete pheromones to attract mates, ensuring the survival of their species.

Observe animals moving their bodies through space, frolicking in the natural sensations of life. Watch a carefree bird gracefully and effortlessly flap its wings as it soars across the open sky. See another bird peacefully float atop the waves on a windy sea, allowing the water to splash upon its feathers, obviously enjoying the experience.

Watch a happy dog go charging, over and over and over again, to retrieve an object tossed by its human companion. See an excitedly barking dog run to greet its caretaker, jumping up to lick it's owner's face, wagging its tail rapidly back and forth, its body expressing total joy in the moment. Feel the softness of a loving cat's fur as it rubs up against your leg. Listen to the soothing sound of the cat purring contentedly as you lift it to rest in your lap.

It's a Sensational World

Join me now on a sensual fantasy into your own mind and body. Imagine yourself being carefree as a wild animal, contentedly enjoying your surroundings and all the sensations of life. Close your eyes. Take a few slow, deep, and full breaths. Allow your body to relax and your mind to be open to new possibilities. Now, imagine you are peacefully lying outdoors on a full-length lounge chair. Feel the warmth of the sun heating up your sunscreen oiled skin. Sense your muscles relax as your thoughts drift away and your mind becomes more and more still. Now, imagine you are walking on a hot sandy beach, tip toeing quickly to avoid burning the bottoms of your sensitive feet. In front of you is a body of cool water. Quickly dip your toes in, feeling a rush of cold tingle along your legs, sending a shiver up your spine. As you slowly sink your whole body down into the cool water, feel the goose bumps in your skin as your body begins to shake. Rapidly move your arms and legs and feel your own blood rushing through your vessels as your body begins to warm up. Soon you emerge from the water, refreshed and exuberant.

Walk back in the sand, forming deep footprints as you walk, the soles of your feet firmly planted with each step. Climb down into a nearby jacuzzi. Feel your aches and pains soak away in the heated fragrant bubbling jet streams. Hold onto a cool glass of ice water as you plunk an ice cube into your mouth. Suck on the ice cube and allow the coolness to numb your tongue and lips and inner cheeks. Take a sip of the water and feel the cooling sensation of fluid flowing down the center of your dry, parched throat. Climb out of the hot tub and enter a steaming hot shower. Feel the prickling goodness of the clean hot water as you lather up your body, part by part, massaging your scalp and hair with fragrant herbal soap. Step into soft cushion slippers as you rub your body briskly with an oversize terry cloth towel.

Slip your body into a comfortable outfit of natural soft cotton clothing. Return to your room and open the wrapper of a small piece of exquisite chocolate. Taste the soothing texture and flavor as the chocolate slowly melts in your mouth. Now, quickly pack your bags, call a taxi, and head for the airport. Listen to the cacophony of sounds as your taxi glides through the traffic and the weather changes to a gentle rain. Listen to the horns blasting, sirens screeching, people yelling, motors running, and cars skidding.

Look at your watch and discover you are running late and may even miss your flight. Notice how your heart is racing and your body is becoming tense. Finally, you arrive at the airport, pay the driver, grab your bags, and go through the baggage check line. Observe your own impatience as you are asked to open your bag while others breeze through undisturbed. Stand on the side, rearrange the contents of your suitcase, close the bag, pull up the handle and roll away as you race walk toward your gate. Breathless and excited, feel a relieved smile spread across your face as you hand your boarding pass to the gate attendant. Board the plane, twisting and turning as you maneuver your body and bag down the narrow aisle until you find your seat. Place your bag in the overhead bin, sit down, buckle your seat belt, and wait in quiet anticipation. Listen to the roaring *sound of the engine as the plane taxis down the runway. Now the plane is positioned for takeoff. Sit back and breathe deeply as you watch the nose of the plane begin to rise.*

Sensation Is The Language Of The Body

This is your life! How do you want to live it? Sensation is the language of the body, reminding us in every moment that we have a body and that our body is alive and breathing and filled with sensation. We live in a world of continual sensation. One of the cruelest forms of punishment is to keep a person isolated, in a dark narrow space, with no room to move about, devoid of light, sound, and other sensual stimulation. In such a state of sensual deprivation, our mind and thought processes will rapidly deteriorate. Children who do not receive adequate stimulation do not thrive. They become depressed, despondent, and eventually die. Studies conducted at The Crêche, a home for orphans in Lebanon in the 1950's, revealed that receiving only minimal amounts of stimulation, the infants, called foundlings, laid in bed without the usual energy and interest in the world that most children display. Their intellectual development was severely stunted and they remained mentally retarded for life. However, those foundlings who were adopted before the age of two years old, regained their full mental capacity for the rest of their lives.

To survive and thrive and develop satisfying productive lives, we require daily stimulation of all of our senses. Internally, we are aware of our need to cough, sneeze, hiccup, scratch an itch, resist being tickled, belch or relieve gas. We feel and even hear our stomach gurgle when we are hungry or when our body is in the process of digesting food we have already eaten. We feel goose bumps cover our body when we are frightened, startled, or have made an important discovery or realization. We are often aware of tension or pain in our body, although we do not always know the exact origin.

Sometimes we are conscious of the way we are breathing. We may notice that we are breathing rapidly, holding our breath in fear or anxiety, gasping in horror and disbelief, or breathing a sigh of relief about some important situation. We are also aware of our emotions as they well up inside of us, forcing a response such as laughter, tears, disappointment, anger, or even rage. Emotion is the language of the soul, nudging us to pay attention to our relationship to the world, to people, to God and to ourselves.

In addition to our own internal stimulation, we are stimulated by external sounds and colors, odors and fragrances, varying qualities of air temperature, sizes, shapes and textures as well as magnetic forces emanating from animals, plants, people and even objects in our environment.

It is impossible for us to pay attention with all of our senses to this continual onslaught of sensual stimulation. Our mind helps us to function, moment to moment, by filtering out of our conscious awareness, much of the sensual stimulation we receive. What our mind pays attention to and focuses on determines what we feel now, in the present moment. Our present feelings affect what our mind focuses on and how the world responds to us, now and also in the future.

We are taught to value our mind more than our bodily sensations. We believe our own thoughts as if they were the absolute truth. But each of us has multitudes of varying and even contradictory thoughts every moment throughout the day, every single day we are alive. Which of these many thoughts should we believe? Which of our many thoughts is the truth? Our mind is truly the most powerful creative force in the universe. What we believe will often eventually appear in physical form. We need to begin to carefully choose the thoughts we are willing to allow into our conscious awareness.

We also value words. We often erroneously believe that by talking, by explaining what we are thinking, we will be able to control our world and at the same time create intimate love with our chosen partners. However, often our partners do not appear to listen to the words we so readily express. And our partners' verbal responses are often not the words we would like to hear. In fact, in many relationships, the more words we use, the less intimate we seem to become.

What Is True Intimacy?

What passes for honest, "intimate" communication is often nothing more than an intellectual exercise, devoid of heartfelt emotion. Sometimes we verbally express what we **think** we feel without paying attention to even the most blatant bodily messages. For example, we might say, "I'm not angry," while holding a tight fist and clenching our teeth in suppressed rage. We might say, "Sex is not important to me anymore," whereupon our throat clogs up in an uncontrollable urge to cough. In some cases, we use verbal communication as a way to justify our position, to whitewash our inconsiderate actions, or to purposely intimidate and belittle our "intimate" partners.

True intimacy implies freedom, freedom to reveal our deepest fears, hurts and insecurities as well as our grandest dreams. Intimacy also implies longevity and commitment within an ongoing relationship. Revealing our deepest self to a stranger in a bar, on an airplane, or in a brief sexual liaison, (someone who we will probably never meet again), does not require the soul searching, compassion and responsibility of true intimacy.

Intimacy implies responsibility. In an intimate relationship, we not only express our thoughts and feelings openly and honestly, we also listen to our partner's concerns, absorb the emotional impact of their words, attempt to comprehend the deeper meanings, and take appropriate action as needed to rectify the situation if possible.

In an intimate relationship we feel safe, not because we expect our partner to always treat us with kindness and compassion, but because we know that our partner truly has our own best interests at heart. We feel safe because, over time, we recognize our partner's style of communicating and responding. We appreciate the ways that our partner is courageous and strong when we feel most inadequate and vulnerable. And we feel acknowledged when our partner appreciates us for the ways we are courageous and strong when our partner feels inadequate and vulnerable.

Intimacy implies a shared history. We understand without words. We are able to be our most natural self, freely talking in our own way or comfortably remaining silent. An intimate relationship allows us to face our self and each other, without the need to hide or pretend. Over time we discover and uncover more and more about our own self in relationship and about our partner.

Copyright © 2009, Revised 2023   *Love Me, Touch Me, Heal Me*   DrEricaGoodstone.com

We know a lot more than most of us realize about people we are meeting for the first time, even and especially before any words are spoken. In fact, words often confuse our original and accurate perceptions, causing us to disregard or doubt what our senses have revealed to us. Discover how much you already know about people you may have never met.

What Do You Know About Others?

On the street, on public transportation, at a restaurant or party, even at your office, observe people you have never met before. Observe the expression on their faces. Gaze into their eyes. Pay attention to their nonverbal behavior, physical appearance, body posturing, and emotional attitude. Listen carefully to not only their words, but the tone and quality of their voices. Compare people to each other. Who appears to be more or less confident, happy, depressed, lonely, angry, or insecure? Who appears to be satisfied with their self and who seems to be pretending and hiding some deep insecurity?

Sometimes our perceptions are wrong or slightly off, but more often than not, we are right on target. How is that possible, if we have not engaged in lengthy conversations and we know nothing about this person's personal history? Without words, how do we know another person?

What Does Your Intuitive Sense Reveal To You?

One major way that we know another is through our five senses. We see, hear, smell, touch, and sometimes even taste, the people closest to us. We learn a lot about others through our five senses. But there is something so evident that most of us do not realize it is so. We know others through our own mind as we receive their thoughts. Thoughts are powerful. They actually have form and substance. If we pay attention, we can sometimes truly read another's thoughts. We know how they feel by the expression on their face, the intensity in their eyes, and the way they carry their body.

We also have an intuitive sense. When we breathe deeply, relax our body, and calm the restless scanning of our perpetually thinking mind, we come to a place of knowing. We have a sense that something or someone is good for us, dangerous, confusing, difficult to understand, or should be avoided.

Blocking Your Senses To Reveal More

There is something more, something indefinable, lying beneath, behind, or between our subtle thoughts, our five physical senses, and our intuitive sixth sense. We might call this place our spiritual sense. This is a place where we connect with all the knowledge that ever was, is or will be. This is the place from which so-called creative genius are able to make their discoveries and create their masterpieces. So often we hear them say, "I didn't create…. It was as if it was dictated to me…." Blocking our physical senses allows us to tap into our spiritual sense, to locate that quiet place within, that place of peace and calm, that place of universal energy, that we share with everyone and everything that exists.

BLOCK YOUR SIGHT

Close Your Eyes.

Place a blindfold or your palms gently against your upper cheek bones, cupping your eyes closed.

>Notice how that is for you to close your eyes.
>
>Observe your inner sight. What do you see?
>
>How do you feel?

Copyright © 2009, Revised 2023   *Love Me, Touch Me, Heal Me*   DrEricaGoodstone.com

Safe, secure, calm, relaxed….

Afraid, anxious, isolated, angry, insecure….

Begin to walk around the room with the blindfold or your palms securely blocking any light from entering your eyes.

Notice how you feel walking around indoors in a familiar room without seeing.

Walk outside into the hallway of your apartment building or onto your front lawn or back yard if you live in a house or condo. Remember to keep your vision blocked.

Notice how you feel walking around outside of your home without seeing.

Open Your Eyes.

View the world around you with new eyes, soft eyes, beginner's eyes, as if you are seeing everything for the very first time.

What do your eyes notice first?

Focus on one object, person, plant or animal at a time. Observe the shapes and colors, textures and designs, movement or stillness, warmth or coldness, or other qualities.

It has been said that our eyes are the windows to our soul. Through our eyes we contact the world. Our eyes observe the wondrous beauty of nature (mountains, oceans, sunrise, sunset, rainbows, flowers, animals) and the monuments of human creation (buildings, cars, computers, airplanes). Through our peripheral vision, we anticipate movement, as in sports, or spot approaching danger. During war, in the midst of battle, some soldiers claim they were actually able to see and dodge bullets coming at them from the front, side, and even behind their backs. Time seemed to slow down. The bullets appeared to be moving in slow motion. In an intense state of fear, as in war or other trauma or when one or more of our senses are blocked or damaged, our working senses may become more acute. We can see, hear, and feel things we would not ordinarily be able to sense.

BLOCK YOUR HEARING

Close Your Ears.

Place ear plugs, cotton, or your index fingers in your ears, your palms resting on your cheeks.

> *Notice how that is for you to block out external sound.*
>
> *Listen to your own inner sound. What do you hear?*
>
> *How do you feel?*
>> *Safe, secure, calm, relaxed....*
>>
>> *Afraid, anxious, isolated, angry, insecure....*

Begin to walk around the room with your ears blocked.

Notice how you feel walking around indoors in a familiar room without hearing.

Walk outside into the hallway of your apartment building or onto your front lawn or back yard if you live in a house or condo. Remember to keep your hearing blocked.

Notice how you feel walking around outside of your home without hearing.

Open Your Ears.

Listen to the world around you with new ears, beginner's ears, as if you are listening to everything for the very first time.

What do your ears notice first?

Focus on one sound at a time. Observe the volume, amplitude, texture, speed, vibration, movement, loudness or softness, or other qualities of each sound..

Sound warns us of imminent danger or the promise of excitement. The sound of a mother's heartbeat comforts her baby and lulls it to sleep. The sound of a purring cat calms us, causing us to smile, or startles us if we're afraid of cats. A barking dog protects us if we are its owner or frightens us if we are about to be attacked. Our lover's voice can thrill us with passionate sentiment or repel us after an unsettling argument.

The sound of music can have profound healing effects upon our physiological functions. In the best selling book, *Sounds of Healing: A Physician Reveals the Therapeutic Power of Sound, Voice, and Music,* pp. 80-82, the author, Mitchell Gaynor, summarizes the findings of numerous studies about the effects of music:

- Reduced anxiety, heart and respiratory rates in patients who had suffered recent heart attacks.

- Reduced cardiac complications among patients who had been recently admitted to a coronary care unit after suffering heart attacks.

- Lowered systolic blood pressure in nine subjects who listened to two albums of music which had average beats of fewer than 55 hertz, the rate at which a sound wave vibrates.

- Decreased systolic and diastolic blood pressure as much as five points and heart rate as many as four to five beats per minute in subjects who listened to recordings of various musical styles.

- Too much noise, setting off the fight or flight response, can increase blood pressure by as much as 10 percent.

- Reduced blood pressure, heart rate, and noise sensitivity in heart surgery patients who listen to music during the first day after surgery.

- Increased immune cell messengers, levels of interleukin-1, by 12.5-14 percent when subjects listened to music that they liked for fifteen-minute periods.

- Decreased levels of stress hormones, cortisol and ACTH, in patients who listened to music while undergoing gastroscopy (insertion of a probe through the mouth and into the stomach).

- Boost in natural opiates, endorphins, resulting in feelings of euphoria, among subjects who listened to various kinds of music.

What is our world like when we have difficulty hearing or are completely unable to hear sounds? Noted feminist physician, Dr. Christiane Northrup, cites studies about hearing loss in middle aged men. For some reason, they are unable to hear sounds specifically within the speaking range of their long time spouses. Imagine the damaging effect this specific hearing loss might have upon their most intimate relationships, the misunderstandings and hurt feelings that might result.

If we begin to lose our hearing, at first, perhaps, we might feel frustrated as we struggle to comprehend what others are saying. People might become impatient as they are forced to repeat their words, sometimes many times. We might gradually lose interest in socializing with others. Even the most ordinary, simple activities, like talking on the phone, watching TV, going to a movie, dancing, or listening to music, can become stressful and unpleasant experiences. Walking on a busy street or driving a car can become dangerous if we cannot hear sounds that might prevent an accident. If we are wearing a hearing aid, we may be jarred or even pained by the static of background sounds.

If we do not wallow in self-pity or become increasingly reclusive, we may discover life has something much more to offer. When we cannot hear, our other senses may become more acute. We can use our sense of sight to read lips, to observe facial expressions and body movements of others, and also to enjoy the beauty of the world around us. Our sense of taste and smell and touch may intensify. We may have to slow down, to pay attention in the moment. And we can tune out the world whenever we choose.

BLOCK YOUR SENSE OF SMELL

Block Your Sense of Smell

Place a nose clip or the thumb and index finger of your dominant hand on either side of your nose.

Press your nostrils closed.

Notice how it is for you to block out the sense of smell. Observe the effect upon your throat. Notice your natural and immediate need to swallow.

How is that for you to breathe only through your mouth?

Pay attention to your own inner scent. What do you smell?

How do you feel?

>   *Safe, secure, calm, relaxed....*

>   *Afraid, anxious, isolated, angry, insecure....*

Begin to walk around the room with your nostrils blocked.

Notice how you feel walking around indoors in a familiar room without smelling.

Walk outside into the hallway of your apartment building or onto your front lawn or back yard if you live in a house or condo. Remember to keep your nostrils blocked.

Notice how you feel walking around outside of your home without smelling.

Open Your Sense of Smell.

Smell the world around you with a new nose, beginner's nose, as if you are smelling everything for the very first time.

What do smell first?

Being able to smell will probably save our life many times. Our nose alerts us to the noxious gas of something burning, the unpleasant odor of moldy food, the stench of filth. Our sense of smell also detects our favorite food cooking, the personal scent of our lover or children, perfume fragrances, and the elements of our natural environment: flowers, grass, trees, the ocean, a gentle breeze.

Each of us has a dominant nostril, the same side as our dominant hand, because of greater nerve sensitivity on that side. A healthy person may be able to detect from 10,000 to 30,000 different scents. Yet, each of us has our own unique scent preferences, based upon our society, culture, ethnic group, experiences, memories, or part of the world we live in.

Our ability to perceive odors seems to peak at around age 40, although studies claim it may decline as early as age 20 in some people. Smoking seriously impairs our sense of smell by actually paralyzing the tiny cilia inside the nasal passages. One out of every 20 head injured people describes losing a sense of smell and/or taste. Even a seemingly mild concussion can affect taste and smell sensibility.

Approximately 4 million Americans have problems with their sense of smell and/or taste, not related to aging. Most complain about a total lack of smell (anosmia) or unusual smells/olfactory hallicinations (phantosmia). Half of those over 65 and 3/4 of those over 80 have a reduced ability to smell (called hyposmia).

If we are constantly or repeatedly exposed to an odor, we tend to adapt to it, that is, our ability to perceive the odor declines. This lowered sensitivity can persist for as long as three weeks after the odor is removed. However, studies show we are more likely to adapt to the same, identical odor if we believe it is a natural substance rather than a harmful chemical. From the moment of birth, a baby recognizes the scent of its mother, especially if nursed. The baby will stop crying if the mother enters the room, even if the mother is beyond the baby's periphery of sight.

Memories triggered by an odor tend to be more emotionally intense than other sensory cues. Some of the worst memories of war-traumatized, bombing-victims, or sexual abuse victims, are caused by their sense of smell. The scent of burning chemicals, body perspiration, or ejaculated semen can cause a previously traumatized person to instantly have a bodily re-experiencing of the trauma. On the other hand, the aroma of freshly baked cookies, pumpkin pie or an oven roast can warm an adult or elderly person's heart, instantly bringing their memory back to an emotionally comforting, happy time in their childhood.

Dr. Alan R. Hirsch, M.D., author of *Scentsational Sex* (April 1998), conducted studies to discover what particular scents caused sexual arousal in men and in women. For men, the scent of a combination of lavender and pumpkin pie showed the greatest measurable arousal, increased blood flow to the penis, while licorice and doughnuts as well as cinnamon buns also had a stimulating effect. But arousal in men increased in response to every odor tested. Not so for women. Arousal for women, measured by increased vaginal blood flow, was highest in response to the scent of Good and Plenty, licorice candy, or licorice Allsorts and cucumber combined, but was also affected by a combination of lavender and pumpkin pie. However, women showed negative responses to several odors, including cherry, charcoal barbecue smoke, and male cologne. Scientists are beginning to find evidence that we may also be aroused or turned off by pheromones, the natural scent or chemicals released by our human partners.

BLOCK YOUR SENSE OF TASTE

Block Your Sense of Taste.

Place your thumbs below and the rest of your fingers above your lips, keeping your mouth closed.

> *Notice how that is for you to block out external taste.*
>
> *Notice how that is for you to breathe only through your nose.*
>
> *Pay attention to your own inner taste. What do you taste?*
>
> *How do you feel?*
>
>> *Safe, secure, calm, relaxed....*

Afraid, anxious, isolated, angry, insecure....

Remember a time when you had a bad cold or flu and were unable to smell or taste food. Remember a time when your stomach felt full or you felt slightly nauseous and were unable to enjoy the sight or taste of food that you usually love.

How does it feel to be unable to taste?

Open Your Sense of Taste.

Taste the world around you with a new tongue, beginner's tongue, as if you are tasting everything for the very first time.

What do taste first?

Imagine the subtle or strong taste as you kiss your pet, your child's cheek, your spouse's lips or as you bite into a juicy apple, a tart lemon, a cube of sugar, ice cream covered with hot melted fudge, mashed potatoes, crunchy almonds, a slice of gooey pizza, or any of your favorite foods.

'It's a matter of taste' may be more true than we have ever realized. The French expression, "chacun a son gout" (to each his own taste), describes it well. Humans are, in fact, genetically, culturally and individually different in their ability to perceive food flavors. Scientists have categorized people into supertasters, tasters, and nontasters, based on the number of fungiform papillae, the structures that hold the taste buds, on their tongues. About 25% of the population appear to be supertasters, 25% nontasters, and 50% tasters. Women are more likely to be supertasters, especially when estrogen is at its highest (ovulation, pregnancy). Supertasters tend to be more sensitive to a bitter compound in broccoli and other vegetables or the bitter aftertaste of artificial sweeteners. Nontasters appear to barely perceive these bitter flavors.

Hormonal levels can alter our sense of taste. Estrogen seems to increase taste sensitivity. Pregnant women are notorious for having intense food cravings, often for such unlikely foods as pickles and ice cream, combinations that they would find unpleasant at any other time. During ovulation, women's taste sensitivity is also enhanced.

Taste buds are not only on the tongue, but also scattered on the roof of the mouth, inside the cheeks, even in the throat. Complex interactions occur within and among the taste buds - each filled with nerve fibers. Thus we are able to differentiate among the four basic flavors - sweet, sour, bitter, and salty. The burn of spicy foods is not a flavor in itself; instead of stimulating the taste buds, it activates the bundle of nerves that wrap around each taste bud. Other taste sensations include, metallic, alkaline, and umami, which is the taste of glutamate, as found in MSG (monosodium glutamate).

Taste is not limited only to the sensory perceptions of taste buds. Taste and olfactory sensations combine to determine how people enjoy food. Scientists have coined the term, "mouthsense" to describe this phenomenon. Limiting the foods we eat does not enhance their taste. In fact, our appreciation of food tends to increase when the sense of taste is surprised and challenged. Indeed, "variety is the spice of life."

Another factor in the sense of taste is the trigeminal system, branches of nerves connecting the brain to the nose and the mouth. These nerves detect irritants such as hot chilies, black pepper, coolness of mint, and carbonation in beverages. The texture of food and its visual appearance also affect taste. Hot food gives off more vapor, increasing the intensity of sweet or bitter flavors; cold seems to reduce the impact of these flavors. Sour and salty foods do not seem to be as influenced by temperature.

Most taste preferences are learned. We can educate our self, through careful study and practice, to discern the unique qualities of various foods. Overcoming our initial aversion to the bitter taste, some of us learn to love the flavor of coffee. Wine connoisseurs are able to distinguish the unique taste of different wines, while gourmet chefs use specific spices to create extraordinary taste sensations for our palates.

Our sense of taste is strongly influenced by our sense of smell. In fact, when we are hungry, our sense of smell intensifies. Detecting the aroma of our favorite foods will stimulate our salivary glands. Studies show that people have **lost weight** merely by smelling their favorite foods. Having their olfactory senses stimulated helped them to overcome their craving, without putting any food into their mouth.

Taste sensitivity and the number of taste buds do not decrease with age. Decreased taste sensitivity may be due to memory loss, changes in the brain's perception of tastes, or chronic illness, rather than to changes in the taste buds. However, the sense of smell, which affects enjoyment of different foods, does tend to diminish with age. Studies show that 50% of people over age 65 and 75% of those over age 80, have a reduced ability to smell. One way to compensate for any loss of taste sensitivity is to eat foods with contrasting textures, temperatures, colors, and flavors. How intricate and delicate is our brain wiring for the sense of taste!

BLOCK YOUR SENSE OF TOUCH

Block Your Sense of Touch.

Close your eyes.

Put on a pair of rubber gloves, the thicker the better.

Touch some different household items, a cup, a spoon, a hairbrush.

Imagine you have lost your sense of touch.

What would you miss touching?

What problems or dangers might this cause for you?

Open Your Sense of Touch.

> *Touch the world around you with new hands, beginner's hands, as if you are touching everything for the very first time.*
>
> *Touch one object, person, plant or animal at a time. Observe the subtle and strong qualities, varying temperatures and sensations you feel as you touch various textures, fabrics.*

Wrapping around our entire body, our skin is the largest and most essential sense organ. If we cannot see, hear speak, taste or smell, we can still survive. But without our skin, our body will cease to exist. Protecting our body structures and internal organs, our skin continually sends messages from the external world directly to our brain and bodily cells. Our skin reflects our age, height, weight, and our state of physical, mental, emotional and even spiritual health or illness. No magical facial surgery can completely mask our inner state.

Touch, even the mere intention to touch, can affect the health, resiliency, texture and responsiveness of our skin and internal organs. How our skin responds to touch is determined by many factors: our genes, gender, health, previous touch experiences, pain threshold, perceptions, beliefs, and memories. Even a light touch on the surface of our skin can have a profound effect: pleasure, pain, irritation, or ticklishness. Each of us responds very differently to touch and we respond differently to the same type of touch at different times and with different people.

Studies show that severe deprivation of touch in the early years can lead to death or lifelong mental retardation. A startling discovery was made in Lebanon in the 1960's when foundlings, infants living at an orphanage, The Crêche, were finally allowed to be legally adopted. Until that point, it was widely believed that these children were mentally deficient and would never develop normal intelligence. To everyone's surprise, those foundlings adopted before 2 years of age developed normal I.Q.'s. Those adopted after age two, maintained some mental retardation, but their intellect level improved somewhat over time. Those foundlings who remained at The Crêche failed to develop normal intelligence because they were deprived of sensory stimulation, including touch.

Recent research indicates that intentional, massaging touch (even 15 minutes, 3 times a week) improves vital signs, activity level and growth of infants, lessens anxiety in adults, and alleviates depression in the elderly. A noted neuroscientist, Dr. James Prescott, suggests that lack of touch and bodily pleasure in the early years is the principle cause of human violence. Harry Harlow's experiments in the 1960's and 1970's showed that infant monkeys deprived of a warm, soft, comforting mother's touch developed inadequate social and sexual skills for their entire lives.

Touch heals. Touch also hurts. And the absence of touch can cause irreversible harm. How do we treat for lack of touch, memories of painful or abusive touch, or our lifelong need to be touched, and hugged and held? Touch can be introduced to a touch aversive person – slowly and very carefully, in a safe and trusting environment, with a safe and trusted person with a lot of patience and compassionn, over a very long period of time.

BLOCK ALL YOUR SENSES

Cover your eyes, with a blindfold, a scarf, or with your hands.

Put ear plugs, cotton or your index fingers into your ears.

Use a nose clip or press your nostrils closed using your middle fingers.

Close your mouth.

Hold your breath.

Notice how that is for you to block off all your senses and hold your breath.

How do you feel?

Open your mouth slightly to allow yourself to breathe through your mouth, keeping all of your other senses blocked.

> *Listen to your own internal sounds.*
>
> *Observe the colors, shapes or visions that appear in your inner sight.*
>
> *Watch your thoughts as they come and go.*
>
> *Observe your own internal tastes and smells.*
>
> *Imagine the sensation of touching and being touched.*

Notice how you feel in your body now.

GO ON A SENSUAL HOLIDAY
OPEN ALL YOUR SENSES

Plan to give yourself a sensual bonanza.

Explore all your senses at once.

Consciously use your eyes to watch, observe and soak in everything around you: shapes, colors, energetic fields, dust particles, body language, facial expressions.

Plan to go to movies, theatre, ballet, sports events, art galleries, horse races, and even while on your computer – pay attention to the sights you see.

Consciously listen to even the most subtle sounds and words with both ears.

Listen to different types of music: vocal, instrumental and electronic.

Listen to different people, children, teenagers, adults, talking, lecturing, laughing, crying, giggling, fighting and playing.

Consciously smell everything and everyone.

Smell the flowers on the table at a restaurant or along your walking path.

Smell the wine or coffee, appetizer, entrée and dessert, before eating.

Smell the food cooking at home.

Smell the food as you bite into each and every morsel.

Smell your pets, your children, your partner, and other people nearby.

Consciously taste a wide variety of foods, cooked in different ways.

Chew slowly.

Attempt to distinguish each and every spice and flavor.

Notice in what part of your mouth you actually taste the food.

Consciously touch and feel the texture, shape, and temperature of objects, nature and people in your environment (being ethically and socially appropriate).

Touch people.

Hug people, your intimate partner, your children, your elderly relatives, your friends and acquaintances.

Allow yourself to be touched and hugged.

Copyright © 2009, Revised 2023   Love Me, Touch Me, Heal Me   DrEricaGoodstone.com

Experience what it is like to live in a totally sensational world! Experience what it is like to block all your senses. No longer aware of sensations, discover the nonphysical, nonmaterial part of yourself, the part that knows and connects with everyone and everything, the part that knows God. Allow your senses to flood back into your life, in every moment, thoughts at bay, judgments gone, aware of only pure, ever-present, sensation. Imagine being with your lover, speaking to your co-workers, standing up for your rights, putting your children to sleep, in that sensational state of heightened awareness of your mind, body and spirit and the mind, body and spirit of others.

TOUCHING MATTERS

THE PROFOUND EFFECTS

OF TOUCH AND BODY THERAPY

TOUCH ME ... PLEASE

CHAPTER 3

TOUCHING MATTERS ...

THE PROFOUND EFFECTS OF

TOUCH AND BODY THERAPY

Touch Me

Your gentle soothing hand
Calms and comforts me
Relieves
My inner longing
I feel safe, secure, connected
Your touch reminds me
I am not alone
I can let go of control
And feel
All there is to feel
Allowing myself to finally be
Me

Copyright © 5/15/01 Erica Goodstone, Ph.D.

Touch Is Powerful

Touch is powerful. Our sense of self, ability to love, attractiveness to others, and sexual passion, often hinges upon the way we touch and respond to touch. Sexual desire may be either stimulated or suppressed by the mere hint of an impending touch. With harsh or abusive touch, we tend to constrict our body, repress our feelings and become less receptive to love. Loving touch assists us to release painful memories and open our heart to others. Touching our self brings a profound sense of inner peace, self-acceptance and self-love.

Research indicates that touch promotes health, healing and general well-being, from pregnancy and birth to every stage of development throughout life. Teachers, psychotherapists, and even waiters are evaluated as more caring, knowledgeable and competent when they casually touch their students, clients, or customers in a non-threatening, non-sexual way. Even in this litigious and touch aversive climate of today's society, caring touch brings us closer to one another.

Touch In Psychotherapy

Research indicates that touch in psychotherapy can be helpful, powerful or destructive depending upon the way it is used, the therapist's intention and the client's perceptions. Undergraduate and graduate college students described a counselor (male or female) they observed touching a client, as more caring than the counselor who did not touch (Driscoll, 1986). Patients' experiences with touch in therapy indicated that touch enhanced self-esteem and fostered a bond that allowed for greater trust, openness and acceptance. Contrary to what most of us might expect, sexual abuse survivors rated therapist touch significantly more positively than did non survivors, emphasizing trust and learning about boundaries in relationships (Horton, 1994). Touch can assist therapists to tap into their clients' deep emotional processes, assisting patients to break unhealthy relationship bonds (Cronise, 1993).

Touch can either assist or interfere with the psychotherapeutic process. Motivations of therapists for touching may include trying to improve physiological functioning, seeking personal gratification of therapist or client, education or interpersonal exploration, somatic/emotional release, sexual and physical gratification, socially appropriate contact, perceived necessity, and intuition (Weisberg, 1992).

Psychotherapy clients found touch in psychotherapy to be beneficial if they were free to talk about the touch, boundaries, and sexual feelings; if they felt control over initiating or sustaining contact; if the touch was not demanded by the therapist; and if the expectations of the therapist for emotional and physical intimacy matched their own reality. Clients felt confused or negative about the touch in psychotherapy if they felt guilty about being angry at their therapist, trapped in having to be close, or were repeating unpleasant childhood dynamics. (Geib,Ph.D., Boston University School of Education, 1982).

Should psychotherapists touch their clients? Yes, perhaps occasionally, to indicate comfort, concern, and compassion. No, in general, unless the psychotherapist can verify years of training, appropriate professional certification and licensure in both touch therapy and therapeutic counseling. Body therapists, on the other hand, who often perform exquisitely intricate body movements, manipulations and muscular tension releases, are not usually trained to deal with emotional issues. Touch within a therapeutic session is extremely sensitive and intimate. Body psychotherapists, certified or licensed as psychotherapists and also certified or licensed in one or more body therapy modalities, are uniquely qualified to introduce touch as an agreed upon component of the therapeutic relationship. Body psychotherapy requires years of training, experience and ongoing supervision.

The Profound Effects of Touch

Touch Research Institute Studies

Touching and being touched has profound healing effects at all ages (from pre-term infants to adolescents, adults and even elderly grandparents) and for a wide variety of ailments and diseases (from asthma, diabetes and fibromyalgia to HIV+ and AIDS. During a one-year sabbatical from my professorship in 1995, I took a brief training at the Touch Research Institute at Jackson Memorial Hospital, Miami, Florida, with Dr. Tiffany Field, psychologist and leading touch therapy researcher in the world. Touch Research Institute studies have been conducted worldwide, for many years, utilizing a simple protocol, easily replicated by other researchers. Subjects receive 15-30 minute massage sessions, 2 times per week for 5 weeks. Control groups receive standard nursing treatment, TENS (electrical stimulation), SHAM TENS (use of the TENS machine without electrical stimulation), or progressive relaxation. Although the TENS treatment and progressive relaxation have some positive effects, massage has more significant and long-lasting effects.

What follows is an overview of the types of studies conducted at the Touch Research Institute and the powerful results attained by a minimal amount of touch (15-30 minutes, 2 times per week).

Copyright © 2009, Revised 2023 *Love Me, Touch Me, Heal Me* DrEricaGoodstone.com

Studies of **preterm newborns**, suggest that infants who are touched at regular intervals, compared to those who are not touched, gain more weight, become more responsive, are discharged from the hospital several days earlier, and upon follow-up 8 months later, are still showing greater weight gain, mental and motor development. **Cocaine-exposed** and **HIV-exposed newborns** who receive touch exhibit increased weight, reduced stress levels, and better performance on the Brazleton Newborn Scale, particularly motor development.

Infants who are touched have greater daily weight gain, more organized sleep/wake behaviors, less fussiness, improved sociability, greater interaction with others, and lower cortisol and norepinephrine indicating lower stress levels and increased serotonin which suggests less depression.

Preschool children who receive massage fall asleep sooner, have more restful nap periods, and have decreased activity levels. For **autistic children**, touch sensitivity, attention to sounds, off-task classroom behavior decrease while relatedness to teacher increases, after receiving massage. **Children who are touched after surviving a natural disaster** show decreased anxiety, depression and cortisol levels. **Diabetic childrens'** glucose levels decrease to the normal range while **asthmatic children** exhibit increased peak air flow, fewer asthma attacks, and less anxiety and depression after being touched. **Juvenile rheumatoid arthritic children** experience lower anxiety and cortisol levels and less pain. Massage therapy reduces agitation and pain levels before debridement in **children with severe burns.**

Adolescent studies show that **anorexic and bulimic girls** have improved body image and decreased depression and anxiety symptoms when touched. Massage therapy decreases anxiety and pain, reduces the length of labor and the need for medication for **teenage mothers in childbirth** and decreases depression and anxiety in **depressed teenage mothers**.

And for the **elderly**, studies indicate that **grandparent volunteers** report less anxiety, fewer depressive symptoms, improved mood, fewer doctor visits, improved lifestyle, decreased pulse rate and improved self-esteem, after giving massage to infants. These effects were stronger after giving than after receiving massages.

For adults, **job performance** studies indicate that after receiving massage, participants experience increased alertness, faster completion of math problems with 50% less errors and lower anxiety levels. Hospital staff members show significantly reduced anxiety, depression and fatigue. **Fibromyalgia** patients experience decreased pain levels, improved sleep patterns, decreased fatigue, anxiety, depression and cortisol levels while chronic fatigue syndrome patients have shown reduced fatigue related symptoms, including emotional stress, somatic symptoms, depression and difficulty sleeping. **Rape and spouse abuse victims** exhibit a decreased aversion to touch, decreased anxiety, depression and cortisol levels.

Dr. Tiffany Field's studies involve mostly traditional massage. She has created a network of franchised Touch Research centers, repeating similar research protocols, throughout the United States and in Europe. However, there are a wide variety of other methods and techniques that utilize touch, from painful, invasive, deep tissue work to gentle, balancing and even lighter energetic techniques. Many studies on other forms of body therapy, until recently, have been conducted in Europe within traditional medical and psychological settings.

The National Institutes for Health, Office of Alternative and Complementary Medicine began awarding research grants in 1993. Several of the grants studied the effects of various body therapies. That same year The American Massage Therapy Association Foundation began offering research grants. The Upledger Institute Healthplex Center, in Palm Beach Gardens, Florida, has been conducting research for years on the use of craniosacral therapy and somatoemotional release to improve conscious awareness of brain function, posttraumatic stress disorder and the bioelectric transference between patient and therapist during therapeutic sessions. Research on body therapy is still in the early stages, but results so far have been quite promising.

Body Therapy

Which One is Right for You?

Although, Touch Research Institute studies have shown beyond a reasonable doubt that massage heals, massage is only one style of body therapy. Most of us are not aware that there are as many ways to touch as there are people to develop methods. Body therapy includes many different styles of touch, movement, and body awareness exercises. Some methods involve direct contact with the skin, some realign the structure of the body, some re-balance the craniosacral rhythm or the meridian system, while others affect the aura or energetic field. A strict code of ethics, developed and established by the national certifying or licensing board or the specialized certification program, is an essential component of body therapy training. Body therapy does not and should not involve sexual contact of any kind and is not for the purpose of sexual release. However, the resulting muscular relaxation and energetic re-balancing of the body often leads to greater ease and pleasure in all aspect of life, including intimate sexual relations.

To help determine which techniques resonate with our own personal bodily needs, each of the various body therapy methods have been classified within seven categories. These categories are not exclusive. Some methods may fit into more than one category. For each descriptive category, a brief summary is presented. For books, videos, web sites, training programs, and how to locate a qualified practitioner of a specific modality in your area, refer to the Appendices at the end of this book.

1. Swedish Massage/Therapeutic Massage
2. Contemporary Western Massage and Body Therapy
3. Structural, Functional, Movement, Alignment Body Therapy
4. Asian Body Therapy
5. Energetic Body Therapy
6. Somatic and Expressive Arts Body Therapy
7. Body Psychotherapy.

Swedish Massage
Traditional Massage Therapy

Probably the most well known, the most thoroughly researched, and one of the few licensed methods of touch therapy in this country, is Swedish Massage or Massage Therapy. In a typical session, the client usually lies on a massage table, totally unclothed, wearing undergarments, or wearing shorts and a tee shirt. Most of the client's body is comfortably draped in sheets and towels, with only the body part being massaged left uncovered. With a combination of oils or creams, herbal and aromatic essences, music, soft lighting, and sometimes colored lights, the massage therapist uses five basic massage strokes (effleurage, petrissage, friction, tapotement, vibration) directly upon the client's skin. The pressure used in the strokes should vary according to the client's preferences.

The goal of massage therapy is to relax the mind and body, relieve symptoms of pain or stress, and sometimes to assist clients to create a healthier, more holistic lifestyle which includes improving diet, exercise, rest and sleep habits. Massage is generally accessible and affordable. Many massage schools have clinics in which advanced students give a series of massages at very reduced rates. The profession of massage therapy has been rapidly gaining respect through state licensing, national certifications, national accreditation of training programs and schools, insurance coverage, and official recognition as an important healing modality at the Olympics.

Contemporary Western Massage And Bodywork

Contemporary Western Massage and Bodywork includes body therapy methods and techniques that alleviate muscular tension, painful nerve constrictions, poor circulation, and chronic aches and pains caused by stress, overwork, overexertion, athletic and other injuries, pregnancy, hormonal imbalances, and illnesses. Expanding upon the practice of Traditional Massage Therapy, these methods include the use of water, ice and heat, massage in the work place or outdoors, massage focused on body parts injured from accidents and diseases, gentle sensual massage, massage to improve athletic performance and to heal athletic injuries, as well as massage specially geared for pregnancy, for infants, and even for animals.

Aquassage/Hydrotherapy (Ice & Heat)
Animal Massage
Chair Massage
Esalen Massage
Infant Massage
Kripalu Bodywork
Medical Massage
Myotherapy
On-Site Massage
Pregnancy Massage
Pfrimmer Deep Muscle Therapy

Copyright © 2009, Revised 2023   *Love Me, Touch Me, Heal Me*   DrEricaGoodstone.com

Sports Massage
Watsu (Water Massage)

Structural/Functional Movement/Integration

Structural, Functional, Movement Integration body therapy methods include techniques to improve body alignment, organ functioning, flexibility of movement, and integration of the body as a holographic system. These methods may involve actual re-sculpting of the connective tissue, improved flow of cerebrospinal fluid, lymph drainage, realignment of vertebrae, release of muscle, nerve and membrane restrictions, inhibition of habitual posture patterns, stimulation of trigger points and reflexes to specific organs, or simply guiding the body to move in an easier, more graceful manner.

Alexander Technique
Applied Kinesiology
Aston-Patterning
Bindegewebsmassage/Connective Tissue
Body Logic
Bowen Method
Chiropractic
Craniosacral
Feldenkrais
Hellerwork
Holotropic Breathwork
Kurashova Method Russian Massage
Laban Movement Analysis
Lomi Lomi

Looyenwork
Manual Lymph Drainage
Mensendiek System
Myofascial Release
Network Chiropractic
Neuromuscular
Osteopathy
Physiatry
Physical Therapy
Rebirthing
Reflexology
Rolfing
Strain/Counterstrain
Touch For Health
Trager & Mentastics
Trigger Point Therapy
Visceral Manipulation

Asian Bodywork

Asian Bodywork includes body therapy methods and techniques originating throughout Asia, mostly derived from traditional Chinese medicine theory. This theory describes the health of the body in terms of the five basic elements (fire, water, earth, metal, and wood) or the functioning of the 12 pairs of primary meridians (lung, large intestine, stomach, spleen, heart, small intestine, bladder, kidney, pericardium or heart constrictor, triple heater, gall bladder, and liver) and the 8 extraordinary meridians (including conception vessel and governing vessel which run directly down the center line of the body in the front and back respectively).

Most of these methods utilize the therapist's fingers and hands, although some techniques use the therapist's shoulders, elbows, knees, and even feet. Acupuncture involves insertion of very fine needles into precise meridian locations. Therapists may determine which meridians to treat by utilizing various diagnostic methods, including differentiating among the 12 pulses in the wrist, examining the qualities of the organs represented on the hara (abdominal area), and observing the client's eyes, ears, throat and tongue.

Some methods involve extensive stretching and twisting movements, an actual physical workout for both the therapist and client. Other methods are more gentle, focusing on controlling and expanding the breath or holding various bodily positions, not unlike yoga postures. The goal of these methods is to release restrictions in the flow of energy or chi throughout the body.

Acupressure
Acupuncture
Amma (Anma)
Amma Therapy
Chi Gong (Qi Gong) (Chi Kung)
Chun Do Sun Bup
Do-In
Jin Shin Do Bodymind Acupressure
Jin Shin Jyutsu
Lomi Lomi

Ohashiatsu
Thai Massagge
Tuina

Energetic Bodywork

    Energetic bodywork includes body therapy methods and techniques from healers around the world, focusing on the energetic fields within and surrounding our bodies. These methods range from direct contact on the skin, to indirect contact an inch to a foot or more above the body, to distant indirect contact from another room, another city, or anywhere on the planet. Training in these methods may be simple or complex, requiring anywhere from a basic one-weekend training to an ongoing series of structured lessons for one to three years or longer. Some methods may involve an initiation process, transferring of healing potential from teacher to student, while other methods teach students to become attuned to their own natural healing potential.

Access
Aura Balancing
Barbara Brennan School
Chakra Healing
Chi Self Massage
Energy Balancing
Intuitive Medicine
Mariel

Multiincarnational Recall
Emotional Body Balancing
Polarity Therapy
Pranic Healing
Radiance Technique
Reiki
Seven Rays
Shamanism
Therapeutic Touch
Zero Balancing

Somatic and Expressive Arts Therapies

Somatic and expressive arts therapies include body-centered therapies and activities that may or may not involve actual touch. Through movement, dance, sports, yoga postures, martial arts, dramatic performances, artistic expression, visualization, as well as through touch, our bodies may express feelings that have previously been unavailable to our conscious minds. Some somatic and expressive arts therapists are trained artists (musicians, singers, actors, dancers, and artists). Others received their major training in one or more body therapy methods. Although some somatic and expressive arts therapists have been educated in graduate academic programs (music therapy, dance therapy, art therapy), many have not received psychotherapy training. Clients would be well advised to seek the assistance of a qualified psychotherapist, to help them assimilate into their daily lives, the powerful emotional experiences that may result from this type of therapy.

Art Therapy
Biofeedback
Dance Therapy
Deep Emotional Release Work
EMDR (Eye Movement Desensitization Reprocessing)
Hypnotherapy
Iridology
Martial Arts
Movement Therapy
Music Therapy
Ortho-Bionomy
Phoenix Rising Yoga Therapy
Pilates Method
Primal Therapy
Primal Integration
Process Acupressure
Psychodrama
Somatoemotional Release
Sports And Exercise
Thought Field Therapy
Visualization

When our bodies move, are touched directly, indirectly or even from a great distance, our emotional equilibrium is often affected. Repressed feelings we didn't even know we had may come bubbling to the surface. Tears, anger, confusion, fear, and childhood memories often emerge unexpectedly.

Many body therapists are highly skilled practitioners. Many are licensed in their state or nationally certified in their specific body therapy modality. However, most do not have adequate, if any, psychotherapy training. Qualified psychotherapists are required to have the following minimal academic credentials:

- Psychiatrist, M.D. degree
- Psychologist, Ph.D. degree
- Clinical Social Worker, M.S.W. degree
- Marriage and Family Therapist, M.A. degree
- Clinical Mental Health Counselor, M.A. degree
- Psychiatric Nurse, R.N. and M.S. degrees.

However, just as qualified body therapists often do not have psychotherapy training, qualified psychotherapists do not usually have adequate, **if any**, body therapy training.

In 1996, The First National Conference on Body Oriented Psychotherapy/The 4th International Congress of Psycho-Corporeal Therapies, met in Beverly, Massachusetts. This coming together of many of the leading body oriented psychotherapists in this country and in the world, led to the creation of the USABP (United States Association for Body Psychotherapy). The first official USABP conference was held in Boulder, Colorado, in June 1998, the second was held in June 2000, and the third is scheduled for 2002. The author of this book, Dr. Erica

Goodstone, was one of the original thirteen steering committee members who steered this important organization into the professional status and international recognition it has today.

The goals of this organization are twofold: * to educate the public about this powerful transformative work and * to create ethical guidelines, educational standards, certification and licensing review boards of this burgeoning profession. **Without exception, every person who has combined touch with counseling reports profound and often seemingly miraculous results happening in sessions with their clients.**

Somatic Body Psychotherapy

Body Psychotherapists (sometimes called Body Oriented Psychotherapists or Somatic Body Psychotherapists) are trained and certified in both psychotherapy and body therapy methods or in specific modalities that combine psychotherapy with touch and body awareness. The counseling modalities used in body psychotherapy are similar to those used in traditional talk psychotherapy (psychoanalysis, behavior modification, gestalt therapy, cognitive therapy, even hypnosis). There are many different types of body psychotherapy. Some are very gentle and respectful of the client's needs and boundaries. Other methods are more forceful, focused on breaking through defenses and body armoring. The common element of all body psychotherapy methods is the use of touch and the focus on body awareness. A body psychotherapy session may include guided imagery, focused breathing, role playing, movement, expressive arts, and emotional release while at the same time counseling clients about the psychological underpinnings and current meanings of the issues and emotions that emerge.

Bioenergetic Analysis
Bodymind Centering
Bodynamics
Calatonia and Subtle Touch (Brazilian)
Core Energetics
Focusing
Hakomi Integrative Somatics
Integrative Body Psychotherapy
Lomi School
Organismic Psychotherapy
Pesso Boyden Psychomotor System
Radix
Reichian Therapy
Rosen Method
Rubenfeld Synergy
Somatics
Somatic Psychotherapy Biosynthesis

Touch Is Essential For Living

Of all the five senses, touch is the most essential. We can lose our sight and hearing and ability to speak, yet still find pleasure in the taste and smell of food, the scent of flowers, animals, and people we love, and the sensation of touching and being touched. If we no longer smell or taste our food, we can still derive pleasure from feeling the various textures with our lips, our tongues and our teeth. We can still enjoy touching and being touched.

Without touch, we do not thrive. Babies, adults, and the aged alike, become angry, depressed, despondent, and eventually get sick and die when deprived of touch and sensual stimulation. Humans are communal beings. We need, desire, and crave contact with each other. People who have lost their mobility have reminded us of the life-saving importance of touch.

Well-known author Helen Keller, blind, deaf and unable to speak from birth, was taught to use her mind, learned to touch and enjoy being touched. She thrived on human contact, without words. Ken Keyes Jr., noted author and workshop leader, without the use of his arms and legs, married and enjoyed touching and being touched throughout his life. After a tragic equestrian accident that left him paralyzed, the popular actor Christopher Reeves, in several intimate TV interviews, tearfully reminded us of the power of touch. His wife stroking his forehead and his son kissing his cheeks kept him connected to feeling human and alive. It is touch that puts Helen Keller, Ken Keyes Jr., Christopher Reeves, and most of us, in contact with our essential humanness and capacity to give and receive love.

The Healing Power of Touch

Touch heals. Touch also hurts. Being touched by someone we love or receiving touch from a skilled and caring body therapist is often a joy. Being touched by someone with an unclear or harmful intention sometimes hurts. Nowadays, touching with even the most honorable intention, has become suspect in this country. In fact, some school districts are taking a very strong stance against teachers who touch students for any reason. Touching a student can be grounds for immediate dismissal. Even among students, if one student claims that touch by another student was inappropriate or abusive, the courts may *now hold the school district responsible. But research about touch in psychotherapy indicates mostly positive effects.

When we are touched, we often feel emotions we have not felt for a long time, as we become more aware of unresolved issues in our lives. When we express our emotions in the presence of a caring and skilled therapist, painful memories emerge, are expressed, and lose their emotional charge. Only then can we begin to enjoy pleasurable experiences and sensations, creating new, positive and pleasant memories.

How Have You Been Touched?

- *How are you touched in your current relationship?*
- *What are your earliest touch memories?*
- *Were you touched frequently, sometimes, or hardly at all?*
- *What was the quality of touch you received: pleasant, unpleasant, gentle, harsh, abusive, intrusive, sensual, sexual, wanted, unwanted?*

How Do You Touch?

- *How do you touch in your current relationship?*
- *What are your earliest memories of touching others?*
- *Did you touch others frequently, sometimes, or hardly at all?*
- *What was the quality of your touch like for others: pleasant, unpleasant, gentle, harsh, abusive, intrusive, sensual, sexual, wanted, unwanted by others?*

Copyright © 2009, Revised 2023   *Love Me, Touch Me, Heal Me*   DrEricaGoodstone.com

TOUCH YOUR BODY

- *What body parts are most sensitive, least sensitive, painful, numb, sensual, pleasurable?*

- *What body parts do you want someone to touch? Why?*

- *What body parts do you want others not to touch? Why not?*

In each of the following touching exercises, notice your thoughts and feelings as you touch each body part. After you become comfortable touching yourself, you can repeat this exercise with a willing partner.

Massage Your Body

Gently and firmly rub, grasp and massage your body, in the following sequence. With your right hand and fingers, massage your left shoulder, upper arm, elbow, forearm, wrist and hand. With your left hand and fingers, massage your right shoulder, upper arm, elbow, forearm, wrist and hand. With both hands massage your lower back, waist, abdomen; upper back and chest, neck and throat. Press your fingers into the base of head and across your entire scalp. Gently rub and caress your temples, ears, chin, jaw, cheeks, forehead and entire face.

Shake and Rock Your Body

Gently and firmly shake and rock your body, in the following sequence: left shoulder, arm and hand; right shoulder, arm and hand; left leg, right leg. Shake your hips from side to side, forward/back, and in circles to the right and circles to the left. Shake your jaw, neck and head. Hold both shoulders and rock yourself like a baby.

Hold Your Body

Rub both hands together to build heat and energy. In a seated position, use both hands to gently hold the following body parts for 30 seconds: Using right palm, hold left shoulder, upper arm, elbow, forearm, wrist, hand. Using left palm, hold right shoulder, upper arm, elbow, forearm, wrist, hand. Place both hands on knees, thighs and then hips.. Place right hand on abdomen and left hand on lower back. Place both hands close together on back of neck, on chin, and then on cheeks. Place right hand on upper chest and left hand on vertebrae in upper back and neck. Place right hand in front of throat and left hand on back of neck. Place right hand on forehead and left hand on base of skull. Place fingertips on eyelids without pressing. Cross arms and place one palm on each shoulder.

TOUCH YOUR PARTNER'S BODY

If you do not have a partner, skip this exercise. You can return to it at some future date with a new partner. If you do have a partner, repeat the previous exercises by taking turns touching your partner and having your partner touch you. Notice your thoughts and feelings, as the toucher or touchee.

Massage Your Partner's Body

Before approaching your partner's body, ask for permission. Throughout this exercise be mindful of your partner's possible sensitivity and self-consciousness. Stop and ask for permission often. If your partner expresses discomfort at any point, remove your hands immediately and only continue with your partner's expressed permission. Now begin to massage your partner's body, gently, firmly, and with utmost respect, in the following sequence. With both hands and fingers, massage your partner's left shoulder, upper arm, elbow, forearm, wrist and hand. Then massage your partner's left shoulder, upper arm, elbow, forearm, wrist and hand. Now, with both hands massage your partner's lower back, waist, abdomen, upper back and chest, neck and throat. Press your fingers into the base of head and across your entire scalp. Gently rub and caress your temples, ears, chin, jaw, cheeks, forehead and entire face.

Shake and Rock Your Partner's Body

With both hands, shake and rock your partner's body, gently and firmly, in the following sequence. Ask your partner to stand. With both hands gently and firmly shake your partner's left shoulder, arm and hand. Now shake your partner's right shoulder, arm and hand. Shake your partner's left leg followed by shaking the right leg. Now, firmly and respectfully, move your partner's hips from side to side, forward/back, and in circles to the right and circles to the left. Gently and firmly move your partner's jaw, neck and head. Wrap both your arms around your partner's upper back and rock gently as if you were holding a tender baby.

Hold Your Partner's Body

Ask your partner to sit with eyes closed. Rub your own hands together to build heat and energy. Place your hands on your partner's body, holding each position for 30 seconds, in the following sequence. Hold your partner's right shoulder, upper arm, elbow, forearm, wrist, and hand. Now hold your partner's left shoulder, upper arm, elbow, forearm, wrist, hand. Place both hands on your partner's feet, ankles, knees, thighs and then hips.. Place your right hand on your partner's abdomen and your left hand on your partner's lower back. Place both hands close together on the back of your partner's neck, on the chin, and then on your partner's cheeks. Place your right hand on your partner's upper chest and your left hand on the vertebrae in the upper back and neck. Place your right hand very lightly in front of your partner's throat and your left hand in back of the neck. Place your right hand on your partner' forehead and your left hand at the base of your partner's skull. Very gently without any pressure place your fingertips on your partner's eyelids. Finish by placing both of your hands firmly on your partner's shoulders.

When you have completed the sequence, repeat this exercise with the receiver becoming the toucher. When you have both been touchers and touchees, spend a few minutes describing what this touching experience has been like for you in both roles.

Copyright © 2009, Revised 2023   *Love Me, Touch Me, Heal Me*   DrEricaGoodstone.com

FOOTNOTES

Chapter 1

4. Pert, Candace, Ph.D. *Molecules of Emotion*
5. Locke, Steven, M.D. , Ader R, Besedovskhy H, Hall, NR, Solomon, GF, Strom, T. editors (1985). *Foundations of Psychoneuroimmunology.* Hawthorne, NY: Aldine Publishing Co.
6. Reich, Wilhelm, Carfagno, Vincent R., Translator. (1973) *The Function of the Orgasm: Discovery of the Orgone.* NY: Farrar, Straus and Giroux.

Chapter 2

1. Wayne, Dennis (1973). *Children of the Creche.* New York. Appleton-Century-Crofts.
2. Gaynor, Mitchell. (June 1999) *Sounds of Healing: A Physician Reveals the Therapeutic Power of Sound, Voice, and Music.* NY: Broadway Books
3. Christiane Northrup (2006) *The Wisdom of Menopause: Creating Physical and Emotional Health and Healing During the Change.* NY: Bantam Books.
4. Alan R. Hirsch, M.D. (April, 1998) *Scentsational Sex: The Secret to Using Aroma for Arousal.* Element Books
5. Prescott, James. *How Culture Shapes the Developing Brain and the Future of Humanity.* (March 2004). Byron Child/Kindred, Issue 9.
6. Harlow, Harry, F. M.D. R "Development of affection in primates. Pp/ 157-166 in: E. L. Bliss, Ed. (1962) *Roots of Behavior.* NY: Harper.

Chapter 3

1. http://www.miami.edu/touch-research/ (Field, Tiffany, Touch Research Institute)
2. http://www.nccam.nih.gov/ (The National Institutes for Health, Office of Alternative and Complementary Medicine)

3. http://www.amtamassage.org (The American Massage Therapy Association)
4. http://www.upledger.com (The Upledger Institute Healthplex Center)
5. http://www.USABP.org (U.S. Association for Body Psychotherapy)
   http://EABP.org (European Association for Body Psychotherapy)
6. http://www.rubenfeldsynergy.com (Rubenfeld Synergy Method)

CONGRATULATIONS!

By finishing *TOUCH ME … PLEASE,* **Part II in the** *LOVE ME*, *TOUCH ME, HEAL ME* **Complete Book,** *y*ou have completed some powerful, life-transforming exercises. You have self-reflected and contemplated how and why you touch and how you might benefit from therapy that includes talk and touch. Stories of individual revelations and transformations may have intrigued you and perked your curiosity. If you have gained personal insight, understanding of your self and others, and you want to continue on this path of loving and healing your life, then you will surely benefit from reading and following the exercises in the next two chapters in this valuable book.

HEAL ME ... PLEASE

PART III

Heal Me…Please, **Part III, is dedicated to**

- **Joel Goldsmith**, whose *Infinite Way* teachings have cleared my spiritual blocks as I continually realized there is only one power
- **Marian Streuken Bachmann**, modern artist Magnifique, who encouraged me many years ago to get my book published and invited me to my first *Infinite Way* group at her home in NYC – and the rest is history
- **Tony Titshall**, for opening his home so that a dedicated group of us can share and strengthen our connection to that one power together
- **Sheila McKinney**, for introducing me to Tony Titshall's group, and supporting me as I struggled to let go og my old beliefs and concepts
- **Ken Lasdowski**, for offering his loving insight, acceptance and joy of living that allowed me to more easily accept my current circumstances without resisting
- **John Delnome**, my friend and confidant, who allows me to share my concerns when the challenges of daily life threaten to disturb my peace of mind.

INTRODUCTION

Heal me ... please

Why me? Why this? Why now?

Heal me, please

What will you do to me?

Heal me, please

What will I have to do?

Heal me ... please.

Erica Goodstone, Ph.D. 1/29/00

Healing Happens In Every Moment

Healing happens in every moment, in every cell and organ of our body. Loving, touching, and being touched with love, we heal. When we heal, our bodies relax and our lives come into balance. In healing, we discover our own truth, face our inner spirit, and we begin to know God.

In **Heal Me … Please**, the third book in this four part series, we examine the healing process: what we believe about healing, how we have healed our self and others, and how we can create healing in our bodies, our intimate relationships, our sexuality, and our lives. You will discover what it takes to heal whatever ails you. You will look at what has helped you to heal and what has hindered your healing in the past. Through writing exercises and closed eye meditations, you will discover new ways to connect with and stimulate your own healing presence within.

Together we will examine our sensual responses, the healing messages revealed to us through our senses, and ways to enhance our sensual responsiveness. As you increase your own sensual awareness, you will naturally become more readily attuned to the unique sensual responsiveness of everyone, including your most intimate partners.

Through stories of real people's lives, we explore the life transforming, healing potential of touch and body psychotherapy. These stories are excerpts of actual case histories, therapy sessions, emotional responses, and eventual healing that took place in seminars and private sessions. Of course, names and identifying personal characteristics have been altered to protect anonymity. None of my clients will be able to say with certainty, "That's me!" Yet, as you read these stories, you may recognize something familiar within yourself. You may even identify with some of these clients' experiences.

We are all voyagers on a life path back to wholeness. Many of us tend to focus on our problems and the possible causes, recalling in detail the many ways we may have felt wronged. In this book we turn our focus toward healing our problems, letting them go, and moving toward creating what we truly desire.

****

HEAL ME ... PLEASE

"Heal Thyself and Do No Harm"

Hippocratic Dictum

Healing happens in every moment, in every cell and organ of our body. When we love and are touched with love, we heal. When we heal, our body relaxes and our life come into balance. When we heal, we discover our own truth, we face our inner spirit, and we begin to know God. In Part III, we examine the healing process: what we believe about healing, how we have healed our self and others, and how we can create healing in our body, our intimate relationships, our sexuality, and our life.

HEAL ME ... PLEASE

Heal Me ... Please

I came to you
Lost in despair
You took me in
With open arms
Welcome
My darling friend
Soul mate
On the path
To unconditional love
Acceptance
Being
Human Be-ing
My words came pouring out
Flooding the room
Intensifying
Exploding
Subsiding
Softening
Subdued

My spirit calmed down
I felt safe
Connected
Affected
Protected
Loved

Copyright © 2009, Revised 2023   *Love Me, Touch Me, Heal Me*   DrEricaGoodstone.com

You listened
Open arms
You spoke
Open heart

My troubled spirit
Found its home
Inside myself
Again

Copyright © 8/27/97 Erica Goodstone, Ph.D.

HEAL ME ... PLEASE

CHAPTER 1

HEAL ME ... PLEASE

Oh My Aching Back!

Lying on the floor. Cold. Frightened. Unable to move. The last time I looked at the clock it was 10:30 A.M. The time now was 2 P.M. Moving or turning even slightly was excruciating, sending my body into a contraction, shooting pain up and down my spine. It all happened because of overexerting my self, pushing beyond my limits, not paying attention to the messages my body was loudly sending (spasms, pain – take it easy) then accidentally falling off a chair. I prayed to God, "Please help me get up." Another hour passed.

Wondering, "What can I do to help myself, I suddenly thought of reflexology. The only body parts I could move without causing unbearable pain were my fingers. Desperate, I pressed the fingers of my right hand along the outer edge of the palm of my left hand in the area corresponding to the spine of my back.. Then I used my left hand to press the same area on the palm of my right hand and fingers. Miraculously, in a little while, I was able to maneuver my body ever so slowly to position my back so that it was facing a portable heater that happened to be on the floor nearby. Finally, I was close enough to turn the heater on. Eventually, the heat relaxed my contracted back muscles just enough for me to manage to stand up. Standing felt like paradise to me.

While lying on the floor for 4 1/2 hours, I prayed to God and my angels to please help me get up and get to a doctor. I believe they were there assisting me, but they had to be sure I would use all of my own resources first. I had the terrifying thought, "What if the pain never ends? What if I can never walk and move and exercise and enjoy life's activities again?"

Every one of us is vulnerable to the unpredictability and randomness of life. Now is the time to face and get on with our life; now, at this moment, while we still have most of our senses and most of our physical, emotional and mental abilities intact. Without warning, we can suddenly meet with extreme good fortune or unanticipated disaster. The untimely deaths (through plane crashes, automobile accidents, murders, assassinations, and other tragedies) people we hear about in the news, or perhaps our own personal experiences, have reminded us again and again about the fragility and preciousness of life.

Many of us complain bitterly and continuously about our life, not realizing that when we have our health and most of our senses are working adequately, we truly have everything we need. If we have lost our lover, failed in school, been fired from a job, or abused by our spouse or parents, as long as we have our senses and our mind, we can re-create our life to fulfill our dreams. As long as we are alive, it is never too late to heal.

Healing happens in every moment of our life. Cells die. Cells regenerate. New cells are born. In fact, we actually have a totally new body, all of our cells replaced with new cells, every seven years. Our immune system continuously works to ward off foreign invaders. But the ultimate healing happens when we are ready to face our Creator, when our body prepares us for physical death. As we die, our body unwinds, letting go of all the stress that binds us, releasing the emotional and physical habit patterns that have ruled our life.

I remember my polarity therapy colleague, Ray, poignantly describing a polarity session with his aging mother. He cradled her head in his open hands, his index fingers gently resting against the sides of her neck in a position that creates a sense of well-being, safety, feeling nurtured and loved. As he held her head, his mother breathed her final breath.

Ray continued to hold her head, pausing only briefly to dial 911. As the emergency crew arrived, Ray observed that, even after his mother was no longer breathing and her heart had stopped beating, her energy continued to unwind. In his gentle grasp, he felt his mother's head and neck, which had always been stiff and almost immovable, beginning to give way in his hands, to soften and to move easily from side to side. As he held his mother's head, he watched her emotional burdens vanish before his eyes. The stress lines on her face diminished and almost disappeared. Her face took on an innocent, child-like, almost angelic appearance. Ray felt assured that her chronic human problems had been removed, that she was healed and at peace and ready to face her creator.

Many people who have been pronounced dead, whose hearts actually stopped beating, claim to have had life transforming experiences. Many have seen a dark tunnel and a bright light, some say they have met with spiritual beings, deceased family members, and old friends. Not everyone who nearly died saw the same visions or felt the same feelings. However, most of these people came to realize that nothing in this lifetime is more important than love. Nothing surpasses love.

- **Believing is receiving.**
- **Believe in love.**
- **Believe in the power of love to heal.**
- **Watch miracles happen.**

The People You Have Loved

Sit quietly and close your eyes. Take a few slow, deep, easy breaths. Now, think about the people you have loved. For each person you have loved, ask the following questions:

What about this person touched my heart and caused me to feel love?

Would I love this person if I first met him or her now? Why?

What did I believe this person could offer me or do for you?

Was I satisfied or disappointed?

How did I respond?

What did I believe I could offer that person?

The People Who Have Loved You

Recall the people who have loved you.

For each person who has loved you, ask the following questions:

What about me touched their heart and caused them to feel love?

Would this person love me if he or she met me now? Why?

What did they believe I could offer them or do for them?

Were they satisfied or disappointed?

Copyright © 2009, Revised 2023   *Love Me, Touch Me, Heal Me*   DrEricaGoodstone.com

How did they respond?

What did I believe they could offer me?

How Have You Loved Your Self?

At the top of one page write: *How I Have Loved Myself.* Make a list of the ways you have shown concern and love for yourself, attempted to satisfy your own needs and desires, put your own needs before the needs and requests of others in the distant past, the recent past and in your current life.

At the top of a second page write: *How I Have Not Loved Myself.* List the ways you have disregarded yourself, ignored your own needs and desires, put others' needs and requests before your own in the distant past, the recent past and in your current life.

How many of us are right here, right now, existing in a place of our own choosing where we can suffer? Some of us have been taught that life is hard, that we don't deserve to feel good, that feeling good is actually bad, or that if we allow our self to feel good, something bad will surely follow. If we believe life is hard, even at those times when it is easy, we will probably find a way to make life difficult. On the other hand, some of us believe that life and people *should* be easy or *should* be a certain way. If we believe life should be easy, when we fall into difficult circumstances, we will probably suffer more than the situation calls for.

Your Suffering

Who or what in your life do you believe has caused you to suffer?

Make a list of every person or situation, including God and including yourself, who you believe has caused you to suffer. Begin with, *"It's his/her fault that ...."* Here's you chance to point a finger and to blatantly blame everything and everyone in your life who you believe has caused you to suffer. When you finish your blame list, answer the following questions:

Where and how did you learn about the way life is and the way people are?

Did you learn that you are good, worthy and deserving?

Did you learn that others are good, worthy and deserving?

In what ways have you interfered with attaining, having, and keeping what you want?

In what ways have you created and participated in your own suffering?

Most of us have not learned to face life as it is. We develop faulty ideas about the way we think our lives *should* be. Often, we have unrealistic and unfair expectations about the way other people *should* be, *should* feel, *should* behave. Sometimes we are unrealistically optimistic about the potential of others, choosing to see them the way we would like them to be instead of truly seeing who they are. Sometimes we make comparisons between the way we live and the way others appear to be living. When our lives seem to be less than the way we perceive others' lives to be, we may become anxious and demanding and actually, through our own actions, sabotage the good that we do have.

Forgiving Yourself and Others

At the top of one page write, *People I Have Not Forgiven*. List the names of those you have not been able to forgive.

What interferes with my ability or desire to forgive this person or persons?

What would have to happen for me to be able to forgive this person or persons?

At the top of a second page write, *What I Have Not Forgiven Myself For?* List the traits or actions you have been unable to forgive yourself for having or doing.

What interferes with my ability or desire to forgive myself?

What would have to happen for me to be able to forgive myself?

Forgiveness is one of the most powerful tools we have in our possession at all times. Just as we can suddenly experience extreme good fortune or extreme disaster, we can just as suddenly choose to forgive a person, place or situation. Forgiving ourselves and others helps us to heal. If we harbor feelings of being an unfortunate victim, of having been irrevocably harmed, of believing that someone or something is unworthy of God's love, we eventually hurt ourselves. Forgiveness is not to please or heal others. Forgiveness heals our own lives. No matter what has happened in the past, when we choose to forgive, our minds and our hearts become more receptive to love. We revive our joy in living and once again discover our true passion.

Where Is Your Passion?

What activities or goals create excitement and passion for you?

What activities or goals keep your mind focused?

What activities, for you, would be dream adventures?

What activities would you like to share with others?

What activities would you prefer to do alone?

What personal traits, emotions, people or situations in your life have interfered with feeling your passion and pursuing those activities that you feel passionate about?

What would it take to rekindle your passion for life?

The Healing Power of Love

There is nothing more real and more powerful than love. We can feel the reverberation of love in every cell of our body. Physicists have measured heart energy. Heart transplant recipients learn the language of the heart, their own and that of their heart donor.

Dis-ease, physical or psychological, is often a sign that we have been ignoring, abusing, neglecting, avoiding or actually hating a part of us. Many of us neglect to take care of our body's needs for nourishing food, regular and proper exercise, good body mechanics, postural alignment, sleep, and relaxation. Our body may tolerate this situation for awhile. In time, however, our body parts will break down.

We may have been indulging in sexual activity without intimacy or commitment, ignoring and denying our heart's need for loving connection. Over time, our heart's message will reach the brain which may signal to our pituitary, the master gland, to stop producing hormones that stimulate desire and lead to orgasm. Our sexual organs, in response to our heart's message, may finally decide to give up the fight and shut down.

All of our organs share the same network of blood and blood vessels, lymph and lymph vessels, nerves, muscles, glands, connective tissue, fat and skin. They all need to receive fresh oxygen from the lungs. Spend a moment to contemplate the holographic nature of our amazing mind-body-spiritual system. Can you fathom that this whole system functions as one cohesive unit of love?

Without love and touch and stimulation, infants as well as the elderly become depressed, chronically ill, and eventually die. Even animals die without love and attention. A friend of mine had two wonderful cats. One summer, while she traveled, she left her two cats home alone, one and off, for a period of two months. She left plenty of food and water for them and she returned once every week or two to check in on them and repack her bags. On one of her visits to her home, she found the older cat lying dead in the middle of her living room. After burying the cat, she went off on another trip. When she returned home a week later, she found her other cat had also died. My friend learned a painful lesson she will never forget. Both of her cats died from lack of love and touch and nurturing.

Your House Pets

Do you have a pet?

If not, why have you chosen not to have a pet?

> *What type of pet/s would you get if your circumstances allowed for it, cat, dog, bird, fish, horse, monkey, other?*
>
> *How do you believe this pet could benefit your life and your health?*

If you do have a pet or several pets, explain why you have chosen to have a pet and why you have selected the particular pet/s.

> *What type of pet/s do you have?*
>
> *What factors influenced your choice?*
>
> *How do your pets show their love?*
>
> *How do you show love toward your pet/s?*
>
> *What type of pet/s would you get if your circumstances allowed for it, cat, dog, bird, fish, other?*
>
> *How do you believe this pet could benefit your life and your health?*

Why would you choose to have a cat or a dog as your pet? They require care, attention, time, and money. They restrict your freedom and curtail your travel and other activities. Research shows that people with pets are happier, healthier and less stressed. Why? Cats and dogs emanate pure love. They live in the moment and they love unconditionally. They respond to your nonverbal cues. They respond to your mood

swings and emotions. They feel deeply and love you completely.

Love Your Body As Your Most Precious Pet

Love your body. Honor it. Nurture it. Be gentle with it. Train it to perform at optimum levels for you. Give it rest. Allow it to relax. Give it rewards - lots of rewards, frequently, at regular intervals. Talk kindly to your body. Listen to its messages. Pay attention to your body just the way a caring mother listens to the sounds of her newborn infant.

Your body's messages are loud and clear, not subtle. Many of us have blocked our hearing, refusing to listen. Ignoring our body's messages and signals will not make the problems go away. They may go into hiding. The signals may get softer and more difficult to decipher. The problems may go deeper and become more pervasive, spreading to distant parts of your body.

Candace Pert's ground-breaking scientific research on neuropeptides reveals that our bodies do, indeed, function as an integrated network system. Her studies show that information is stored, processed and exchanged through information carriers known as neuropeptides. These special substances are stored in the bone marrow, the place where immune cells develop. Neuropeptides have receptor sites in many different parts of the brain and in our body organs. Hormones and neuropeptides are also distributed throughout the body through the master gland, the pituitary, located at the base of the brain.

The ignored body parts or organs may lay dormant, isolated and neglected for a long time, perhaps years and even decades. However, at some point, your organs will begin to seek attention, each organ fighting for control. Imagine that? Imagine your mind demanding respect, your heart crying for compassion, your liver raging to eliminate its negative debris, your lungs gasping for more breathing room, and your stomach filling your abdominal cavity against the will of your intestines.

In a happy, cohesive family everyone has a chance to thrive. But, if family members are upset, fighting with each other, and become distant and isolated, each person is affected. Isn't it much wiser for family members to talk to each other privately, regularly, and sometimes at family meetings to air any grievances, and to reinforce the love of happy family life. Our bodies, when healthy, function like one big happy family. But when communication between our body cells breaks down, we become like a dysfunctional family, our individual organs starving for love and nourishment.

A FAMILY AFFAIR

Bring your body to your own family party. Let all your internal members greet each other, hug and have a quiet conversation. Let each part express its needs, desires, dreams and feelings. Let each part respond to every other part. Imagine all your organs and body parts having a meeting where they make an agreement to listen and respect one another's needs. In your journal, list the statements your body parts agree are essential for the healthy functioning of your entire bodily organization.

How Have You Been Treating Your Body?

How have you been treating your body as the container and home of your internal family?

How have you been treating each of your body organs?

Have you maintained contact with every part of your body?

Have you ignored or responded to your body's messages?

Have you handled problems by cutting out the offending body part, removing it, sending it away?

What has been the effect of actions you have taken toward your own body?

Copyright © 2009, Revised 2023   *Love Me, Touch Me, Heal Me*   DrEricaGoodstone.com

When Your Body Is Healthy

When your body is healthy, your emotions stable, and your five senses working, you expect you will always remain this way. Most of us don't realize that in one instant, any moment, our lives can change dramatically. A car accident, a sports injury, even an accidental fall can leave us bedridden, or walking around with unsightly bandages or a clumsy back or neck brace. Suddenly we may become self-conscious and inhibited, feeling disabled and different. In our Marlboro Man, Super Woman, Body Piercing society, being physically challenged, ill, or dependent on others, is not okay.

There but for the grace of God go I. Every one of us is vulnerable to the unpredictability and randomness of life. Without warning, on any day of our lives, we can meet with mild or extreme good fortune or life-threatening disaster.

The Hospital Bed

Close your eyes. Imagine you have just awakened from a deep sleep. Nurses are standing nearby. The doctor who examined you asks, in a concerned voice, *"How are you feeling?"* All you feel is groggy, sleepy and bewildered. You don't know why you're here or where you are. The doctor explains, "You were in a terrible accident. We didn't think you were going to make it. You must have a strong will to live." You want to sit up. That's when you realize, *"I can't move. I want to talk but the words won't come out. A tear drips down your face."* The doctor notices and tells you the words you are dreading. *"You are paralyzed from head to toe. You have a rare condition called "Locked in Syndrome."* We see that your right eye tears and your eyelid opens and closes. We will set up a special gadget for you. By moving your right eye, and selecting letters of the alphabet, you will be able to communicate with us.

Sound farfetched and not possible? Two astounding books were written by victims of this horrible affliction. Using only the blinking of his left eye, Jean-Dominique Bauby, editor in chief of *French Elle*, selected letters of the alphabet to write a book about his ordeal. Julia Tayson Tavalaro, a beautiful, happily married, 32 year old woman, living in her dream home with her beloved husband and 14 month old daughter, after a series of sudden strokes, was only able to make small movements with her head, neck and eyes and eventually some groaning, grunting sounds. A specially constructed pointer attached to her head allowed her to select letters, one by one, to write lengthy poems and complete her memoirs.

Life Is Precious

Life is precious. Every moment counts. Savor every moment. Ken Keyes, author of *The Handbook for Higher Consciousness* (Living Love Center, 1975), tells a beautiful story about living in the moment. *A young man in the jungle, pursued by a tiger, quickly climbs a tree. The tiger rapidly approaching, the young man is hanging onto a branch that he knows is about to break off the tree. At that moment, he notices a beautiful, ripe strawberry. As his branch is breaking and he is about to meet his fate in the jaws of the hungry tiger below, the young man reaches out, plucks the strawberry, eats it, and enjoys the sweet taste.*

That young man was living in the moment, enjoying the most that was possible even as he faced a certain death. Perhaps you have personally experienced a devastating physical illness. Perhaps you are currently living with chronic physical or emotional problems, that may never go away. If you are currently in a physically challenged state, how are you handling it? What are you telling yourself and others?

A useful thought for you might be: **It is not what life hands us that counts, but what we do with the life we are handed.** A beautiful healing statement that someone wrote is: *Life is not freedom from the storm but peace within the storm.*

For those of us currently living in good health, imagine how you might cope if your active, healthy life came to a screaming halt, unexpectedly? Would you wallow in self-pity, anger, rage and helplessness? Would you slide through the center of a crowded subway clanking a jar of coins, begging total strangers to give you money for having no legs? I saw such a man, groveling in the midst of stressed out, disinterested working people.

As long as we are healthy, we can choose to ignore body signals, the meaning of life, and the purpose of relationships. We can ignore the power of love. However, no matter how much pride and self-sufficiency our ego pretends to have, when we become ill we need other people -- doctors, nurses, close family members, friends, neighbors, or acquaintances.

Becoming ill interferes with our normal routine in life. We are forced to curtail our activities, sometimes to remain perfectly still in bed for an indefinite period of time. During that quiet time, we have an opportunity to review our lives and to learn lessons that our illness can teach us.

Lessons From Your Illness

Remember a time when you were ill. That time could be right now. If you are currently ill, use your current situation for this exercise. Write a brief memoir of your illness.

Describe your illness.

Where were you when you first became ill?

Who was there with you at first and as the illness progressed?

How did that person treat you and how did you feel about that?

What were your told about your illness? By whom?

Did you ignore or deny your illness for any length of time? What effect did that have?

Describe your experience with health practitioners, medical doctors, nurses, hospital workers, alternative and complementary health practitioners and others who assisted you.

What were you told about your illness: diagnosis, symptoms, and prognosis for healing?

How were you treated? Describe what that person said or did.

How did you feel about the way you were treated?

Did you have a spiritual experience? Describe what happened.

Copyright © 2009, Revised 2023   *Love Me, Touch Me, Heal Me*   DrEricaGoodstone.com

How long has your illness lasted? Have you fully recovered yet?

What lingering effects are there in your body, mind, spirit, relationships?

How Have Your Health Practitioners Treated You?

Research shows that loving kindness, attention, warmth, touch, and belief in your ability to heal actually assist you in your healing process. Have your medical doctors or other health practitioners kept you waiting for very long periods of time? Have you been treated as a less important patient because you're affiliated with Managed Care, Medicaid, Medicare or other insurance that pays less than the doctor's preferred fees? Have you been examined carefully, tested adequately, listened to, and have all your questions been answered to your satisfaction? Is your doctor or health practitioner reachable by phone? How long does it take for you to schedule an appointment? Are you satisfied with the health care you have been given?

Your Healing History

Let's begin a life healing review, as far back as you can remember.

What has happened to your body, mind and spirit during your life?

What diseases, traumas, injuries and emotional hurts have you experienced?

What medications, shock treatments, surgeries or other professional medical or psychological treatments have you received?

What problems of yours were inherited, what was acquired, and how?

What have you done to cause your health problems, to make the symptoms worse or to alleviate symptoms and improve your health? What was the effect?

What have others -- health practitioners, friends, family, clergy -- done to cause your health problems, make the symptoms worse or to alleviate symptoms and improve your health? What was the effect?

How did you feel about yourself while you were ill?

How do you feel about yourself now, in relation to this illness?

What have been the long-term effects of your health problems and the way they were handled?

Your Healing Needs

Where in your life and body do you currently need healing?

How would you describe your current health, body image, and general emotional state?

How are your current relationships with friends, family, co-workers and lovers?

How is your financial situation, work, education, and career?

How do you spend your leisure time?

How comfortable is your current home?

How do you express yourself creatively?

Your Health Habits Inventory

List each of the following at the top of a page in your journal:

- **My Physical Health**
- **My Emotional and Mental Health**
- **My Social and Relationship Health**
- **My Sensual Health**
- **My Sexual Health**
- **My Spiritual and Intuitive Health**

Now, do take an inventory of the current state of your health: physical, emotional and mental, social and relationship, sensual, sexual; spiritual and intuitive. List words, phrases, sentences or entire descriptions in each category.

Change and Healing

Change and healing require faith and also conscious effort. If we continue to do what we've always done, we'll probably get what we've always gotten. As we age, we will experience diminishing returns on a poor health investment. **Let's do something different, do something positive for our own health - now!**

Your Health Investment Portfolio

In your journal draw a large circle. Divide the circle into parts, like the pieces of a pie.

Using different colored pencils, indicate the following:

What portion of my life do I devote to self-care?

What portion of my life do I devote to caring for others?

What portion of my life is filled with meaningful work and career?

What portion of my life is filled with basic chores and tasks?

What portion of my life is filled with leisure activities and play?

What portion of my life is devoted to rest, relaxation and rejuvenation?

What portion of your life is spent in meditation, prayer and spiritual practices?

Return on Your Health Investments

Maintaining good health represents a return on your investment.

What actions have your taken or not taken today and this week that are long-term investments in future ill health (unexpressed angry feelings, 3 cups of coffee for breakfast, procrastinating and worrying)

What actions have you taken today and this week that are positive self care habits and long-term investments in your future health (eating a well-balanced breakfast, remembering to breathe deeply, doing some aerobic exercise)?

YOUR COMMITMENT TO HEALING

Sit quietly, close your eyes and take a few long, slow, deep breaths. Read these the following questions a few times. Silently contemplate the meaning in your life. When you are ready, begin to write in your journal. Let your answers be as honest and thoughtful.

Remember, this is about your life, what you are willing to do to create the life you want.

Am I willing to end my commitment to suffering and begin my commitment to healing?

Is my commitment to healing my life great enough to do whatever it takes to eliminate my own inner obstacles, fears and blocks?

Am I willing to accept the power of my mind to create, my heart's knowledge of truth, and the spiritual being that exists inside of me?

Am I willing to accept, with humility, my own smallness in comparison to the universal powers that exist?

What Does God Mean To You?

Open your eyes and begin to write - automatically - as the thoughts come to you. Do not stop to think or ponder or censure. Answer this simple question, *What does God mean to me?*

Following Your Own Spiritual Path

Sit comfortably. Take a few slow, deep and easy breaths. Imagine yourself as young child. In your mind, answer the following questions:

What did you believe about God and love, angels and spirits, mother, father, and life?

As you became more conscious, perhaps before you were able to form words, what did you know about spirits and spirituality?

What is your earliest memory about religion, spirituality and God?

With what religion were your mother, father or early caretakers raised?

What did your mother, father and earliest caretakers teach you, show you or believe themselves about God, church, religion and spirituality?

In your home was there a unified belief or divergent and conflictual beliefs?

Did God, angels, higher power, entities or anything otherworldly affect you as a young child?

Did you have a spiritual crisis at any point in your early years?

Did you ever turn away from God? If so, what caused this to happen?

What do you currently believe about God, religion, and spirituality?

What do you currently believe about reincarncation, psychic phenomena, ghosts, angels, entities, clairvoyance, witchcraft, spirits, spells, seances, energy transfers?

What religion or religious beliefs and concepts do you currently follow? Describe those beliefs.

What Does God Have To Do With Your Healing?

Young children are often quite spiritual. Children are likely to see, hear and claim to connect to spirits, angels and entities from other realms of existence. Some even appear to remember previous lives. Children who are abused, isolated or abandoned may retain their connection to this other world indefinitely. But as most of us become actively involved with friends, school, and social events, we tend to leave behind our earlier spiritual connections in favor of belonging and being accepted. Joining our parents' church or synagogue, we look there for our spirituality and redemption from pain and suffering. If we are lucky, our spiritual leaders are sincere, we feel connected to a higher power, and we learn to trust in life, ourselves, each other and in God.

Many of us are not so fortunate. Perhaps our parents or our pastors have instilled in us the fear of a wrathful, vindictive God. Perhaps our parents have taught us that God is a myth, does not exist, and that humans retain within themselves the ultimate power in life. Perhaps one of our parents believes in God while the other parent does not. Perhaps our parents follow different religions, each with entirely different beliefs, code of ethics, traditions and prescriptions for happiness.

Many of us experience a spiritual crisis, at a young age, that turns us away from God. For me, it was in my adolescence. Going to temple always reminded me of the early days with my father, who was deeply religious and internally spiritual. But my friends at the time were more interested in socializing and flirting with the boys. They did not share the sense of spiritual awe that I had always known. They did not seem to care about significance of the holy days or the power of prayer.

That day, I turned away from God, my religion, prayer and spirituality, for many years to come. Fortunately for me, my connection to God was eventually reawakened. My reawakening began with the consciousness raising groups of the 70's and 80's and intensive study of different spiritual and mystical traditions: Rosicrucians, Siddha Yoga, Kabbala, breathwork, and body therapies.

A weekend experience with my mentor, Ilana Rubenfeld, and my training in Rubenfeld Synergy and polarity therapy led me to my life's work, the complex and powerful integrative work known as body psychotherapy. For me, body psychotherapy brings together all the elements of a full life. Releasing whatever blocks us from experiencing the unity within our own body, mind and spirit, body psychotherapy helps us to open our hearts to love and be with others in meaningful relationships, and to feel our connection to a higher power or God.

Your Connection To God

Close your eyes. Take a few slow, easy, full breaths as you allow your body to relax.

Imagine that you have a direct connection to a higher source with the definite knowledge that you are safe, supported, and loved.

What if all you had to do in you life was to follow this higher guidance?

How would your life change?

Would you be more demanding or more forgiving of yourself and others?

Would you expect life to be a certain way or would you find wonder and acceptance in living life, the way it is, moment to moment?

Imagine living as if there is nothing you have to do, be, or become. Allow yourself to open your heart and mind to your own personal connection to all the knowledge that exists. Imagine that all answers will be provided for you if you ask and patiently wait to receive. Pause to examine your current life situation. Ask a question about what you want to change, improve, attain, or become. Sit quietly and listen for the answer.

The Joy of Suffering

Sometimes you choose to visit a professional for help with a problem in your life. You may go to a physician and find you are not being seen for who you are, not listened to, and not really heard. You may go to a psychotherapist, speak what is true for you, and find that the therapist does not really understand you and perhaps offers advice you are not ready or willing to follow. You may choose to see an alternative and complementary practitioner who promises to offer what the traditional doctors could not. Once again, you may find you are not seen for who you are, not listened to, heard or understood.

Ultimately, you need to find a way to heal your own self. The joy in suffering is that your suffering, painful as it is, brings you closer to knowing your self. Nobody else can remove the stressors in your life, improve your diet, increase your exercise, get adequate sleep and rest, heal your thinking, balance your emotions, or forgive yourself for you. Each of us must find our own connection to God or something greater and beyond our own self. Some religious groups believe that disease, illness and mental problems do not come from God and with proper thought alone, healing can and will occur.

Is your life exactly the way you always dreamed it could be? If the answer is "Yes," congratulations! Close the book now and continue enjoying your life. But if you're like the vast majority of us, even if your life is relatively good, in some ways you are not quite happy, not quite satisfied. Perhaps you're not happy with your work, your relationships, your appearance, your family, your friendships, or your health. Perhaps you seem to have everything you *should* want yet you find yourself sabatoging your good fortune, disappointing and hurting those closes to you.

Sometimes the most devastating events - death of a loved one, life-threatening illness, even complete mental breakdown - can be a gift for the healing of our soul. Unable to run and escape in our usual manner, we are forced to remain still, to face our true selves, reveal ourselves to the world, and to reconnect with our inner knowing.

The life we are currently living is not going to last, no matter what we do. The question is: How do you want to spend the limited time you have? What is your passion, your deepest desire, your life's purpose here on earth? Are you currently fulfilling your life's goals, following your heart's desire? If not, what are you waiting for?

LET ALL YOUR SENSES

SPEAK AS YOU HEAL

HEAL ME ... PLEASE

CHAPTER 2

LET ALL YOUR SENSES SPEAK

AS YOU HEAL

Touch Me Today

Touch me ... today
Feel me
With your hands
Hear me
With your heart
Speak to me
With your eyes
Love me
With your ears

Listen to
My silent voice
The one
That hasn't spoken
For a long time

Smell and taste
My memories
The ones I shared
With you
In some forgotten
Distant past

Allow your fingers
To explore
My inner being
Those secret places
That even I
Dare not go
Those held together
Tight spots
That lock the truth
Entombed
Inside of me

Touch me now
Let all our senses
Meet
Rejoice together
Now
As we explore
The depths
And heights
Of our connection
To each other
To life
To the source

Copyright © 9/20/97 Erica Goodstone, Ph.D.

Let Your Senses Speak To You

What Are Your Five Senses Revealing?

Every moment of every day we touch and are touched by all of our senses. View something our mind tells us is beautiful. Watch innocent children or carefree animals romp and play. Our mood may instantly change from gloomy, agitated or angry to peaceful and calm. Taste delicious food or sip a cool drink of water. Our mood may lift and we find we can somehow cope more easily with our problems. Sniff familiar and favorite scents, suddenly recalling people we have loved or earlier happy times. Our spirit may calm down in the moment. Hearing loving words can soothe away our physical aches and pains. Listening ears of one who cares may alleviate our longing for love, relive our sorrow, assuage our guilt and encourage us to persist in our struggles toward attaining our dreams.

Physical touch is the most powerful aphrodisiac in the world. Intentional loving touch heals. It heals our physical wounds, unbinds our psychological scars, and reminds us of our spiritual essence. Sensual touch makes all our sense come alive with new vitality. And intimate sexual touch can lead us to union with ourselves, our partner, and with God.

Copyright © 2009, Revised 2023   *Love Me, Touch Me, Heal Me*   DrEricaGoodstone.com

Physical touch is intimate. When we touch another person we discover who they are. When we are touched we cannot hide. Perceptive hands know all there is to know through touch.

You cannot know someone without touching them. You cannot touch someone without knowing them. You may choose not to consciously know what your body and mind sensed when you touched or were touched. And you can touch another person with any of your senses, not just physical touch.

If you believe words but do not believe your touch sensations, then you are favoring your sense of hearing. If you believe what you see but do not believe your touch sensations, you are favoring your sense of sight.

Your other two senses, taste and smell, are closely related to touch. We are all naturally attracted or repelled by the odor of another person's body. A person's state of physical and emotional health will affect the odor they emanate and the taste of their skin. The taste of another person can usually only be discovered in an intimate encounter.

So we have an order of intimacy from least intimate to most. Sight and sound and smell can be the least intimate. (A perfume or a body odor so strong that you smell it from a far distance; seeing someone who doesn't know you see them; overhearing a conversation not meant for your ears). Or these senses can be extremely intimate. For example, a partner seductively undressing for your eyes only; whispers of sweet nothings directly into your ears; the scent of a special perfume that you love.

Touch and taste are always intimate. Recall the feeling of sitting too close or being touched in a private place by a stranger. Yet, all the senses are intimate. That's why we hide our head in shame (after a wrongdoing) or children hide behind mommy's skirt - not to be seen. Maybe we are afraid to speak or sing in front of large groups of people, or afraid to voice our opinions assertively - afraid to be listened to and heard. Americans often use deodorant or after-shave and cologne, afraid to allow another to smell us "au naturel". In many other countries, men and women to not attempt to cover up their natural bodily scents.

Of all the senses, taste is one we often share through tasting and sharing food together. However, most of us reserve the tasting of each other's bodily fluids to our sexual partners (and with the prevalence of disease to only a handful of select partners). And some of us choose not to share the intimacy of taste at all. Many abhor deep mouth kissing and refuse to engage in oral-genital contact. Many women are repulsed by the taste of a man's ejaculatory fluid. Many men dislike the taste or smell of a woman's vaginal fluids. Most of us would be repelled by fluids that emanate from the nose or ears or anus. Yet animals delight in sniffing and licking each other's entire bodies, anus and nostrils alike.

A developing fetus, still in its mother's womb, feels sensations, responds to sound and light, and becomes physiologically aroused. In fact, male fetuses have penile erections and female fetuses have vaginal lubrication, while still developing in the womb.

Reawakening Through Sensual Awareness

What is spiritual and sexual reawakening if not the exploration of our own bodily sensations and our inner voice and vision? We can begin by paying attention to all of our senses, one by one. Gradually increasing our sensual awareness through our eyes, ears, mouth, nose and skin will help us to become more receptive to the unique senses and scents of our most intimate partners. We will also find, in the still quiet of mindful attention, that we connect with something way beyond our own self, something infinite, powerful and the source of all that is or ever was.

WHAT DO YOU SEE?

OPEN YOUR EYES AND LOOK

Open your eyes wide and take a good look around you. Develop an artist's eye for detail.

Imagine wearing clear, neutral, objective, non-emotional glasses.

What do you see in your indoor environment every day?

Colors, shapes, patterns, arrangements, structure, cleanliness (or lack of).

At home

At work, school or leisure activity center

At senior citizen center, prison, hospital, or other place you spend time at often.

What do you see in your outdoor environment every day?

Places, nature, stores, houses, buildings, destruction, construction

What do you notice about people in your everyday life?

Physical appearance (beauty, height, weight, body shape, posture)

Clothing (style, cost, color, fabrics, fit)

Attitude, emotions, character traits, behavior

Financial and professional status

Individuality, creativity or conformity

What do you notice about yourself?

Physical appearance (beauty, height, weight, body shape, posture)

Clothing (style, cost, color, fabrics, fit)

Attitude, emotions, character traits, behavior

Financial and professional status

Individuality, creativity or conformity

JUDGE WHAT YOUR EYES SEE

Imagine wearing dark, negative, judgmental glasses.

Critique and criticize what you see in your indoor environment every day.

Colors, shapes, patterns, arrangements, structure, cleanliness (or lack of).

At home

At work, school or leisure activity center

At a senior citizen center, prison, hospital, or other place you spend time at often.

Critique and criticize what you see in your outdoor environment every day.

Places, nature, stores, houses, buildings, destruction, construction

Critique and criticize the people you see in your everyday life.

Physical appearance (beauty, height, weight, body shape, posture0

Clothing (style, cost, color, fabrics, fit)

Attitude, emotions, character traits, behavior

Financial and professional status

Copyright © 2009, Revised 2023   *Love Me, Touch Me, Heal Me*   DrEricaGoodstone.com

Individuality, creativity or conformity

What do you notice about yourself?

Physical appearance (beauty, height, weight, body shape, posture)

Clothing (style, cost, color, fabrics, fit)

Attitude, emotions, character traits, behavior

Financial and professional status

Individuality, creativity or conformity

Imagine wearing rose colored, positive, loving and unconditionally accepting glasses.

Praise and enjoy what you see in your indoor environment every day.

Colors, shapes, patterns, arrangements, structure, cleanliness (or lack of).

At home

At work, school or leisure activity center

At a senior citizen center, prison, hospital, or other place you spend time at often

Praise and enjoy what you see in your outdoor environment every day.

Places, nature, stores, houses, buildings, destruction, construction

Praise and enjoy the people you see in your everyday life.

Physical appearance (beauty, height, weight, body shape, posture0

Clothing (style, cost, color, fabrics, fit)

*Attitude, emotions, character **traits**, behavior*

Financial and professional status

Individuality, creativity or conformity

What do you notice about yourself?

Physical appearance (beauty, height, weight, body shape, posture)

Clothing (style, cost, color, fabrics, fit)

Attitude, emotions, character traits, behavior

Financial and professional status

Individuality, creativity or conformity

SET YOUR SIGHTS

Close your eyes.

Imagine a present scene, a picture of your world the way it is right now.

Your Environment

People

Yourself

See beneath the surface.

See beyond people's egos, defenses, fears, separating actions

See beyond your own ego, defenses, fears, separating actions

Copyright © 2009, Revised 2023   *Love Me, Touch Me, Heal Me*   DrEricaGoodstone.com

> *See your dreams, your potential, your capabilities*

Imagine living in your ideal world.

> *Describe your indoor and outdoor environments.*
>
> *Describe the people in your life.*
>
> *Describe yourself.*

Imagine a future scene, as if it were occurring right now.

> *Your environment is clean, exciting, peaceful, and everything you want it to be.*
>
> *People are loving, accepting, beautiful, and everything you want them to be.*
>
> *You are loving, accepting, beautiful, and everything you want to be.*

Now, hold a vision of your present world, the way it is right now

And at the same time…

Hold a vision of your ideal world, the way you would like it to be in your future.

Hold these two visions simultaneously for 30 seconds.

Then let the visions go, open your eyes, and go for a walk for a few minutes.

Do this every day, preferably morning and evening. Watch miracles happen!

DO YOU HEAR WHAT I HEAR?

Many of us often do not really listen. Our ears are hearing but our minds are busy calculating and interpreting, sometimes even before the speaker has begun talking. I call this defensive listening. You are listening with a closed mind, perhaps to protect your mind, to protect your genitals, to protect your heart, or even to protect your most valued spiritual beliefs.

OPEN YOUR EARS AND LISTEN

What sounds do you hear in the background?

What sounds irritate or annoy you?

What sounds or music make your smile and feel warm all over?

How Do You Listen To Yourself?

What bodily sensations do you pay attention to and what do you, ignore?

How do you respond to what you hear?

Copyright © 2009, Revised 2023   *Love Me, Touch Me, Heal Me*   DrEricaGoodstone.com

Brace yourself, hold it all together, stand up to, stand my ground, dig my heels in,

Keep a stiff upper lip, lift my spirits, put up a good front,

Get my back up against the wall, keep a smile on my face, reach out, hold it in?

How Do You Listen To Others?

Do you hear what you want to hear and ignore the rest?

Do you listen to the words and the nuances of meanings?

Do you listen to the nonverbal messages - body language and facial expressions?

Do you listen to the tone, attitude, pitch, and quality of voice?

Do you consider who is speaking, the source of the words you hear - the speaker's background, experience, prejudices and perspectives)?

Do you pay attention to you own bodily feelings as you listen to the words of others?

Who Do You Hear When You Listen?

Do you hear your mother, father, sister, brother, aunt, uncle, grandmother, grandfather, teacher, minister, school bully…?

Do you hear someone who is about to tease you, abuse you, ignore you, humiliate you, appreciate you, play with you, love you….?

Do you listen for acceptance, love, rejection, approval, safety, denial, disrespect, disregard, judgement, criticism, praise, insult, abandonment?

Do you expect to hear intellectual content, emotional understanding, criticism, sarcasm, drama, or worldly wisdom?

Do you feel heard, understood and connected or ignored, put down and alone?

How do you think, feel and respond when you hear what you are expecting to hear?

How do you think, feel and respond when you don't hear what you expect to hear?

What Are Your Listening and Speaking Goals?

<u>My</u> listening and speaking goals are to

- connect to my truth, what is true for me, in every moment of my life.

- listen and respond to the wisdom of my body and all my senses.

- respond to the world and the people in it from my own truth.

What Are <u>Your</u> Listening and Speaking Goals?

What Do <u>You</u> Want To Say … And To Whom?

Allow your beliefs to live, breathe, and to change form as life shows you another way. **Don't sell yourself short.** Each of us is unique and has our unique logic, beauty and wisdom. Maybe you've been put down, criticized, or judged and you believe you are less valuable and know less than others. You probably have much sharper antennae to recognize signs of impending abuse. You may know more about how to leave your body, to dissociate, so that you do not have to feel the full effect of the pain. You may know more about how to compulsively complete a task regardless of how your body feels.

We can help each other. None of us sees the whole picture. Even the most enlightened Guru is not living your life, with your friends, your parents, your lovers, or your spouse. The enlightened Guru meditates and chants in an environment surrounded by devotees and followers.

I often wonder what would happen to the Guru's perfect sublime state if he or she lived with your parents or spouse and was in close contact with your friends. Would the Guru maintain that state of calm and peace and wisdom and transform everyone else? Or would this enlightened master become frustrated, angry, agitated, without the time, space and clear energy to meditate.

I remember Hilda Charlton, an enlightened master in New York, could no longer be around beginners' energy. Another well-known guru stopped having darshan with beginning followers because of a back problem. Another wonderful, enlightened meditation group was unable to remain in New York City because of the intense negative energy they felt.

We are all human beings with bodies that utilized our five senses. We all need to listen to each other and especially, to listen to our own self.

OPEN YOUR SENSE OF SMELL

BREATHING

Sit quietly and close your eyes.

Keep your mouth closed, lips touching, teeth apart inside your mouth.

Breathe slowly, softly and easily through your nose 10X.

Breathe through your left nostril.

    Squeeze your right nostril closed with your right thumb.

    Inhale and exhale through your left nostril 10X.

    Remove your right thumb and rest.

    How do you feel?

    Did you feel any difference breathing through only one nostril?

Breathe through your right nostril.

    Squeeze your left nostril closed with your left thumb.

    Inhale and exhale through your right nostril 10X

    Remove your left thumb and rest.

    How do you feel now?

    Did you notice any difference, breathing through your right or left nostril?

Breathe through both nostrils 10X.

> *How do you feel?*
>
> *Did you notice any difference, breathing through both nostrils?*

Alternative breathing through right and left nostrils.

> *Place your right thumb against your right nostril.*
>
> *Place your left thumb against your left nostril.*
>
> *Squeeze your right nostril closed as you inhale and exhale through your left.*
>
> *Squeeze your left nostril closed as you inhale and exhale through your right.*
>
> *Continue alternating until you have completed 5 rounds on each side.*

SMELLING

Take a smelling tour of your kitchen.

Begin in the cabinets.

> *Open the jars or cans and smell the different spices, sauces, condiments, beverages, cereals, crackers, vitamins, herbs, other foods.*

Open the refrigerator.

> *Open the jars and packages and smell the different fruits, vegetables, dairy, juices, leftovers, beer, soda, meats or meat substitutes.*

Take a smelling tour of your bathroom. Yes, even if it has a malodorous residue.

Open the jars and tubes.

Smell the various oils, creams, lotions, soaps, toothpaste, detergents, medications.

Take a smelling tour of your closet.

Smell your dirty laundry.

Smell your freshly cleaned clothing, still hanging with the cleaner's tags or recently removed from the washer and dryer..

Smell your body.

Scan through your body.

Notice the different scents and odors emanating from different parts of your own body.

Take a walk into town.

Before you leave, pay attention to the scent of your own apartment or house.

Intentionally walk past coffee houses, bakeries, fish markets, meat markets or different sections of your local supermarket.

Find the bath, cosmetics, and drug departments.

Go to a linen shop and a clothing store.

Consciously smell the variety of scents and odors.

When you return home, notice the scent in your apartment or home.

OPEN YOUR SENSE OF TASTE

Taste Your World

Take a tasting tour of your kitchen.

Begin in the cabinets.

> Open some boxes, jars or cans and taste different spices, sauces, condiments, crackers, cereals, other foods.

Open the refrigerator.

> Open the jars and packages and smell the different fruits, vegetables, dairy, juices, leftovers, beer, soda, meats or meat substitutes.

> Take a tiny taste of a wide variety of different foods and condiments.

Taste yourself.

> Taste your fingers, wrists, forearms, knees, ankles, palms, hair - whatever bodyparts you are able to reach and feel safe enough to taste.

Take a walk into town.

> Before you leave, recall the tastes available in your own apartment or house.

Intentionally walk past restaurants, coffee houses, bakeries, fish markets, meat markets, different sections of your local supermarket.

Intentionally taste foods of many different types, shapes, colors textures and drink a variety of different beverages.

When you return home, compare the outside tastes to those available in your apartment or home.

Spend an entire month consciously tasting as many different foods and drink as many different beverages as you can.

Keep a running list of every type of food and drink you have tried - and your sensual reactions.

OPEN YOUR SENSE OF TOUCH

TOUCH YOUR WORLD

How do you feel about touching yourself?

How do you feel about touching others? Who? Why?

How do you feel about others touching themselves?

How do you feel about others touching you? Who? Why?

Touch your own hands.

> *Feel the texture, warmth, quality, roughness, smoothness, energy*
>
> *As if your right hand and left hands are two different people*
>
>> 1. *Which is male, which is female?*
>> 2. *Which is aggressive, which is more passive?*
>> 3. *Which is parent, which is child?*
>> 4. *Which is playful, which is serious?*
>> 5. *Which feels good, hurts?*
>
> *Caress each hand with your other hand, with your lips, your teeth*

Touch as many different parts of your body that you feel safe and comfortable touching.

Touch some body parts that you usually would avoid touching.

Take a touching tour of your kitchen.

Begin in the cabinets.

> *Open the jars or cans and touch the different spices, sauces, condiments, beverages, cereals, crackers, vitamins, herbs, other foods.*

Open the refrigerator.

> *Open the jars and packages and touch the different fruits, vegetables, dairy, juices, leftovers, beer, soda, meats or meat substitutes.*

Take a touching tour of your bathroom.

Copyright © 2009, Revised 2023   *Love Me, Touch Me, Heal Me*   DrEricaGoodstone.com

Open the jars and tubes.

Touch the various bottles, oils, creams, lotions, soaps, toothpaste, detergents, medications.

Take a touching tour of your closets and drawers..

Touch the different fabrics, textures, shapes, materials.

Touch the hangers and cleaners cellophane wrapping.

Take a walk into a nearby town.

Intentionally walk past different stores: coffee houses, bakeries, fish markets, meat markets, different sections of your local supermarket.

Find the bath, cosmetics, and drug departments.

Go to a linen shop and different clothing stores. Feel the quality of the different materials, scarves, hats, gloves, shoes, socks, panties, bras, belts, handbags, suits, shirts, blouses, sweaters, furs

Go to a bedding store. Lie down on different mattresses. Compare the effect of hard and soft mattresses, feather and polyurethane pillows.

Go to a hardware store, a picture framing store, a novelty store.

Feel the various textures, shapes and qualities of the store's items.

The questions and exercises in this chapter were designed to help you expand your sensual awareness and responsiveness. If you have completed all the exercises, you have also learned how to tune into your own body and allow your body's wisdom to speak to you. As you continue to increase your own sensual awareness, you expand your healing potential exponentially and you also become more readily attuned to the unique sensual responsiveness of everyone, including and especially, your most intimate partner/s.

TOUCHING STORIES

HEALING THROUGH TOUCH

AND

SOMATIC BODY PSYCHOTHERAPY

HEAL ME ... PLEASE

CHAPTER 3

TOUCHING STORIES

Healing Through Touch

And Somatic Body Psychotherapy

The Story of My Life

The story of my life
Unfolds
In your presence
Private burdens
Shameful secrets
Held within my lonely
Heart
Come pouring out
I cry
I laugh

*I kick and scream
You understand
You know the price
Of long held pain
The half-lived life
In fear
In shame
I let you see me
As I am
No judge
No jury
No pretense or sham
You make it safe
For me to be
As I slowly open
Becoming free.*

Copyright © 8/20/99 Erica Goodstone, Ph.D.

Touching Stories

In this chapter, we explore the healing potential of body psychotherapy through stories of real people's lives. These stories are excerpts of actual case histories, therapy sessions, emotional responses, and eventual healing that took place in my office. Names and identifying personal characteristics have been altered to protect anonymity. None of my clients will be able to say with certainty, "That's me!" Yet, as we read these stories, each of us may recognize something familiar within ourselves.

As you read this chapter, ask yourself the following questions:

About The Stories:

How do I feel about this person, situation, or emotion?

Does anything about this story feel familiar or cause me to feel uneasy, anxious, angry, or sad?

About Body Psychotherapy:

Is this something I could use?

What would happen if I freely expressed my emotions and paid attention to my bodily sensations?

What would happen if I was willing to face the truth about my own life?

George's Handshake

George walked into my office, sat in his chair and immediately said, *"I'm not sure if I should be here, if this is what I need, if I even need therapy."* Describing his marriage as better than ever, he insisted, *"I love my wife. Sex with her is wonderful. It's just that ... well ... I look at women everywhere. I get turned on and even masturbate thinking about other women. Sometimes I go for massages ... you know ... the sensual ones. Lately I've been hanging out at topless bars - not the seedy kind. These are high class places, of course."*

Throughout the session, George's statements sounded believable until, as he was leaving, he shook my hand. **His handshake said it all!** I had the sense that he was not really there. Given his body size and structure - tall, lean and muscular - I would have expected a strong, solid handshake. But when I shook his hand, I felt as if there was nothing there to hold onto. Not completely limp, it was just hardly there.

George's body holds the key to understanding his insatiable desire for variety and new sexual stimulation. Not being conscious and actually suppressing his own internal sensations, he has difficulty connecting openly with others.

Being intimate with another person, physical and emotional as well as sensual and sexual, requires that we accept our own totality, including limitations and insecurities. It is not necessary to live a life of quiet shame and discontent or disdainful superiority, thinking we are less valuable or more worthy than others. We do not need to keep others from seeing our imperfections. We do not need others to be our own ideal of perfection.

When we are touched in a sensitive, healing way, communicating to us that we are seen, heard, understood, and okay as we are, miraculous changes occur. Our problems take a back seat to a sense of connectedness to all of humanity. We discover how powerful we really are and how much we affect others peoples' lives every day.

Lana's Unconsummated Marriage

At her first counseling session, Lana explained, *"I never enjoyed sex …even before I met my husband. If he left me alone, I'd be perfectly content to never do it."*

Her history revealed a painful, traumatic upbringing with a cold and often sadistic mother who had shown disgust with Lana's bodily functions, a gentle but unavailable workaholic father, and an older brother who sexually molested her over many years. It became Lana's lifelong quest to prove that she was beautiful and clean enough to be loved. Years of talk therapy and the pursuit by numbers of men, could not erase her deep-seated belief that she was unclean, ugly, and unworthy of love.

Although she loved her husband and knew he was a good man, extremely kind, patient, and nothing like her abusive brother, she just couldn't allow herself to feel pleasure when he touched her. Her mother's disgust and disapproval remained palpably locked inside her body, along with the painful memories of her brother's unwanted advances.

The pain and sadness of Lana's early touch memories prevented her from being able to enjoy pleasurable sexuality with her loving husband. As her body was re-touched in a healing way, she allowed herself to express her deepest emotions and her body posture became noticeably more relaxed. Eventually, over time, Lana actually began to feel desire and sexual pleasure with her husband.

Having intimate physical and emotional contact with another person, requires self-acceptance and emotional freedom. We forgive those who have caused us pain and we forgive our self for our weaknesses, insecurities, and self-indulgences. We no longer expect our self to be perfect to please others.

The Revitalization of Steven's Life

As Steven entered my office, I noticed his breathing was shallow and the movement in his neck and shoulders was limited. His symptoms included high blood pressure, severe anxiety, and difficulty sleeping. Without much emotion, Steven explained his predicament, *"I've been at the same job for over 10 years. They're downsizing, piling more and more work on the people who are still here. I can't afford to quit, but I'm miserable going to work. I take medication to lower my blood pressure and lately I have trouble sleeping. I've been with my girlfriend Paula for years, too long. I think I want to break up, but I can't make up my mind. Lately we've been fighting a lot. She's bothers me with her doubts and insecurities which makes me feel more anxious. And she complains I don't listen to her."*

During the first few sessions, Steven alternately complained about his job and about his relationship with Paula. In the third session, as he pounded his fist into a pillow and yelled at his girlfriend as if she was present in the room, something different happened. He screamed, *"You selfish bitch. You don't stop complaining about your problems. What about me?"* Suddenly he stopped! Tears filled his eyes.

In that moment he realized these were his father's exact words. He realized he was repeating his father's pattern with his mother. An imaginary dialogue with his girlfriend, in my office, enabled him to realize that he had been repeating a family pattern. He now wanted to change the negative way he had been treating and responding to Paula.

After a few more body therapy sessions, Steven's breathing was becoming apparently fuller and easier.. In his seventh session he told me, *"I'm sleeping better at night. I even took a few days off from work. Now it doesn't seem so bad to be there."* In that session, I worked to release the tension in his neck and shoulders, encouraging him to move his neck into the yoga fish position, lying on his back with the top of his head on the body therapy table and his chin pointed up in the air.

At first, he complained that this was an impossible maneuver. But over the next few weeks, he was able to actually move his head and neck separately from his shoulders. A few weeks later he told me, *"I feel like a new man. I never knew I could move like that."*

As his habitual bodily tensions lessened, Steven's energy level and creativity increased. He showed me an article he had recently submitted to a few magazines for possible publication. At the same time he expressed a renewed sense of passion and desire for his girlfriend. For the first time since the very beginning of their relationship, he was taking Paula on a vacation to a tropical island resort.

The Truth About John

When John enters a room, it is difficult not to notice him. Over 6 feet tall, with broad shoulders, a well-developed muscular body, and a warm, engaging smile, he would appear to be highly appealing to woman. However, by the time he arrived in my office at age 33, he had dated only a few women in his entire life and had never attempted any sexual contact beyond a simple kiss and only the briefest of hugs. During his first date with a woman, he would tell her he was afraid of sex and being close. Rarely did his relationships last beyond a second or third date. Although he claimed to have a few close male friends, he did not share his inner thoughts or true feelings with anyone. Afraid of letting others know how insecure he really was, he walked around with a chip on his shoulder, easily angered into violent behavior. As a young child he had been abused by older boys in the neighborhood, humiliated by teachers about his poor study habits, and teased by his family about his shyness around girls.

John's work in therapy involved letting go of his pretenses and letting down his guard. It took quite a while before John stopped censoring every thought to make sure it was acceptable. He needed to be reassured over and over that it was safe for him to express his thoughts and feelings in the moment. At one point, he admitted a lifelong fear he had that he might be gay. John's major overhaul came when he recovered his childhood sense of shame at not being "man enough" to defend himself against all the people who had humiliated and abused him. He also expressed some anger toward his parents, his mother for not protecting him and his father for not being a strong masculine figure in his life.

As John's familiar armored posture and frozen smile gradually softened, he began to feel vulnerable, exposed and more frightened out in the world. His familiar defenses, relying on his muscular physique, distancing himself, or playing the victim, no longer shielded him from his own painful feelings.   It took a long time, several years of exploring his life issues and feeling his underlying emotions, before John was able to finally feel safe in the world. For a while, he needed almost daily reassurance that he would survive the demise of his defenses and be able to enjoy life being himself. Eventually he overcame his fear of connection and began to date women – and enjoy it.

Carol's Vagina Speaks

Carol, an attractive woman in her early thirties, began by telling me, *"I never really enjoyed the sexual act, but I wanted a boyfriend and I knew men wanted sex. So I guess I just did it to please them."* She explained, *"We were always in a hurry. His parents were about to come home or we were in the car and somebody might see us if we lingered too long. So I guess I was never very stimulated or turned on."*

In one session, Carol talked about the pain she had always felt in her vagina. I asked her to imagine what this body might say if it had a voice and could speak. After some initial hesitation, these words emerged from Carol, *"Why did you ignore me? Didn't you know I hurt? I needed you to pay attention to me, to treat me gently."*

As we explored further, we discovered that Carol came from a long line of highly educated, intellectual women who valued their brains and devalued their bodies. Despising femininity, the women in Carol's family were not proud of the body parts that distinguished them as female.

Carol's lifelong sexual problem could not be treated with medication, counseling, or even traditional sex therapy. It was not mechanical stimulation, external lubrication, or behavior modification that was needed. Internal dialogue, gentle, caring touch, and reconnection to the sensations in her body helped Carol to recover pleasurable feelings.

Lifelong shame about her intimate body parts gave way to an appreciation of her female body. As Carol learned to accept and love her own body, she began to enjoy and even crave the attention she received from men. Her body responded with heightened sexual desire. As a result, she dressed more stylishly, no longer hiding the natural curves of her body. To her surprise and delight, she received more male attention than ever before and more invitations to go out on dates than she could handle.

Louis' Panic Attacks

Louis, a part-time student in his late twenties, had experienced panic attacks all his life, but previously only in really frightening situations like speaking in front of his class or taking an important exam. *"Now the panic is occurring more often,"* he said. *"Lately I feel panicked when I walk into my office building, when I get on public transportation, even while I'm standing on line at a supermarket. There are beautiful women everywhere. If I look at a woman and she looks back at me, my body freezes. I feel as though I will pass out. I try to get out of there as fast as I can. By the time I'm outside, I can hardly breathe. Can you help me?"*

With Louis, the immediate task was to expand and increase his natural breathing pattern to lessen the possibility of another panic attack. Together, we observed the way he was holding his body in a state of defensive alertness, barely inhaling and exhaling, as if he is perpetually preparing to attack or be attacked. Through gentle touch, he was encouraged to progressively relax his body, part by part.

After many months of sessions, one day Louis spontaneously curled into a fetal position and began rocking. When I placed a hand lightly on his back, he began to whimper. Tears came, followed by deep, full belly sobbing. When he finally quieted down, his body appeared more relaxed than I had ever seen it before. For the first time in our work together, he was breathing deeply, inhaling and exhaling fully. When he sat up, a shy smile crossed his face. All he could say was, *"Thank you."*

Louis' panic attacks gradually diminished. Now, whenever he felt a panic coming on, he turned inward, observing which part of his body was tense. At the moment when he felt most afraid, Louis would inhale deeply and exhale slowly, allowing his body tension to naturally dissipate.

As he gained control over his breathing, Louis was finally ready to talk about the painful childhood experiences that had kept his body "on guard" for life. Raised by a controlling and angry father and a mother who played a traditionally submissive housewife role, Louis admitted he had not cried since he was very young, when his father beat him with a strap if he did not behave "like a man". For Louis, not behaving like a man was humiliating. But behaving like a man was also terrifying since his father had not taught him how. **It was the breath of life that saved Louis.** As he breathed more easily, he became less fearful of life and more comfortable in the presence of women.

Henry's Tears

Henry, a silver-haired stately businessman in his mid-fifties, took immediate control of the situation. He informed me that he had no time to waste. Looking over at the bodywork table he asked, *"How do I get from here,"* pointing to his less than functioning groin, *"to there?"* indicating the future, free from sexual impotence. *"I've already tried Viagra,"* he said. *"It worked all right for awhile. But I never needed to take anything before. I don't want to be dependent on a drug for the rest of my life."* He explained that he was curious about the way I work, but really doubted that allowing his body to be manipulated and feeling his feelings was going to cause his erection problem to disappear.

Henry described his marriage of many years. *"I love my wife so much. Denise is the best. She's beautiful and so intelligent. We have two great kids. I have a great life. Sex with my wife has always been wonderful. Sometimes I would come home in the middle of the day just to be with her. She was always hot and ready for me. I don't want to be with anybody else and I don't want to push her away. But lately I don't know what's happening. I get started, things seem great, and then poof. It goes down and won't come back. I'm scared. My wife tells me not to worry, but I'm sure she's been wondering what's wrong with me. I was at my wit's end when I took Viagra for *the first time. Luckily it worked. But I never did tell Denise about it. I don't know what to do."*

Henry decided to go for it and signed up for a series of sessions. Many men in his position, afraid of losing their potency, might choose instead to turn to massage parlors, hookers, pornography, phone sex, and online relationships for sexual reassurance. But they are living precariously. If their private sexual activities are discovered, their unsuspecting, betrayed partners may respond strongly and even choose to end the relationship.

During the history session, Henry described a rather idyllic childhood. His parents were deeply in love, expressing affection and sexual desire for each other openly. He grew up close to his younger sister, with lots of friends and even girlfriends from the earliest age he could remember. His sister and he had been given every advantage, from attending Ivy League universities to socializing with an elite crowd.

Then Henry talked about Lucy, his high school sweetheart, his first love. Having shared wonderful, loving and exciting times together, they had planned to marry as soon as he graduated from college. Henry's father believed that Lucy, from a working class family, would not be an asset to his upper class, cultured lifestyle. When Henry went away to college, his father contacted Lucy to tell her it would be best for all concerned if she stopped seeing his son. Brokenhearted but still hopeful, she had called Henry to discuss the matter. Not paying much attention, he brushed her off with a sarcastic comment. Believing, erroneously, that Henry agreed with his father and would eventually break up with her, she decided to be the one to end the relationship first.

When she told Henry she no longer wanted to see him, he did not pursue her. He just let her go. That was the first and last time Henry remembered crying, except once in his early childhood when he had come running to mommy for comfort and she had scolded him, saying that boys must be strong.

Stopping to clear his throat and showing his obvious annoyance, he said to me, *"I don't understand what any of this has to do with losing my erections now. That happened when I was 18. I'm 54 now and I haven't thought about Lucy in years. I've been with Denise all my adult life and we love each other. Our sex life has always been wonderful."*

A little more probing, however, revealed that his wife, Denise, was quite a perfectionist and liked her life to remain in perfect order. Henry had enjoyed complying with Denise's demands, convinced that it kept him on his toes and fueled his continual passion for his wife. On top of the world for over twenty years, his businesses had been flourishing and expanding. Lately, however, business was slowing down, and for the first time he had to downsize. Instead of using his creative talents toward establishing new business ventures, he now had to close some offices and fire a few trusted employees. A few sessions later, as he relaxed on the body therapy table, a tear appeared in the corner of his right eye. The realization came to him, "All my life I've been in control. I chose the college I wanted. I got almost straight A's. I married the most beautiful woman and my children grew up exactly as I would have wanted. I had control of all my businesses and it felt as if nothing could stop me - until now. Everything is changing. I have to curtail my business and I could lose a substantial amount of money. I'm terrified of telling Denise. This is the second time in my whole life I remember feeling such fear and a sense of impending doom. The last time this happened was when I was away at college and Lucy told me on the phone that she had to stop dating me, that she was seeing someone else, and that she no longer loved me. I couldn't believe my ears. My body went numb. I felt a knot in my stomach. **That's when the tears came!** My roommate asked me what was wrong. For a few minutes I was unable to speak and then my heart literally closed up. I never cried again! A few years later I met Denise, took her on a whirlwind of exciting dates and never let her get off the whirlwind until now. I'm afraid if I don't keep her life exciting and busy and passionately sexual, she will suddenly leave me just as Lucy did, so many years ago."

Henry's insight transformed his marriage. He began to tell his wife the truth about his declining businesses and his fear of her deserting him if times got bad. He even brought her with him to therapy to improve the way they communicate with each other.

After years of hiding his emotions and striving to please his critical, demanding mother first, and then his equally critical wife, he finally discovered the joy of letting himself feel and express his real feelings. After years of marriage, Henry had finally revealed the sensitive, not so strong, even vulnerable and frightened side of himself. Much to his surprise, his usually critical and demanding wife did not desert him. Instead, she actually touched him more tenderly than he had ever remembered. Realizing his marriage was on solid ground, no matter what happened to his finances, his erections naturally returned to normal. Their sex life took on a new, more sensual and romantic style.

Henry's emotions were his ally. Without the anxiety, fear and breaking down into tearful sadness, Henry stood to lose everything dear to him, his wife, his self-respect, and his wonderful family life.

What Is Body Psychotherapy?

Body psychotherapy is a life transforming, therapeutic experience. The counseling is similar to psychotherapy that is not focused on the body and does not involve touch. But when our bodies are touched as we are talking about our life issues, there is a powerful synergistic effect. Even very gentle touch re-connects us with memories of sensations and emotions stored within our body tissues. Unexpectedly, we might find ourselves crying, yelling, or even laughing uncontrollably. As we feel emotions we haven't felt in a long time, we may have a life-changing realization.

Professional certification and licensing boards have specific guidelines and strict ethical codes for the practice of body psychotherapy. Before receiving any sessions, we are entitled to be told what to expect during a session. The therapist must have our agreement before engaging in any verbal dialogue, touch, or other therapeutic processes. If we feel uncomfortable at any point, it is important to immediately inform the therapist. Remember, we always have the right to say, "No." We must trust our own reactions and responses. Nobody is a more qualified expert on how we feel in any given moment. Healing happens most easily when we feel safe, respected and heard.

The common element of all body psychotherapy methods is the use of touch. Touch is used differently and for different purposes within the various modalities. Some body psychotherapists (Bioenergetic analysts, Reichian therapists, Core Energetic therapists, Radix practitioners) may at times use forceful, deep, even painful pressure, in an attempt to break through bodily armoring and emotional resistance. Organismic body psychotherapists sometimes actually use their own physical bodies to touch and support their clients to let go of habitual tension patterns. Other body psychotherapists (Hakomi, Focusing, Rosen

Method, Integrative Body Psychotherapy, Rubenfeld Synergy therapists) utilize guided imagery, gentle touch and even touch that is off the body in the energetic field. If one style of body psychotherapy does not feel right, for any reason, choose a different therapist whose style of working feels more comfortable.

For me, body psychotherapy is gentle and always respectful of the client. Although my certification and the framework for my sessions is Rubenfeld Synergy, Somatoemotional Release and Polarity Therapy, I have incorporated many techniques from other counseling, body therapy, and body psychotherapy modalities. It is like having a bag of tricks at my fingertips, literally.

How Does The Body Psychotherapy Process Work?

Our body does not lie. The way we hold and move our body is the key to understanding ourself and reaching our full human potential. When we recognize and express our deepest feelings, the cells in our body respond accordingly. Our tissues soften, our posture lengthens and widens, and we view our world with greater clarity.

In body psychotherapy, both therapist and client are on a sacred healing journey together. We not only touch each other, we also explore together the deeper psychological, symbolic and interpersonal meanings in our life. When we are touched, we are no longer the person we pretend to be, want to be, or perceive our self to be. Feelings sometimes intensify, but over time the intensity gradually diminishes. We build a solid base of self-awareness, self-acceptance, and self-love.

Body psychotherapy is about life, your life, my life, and our lives together on this earth. Being willing to feel and express our raw emotions, we have the rare opportunity to release the pain and anguish inherent in the human condition. We can actually live the remainder of our lives in a state of peaceful joy, more readily willing to acknowledge, accept, and love our most intimate partners.

Body Psychotherapy Energizes Our Brain

Touch enhances our body awareness and assists us to relax. Our brains receive, interpret, and transmit to our bodies the information received by our senses. Chemicals in the form of neurotransmitters travel along pathways of the brain searching for a home in specific neuroreceptors, located within our brain and throughout our body. Our circulation improves, our breathing increases, our posture re-aligns, our face softens, our voice deepens, and our internal organs function with less restriction. Energy flows within our own bodies and also flows outward, connecting us in unseen ways with people, animals, plants and even nonliving objects. Our energy flow can be blocked, stimulated, drained, sedated or even depleted. Our "electromagnetic field" has been measured and documented through Kirlian photography. Asian healing methods track this "chi" energy through the "meridians" (energy channels) in our body. Yogis have observed this "kundalini" energy traveling upward through the "nadis" (small energy pathways) to the "chakras" (energy centers). As we are touched in body psychotherapy, our energy flows more freely within our own body and outward to the world around us.

Body Psychotherapy Allows Us To Breathe in Life

Breath is life. When we breathe our first breath, we are alive. When we gasp our final breath, we are no longer alive. Many of us are living every day in an almost "near death" state. Although we are breathing enough to remain alive, we are not breathing enough to feel. Restricting our breathing restricts our life. We hold our breath to hold in our emotions. We hold our breath to not feel pain. But when we don't allow ourselves to feel pain, we also do not feel pleasure and joy. **Body** psychotherapy helps us to regain the fullness of our breath and the fullness of our life.

Body Psychotherapy Reveals And Uncovers Our Truth

Truth heals - when realized, acknowledged, and accepted. Every bodily sensation mirrors our thoughts, emotions, desires and disappointments. Through conscious awareness of our these sensations, moment to moment, we discover what is true for us. As we face and admit our personal truth, the path is finally clear for our pain and sorrow to dissolve. We recognize our responsibility to thrive in this life, to shine our own light brightly for ourselves and for others who may be hiding in the dark. **Body psychotherapy helps us to know our own self as we remove the armoring that hides the truth of our being from our own consciousness.**

Body Psychotherapy Helps Us to Heal

In body psychotherapy, memories of our past experiences emerge into our current awareness. We scrutinize the details of each crucial segment of our life until this piece gradually recedes into the background, merging into the core of our being. New pieces emerge into our awareness and the process continues. Rough edges of our personality reveal themselves and slowly dissolve as we examine the hidden meanings. We become exhibitionists, revealing our most intimate and shameful secrets to another human being. We become voyeurs of our own life. We watch our responses as our fears, thoughts, desires, compulsions, and not so acceptable emotions, are exposed. The long, slow process of healing begins as we bring our demons into the light, shine our mental flashlight on our problems, and forgive our self and others for being human. **As we heal through body psychotherapy we are able to integrate positive and negative aspects of our self and the world in which we live.**

Body Psychotherapy Reopens Our Heart To Love

Emotions are natural human gifts, revealing our innermost desires. We respond emotionally to our own internal sensations and to the physical and emotional states of people around us. With intensely painful stimulation that we cannot eliminate or control, we adapt by closing off our emotions and closing our hearts. Sharing heart talk, honest emotional responses, while being gently touched by an accepting and caring therapist, we allow our self to experience the full range of our emotions. **Body psychotherapy assists us to feel our emotions as we heal our bruised or broken hearts.**

Body Psychotherapy Reawakens Our Sensual, Sexual and Spiritual Aliveness

Our sexual problem can be the gift that sets us free. Our body provides us with all sorts of messages reminding us to slow down, rest, change our habits, speak up, run away, hide, nurture ourselves, or to seek help. When we pay attention to the sensational world around us and inside of us, we see beautiful colors, hear pleasing sounds, smell fragrant essences, savor the taste of food, and touch with pleasure the people and textures that surround our life. If we choose to, and if a partner is available to us, we explore our sensuality and sexuality with another. We are open, loving, and willing to share our self fully. **Body psychotherapy enhances our senses so that we are free to explore our sensuality and sexuality in our own way.**

Body Psychotherapy Reconnects Us To Our Soul

We meet with our body psychotherapist at the level of our soul. There is no judgment, shame, good or bad, weak or strong. There is only love, truth and pure connection. The forces that have kept us in a state of fear seem to miraculously lose their power and disappear. **Once we have experienced soul connection in a private body psychotherapy session, we can then go out into the world transformed, seeking that same soul connection with others.**

Body Psychotherapy Reminds Us To Play

We learn from a very early age the way the world is. Children play. Adults work. Children giggle. Adults are serious. Children feel emotions. Adults feel only a few acceptable emotions and repress the rest. Children are fully alive. Adults are careful and mature. In body psychotherapy, we discover we have choices about the way we want to live our life. We can choose to be serious, heavy-hearted, angry or depressed. Or we can lighten up and play and laugh at the absurdity of even the worst of our life circumstances and dilemmas. We begin to cherish the ever-present moment of now. **Body psychotherapy reminds us to**

lighten up, play, laugh and enjoy, from moment to moment, the simple pleasures of life.

A Body Psychotherapy Session

For individuals, the first session involves an in-depth history. Couples, begin with a joint session, allowing both partners an equal opportunity to explain how they view theirrelationship issues and problems. At a later date, each partner returns privately for a history session. During the history sessions, I encourage clients to tell their personal stories in their own words. Scanning chronologically through the earlier years of their lives, we end by focusing on current relationship issues and what they hope to create in the future. Clients then have an opportunity to ask me how I work and what they might reasonably expect to experience in the therapy process.

Subsequent sessions are divided into a talking portion and a body therapy portion. Beginning with casual conversation about the past week and reactions to the previous session, any pressing issues or problems are brought out for discussion. When the salient issues have been addressed, at some point I will ask "Would you like to get on the table now?" Sometimes, clients are deeply involved in talking about something important and would prefer not to disrupt their train of thought. In such sessions, the bodywork may be delayed or there may be no body therapy at all.

When clients are ready to lie down on the body therapy table, they are asked to remove their shoes, glasses, and any bulky items in their pockets. Clients are never asked to remove any clothing! Once the client is lying on the body therapy table, I observe the tension points and breathing patterns. Slowly, carefully, and respectfully, I begin to approach touching.

Starting far from the center of my client's body, usually at the feet or head, I keep my palms a distance of about 12" above the body. Sitting quietly, allowing my own body to relax, I pay attention to the sensations between my hands. As I allow my hands to very slowly approach the surface of my client's body, I usually feel the heat and sensation of that person's energetic field. Depending on the physical and emotional state of the client's health, I may feel the sensation as far as 12" away or I may not feel it at all until my hands are actually touching the body.

Every client is unique. Every session is different. Sometimes I spend a long time at a person's feet, moving the legs, one at a time, rocking, shaking, stimulating meridian points and observing the movement from the leg into the hip joint and above. At other times, I spend a long time cradling a client's head in the palms of my hands or gently rocking it from side to side. I listen with my hands for places of restricted or easy movement. As I work, I continually look for changes in facial expressions and breathing.

Often, I check whether the person on the table feels comfortable and safe. **There is never, at any time, any contact with sexual organs or intimate body parts nor any touching for the purpose of sexual arousal.** Should the client express discomfort or a desire not to be touched at a specific time or in a particular place, I will always honor the client's request and immediately refrain from touching.

After the initial contact, I usually move closer to the center of the client's body. I may place one hand under the lower back and one hand gently resting on the abdominal area. This begins the energetic opening of the body through sustained holding with both of my hands. As I feel bodily tension diminish and the skin become tingly and warm, I may move my hands to another position, usually moving upwards to the rib cage, shoulders and neck, eventually cradling the head once again.

Sometimes I focus on opening the energy channels along specific acupressure meridians. At other times, or within the same session, I may do some gentle release techniques. These involve placing my hands under the client's hip, shoulder, or ankle, on one side of the body, to heighten awareness of the sensations in this body part. I will then slowly move my hands away as I feel the body part begin to let go of tension. Often, there is an obvious difference in the way this side of the body looks to my eye and feels to the client when compared to the opposite side of the body.

Differences in one side of the body compared to the other side, often leads to awareness of internal conflicts. At this point, we may begin some verbal dialogue. Depending upon the specific emotional and psychological issues that surface, movements (kicking, hitting, pounding fists) or emotional releases (crying, sighing, screaming) may spontaneously arise. To alleviate certain tension patterns, I sometimes guide the client's body to move into an unfamiliar and maybe uncomfortable position, perhaps a yoga posture, such as the fish or the cobra.

As the client's body releases chronically held tension, the logical, thinking mind may give way to a more intuitive, creative, non-linear way of thinking. Special chemicals in the brain and body cells, called neuropeptides, are released. New pathways are established in the complex body mind system. Images, memories, and powerful insights may emerge. New perspectives about life become integrated into ordinary thoughts and behaviors. **This is the miracle of body psychotherapy.**

Your Body's Messages

Sit quietly. Close your eyes. Take a few deep breaths and allow your body to relax. Pay attention to the changing thoughts in your mind. Notice whether any parts of your body feel uncomfortable, tense, painful, or seem to be calling for your attention. Pay attention. Continue to focus on the thoughts in your mind and the sensations in your body.

Think about the part or parts of your body that are in the foreground of your attention.

- *If these body parts could communicate, what sounds would they make?*
- *What colors would they be?*
- *What would be their quality or texture?*
- *Do the sensations you are currently feeling remind you of anything in nature or in your life?*
- *Is somebody or something in your life disturbing your emotional state?*
- *Are you causing your body to tighten or tense up in response?*

- *What messages about your life, your relationships, and your sexuality, are being offered to you by your bodily sensations?*

Body Psychotherapy Clears The Path For Love, Relationships And Intimacy

Our body reveals us to the world, to each other, and to our self. Through our energy and through touch, with or without words, we are known. As we discover that hiding is an illusion, we begin to relax our defenses. We discover that we are all longing to be accepted and loved. Scientists who study the universe, from the tiniest particles to the vastness of infinity, ultimately discover that love, attraction and repulsion rule the universe. **Through body psychotherapy, as we learn to love and accept our self and others, intimacy becomes our natural way of being.**

CONGRATULATIONS!

By finishing *Heal Me…Please*, **Part III** in the *LOVE ME, TOUCH ME, HEAL ME* **Complete Book,** you have completed some powerful, life-transforming exercises. You have self-reflected about the ways that healing has occurred in your life. You have reviewed and contemplated how your thoughts, behaviors, attitudes, and responses to the world and others' opinions may have blocked, interfered with, or enhanced your own healing process. You have discovered how powerful each of us really is and how important it is to tune in to your own inner knowing.

SEXUAL AND SPIRITUAL REAWAKENING

Part IV in the *LOVE ME, TOUCH ME, HEAL ME*

Complete Book

The Path To

* **PHYSICAL**
* **EMOTIOAL**
* **SEXUAL**
* **SPIRITUAL**

REAWAKENING

Erica Goodstone, Ph.D.

Sexual and Spiritual Reawakening, **Part IV**
is dedicated to:

* Bryce Britton-Kranz, my friend, colleague and mentor in this powerful work that is so close to the human soul
* Dr. Alice Ladas, Grande Dame of research in female sexuality and body psychotherapy, who stepped out into a man's world as a pioneer and advocate, lighting the way for all the women that have and will follow
* Dr. William Masters and Virginia Johnson, who pioneered sex therapy, leading to the creation of a unique and gratifying profession
* Dr. Deryck Calderwood, my creative and courageous teacher, who taught me to stand on my own in the face of criticism and cynicism
* Dr. Mary Calderone, who reminded me that sexuality and love, are not and need not be, separate from love and the rest of our life
* American Association of Sex Educators, Counselors and Therapists, AASECT, for providing leadership, certification, and a place to call home among colleagues when I was a fledgling therapist
* Society for Sex Therapy and Research, SSTAR, for bringing together the leading authors, researchers, educators, psychotherapists, psychiatrists, and medical professionals to dialogue and explore sexual issues, concerns and treatment possibilities, through presentations and case studies
* Ilana Rubenfeld, my teacher and mentor, who encouraged me to forge my own way and create my own unique style of healing therapy, which I originally called *Sexual Reawakening*

SEXUAL AND SPIRITUAL

REAWAKENING

INTRODUCTION

We are all sexual beings. Sexuality teaches. Sexuality heals. Sometimes our sexuality hurts. When we allow our hearts to feel love and our bodies to feel pleasure, we are sexual. Being sexual is being alive. Feeling our sexual aliveness reawakens us to who we are. By allowing full sexual expression into our life, we cannot help but discover our spiritual nature.

We are all spiritual beings. Connecting to our spiritual nature and spiritual potential brings us an accepting appreciation of life. The path of discovering our spiritual connection can be difficult, painful and may reveal to us our deepest, darkest, most unloving personal attributes. Following a spiritual path also connects us to the highest values and the most life affirming self we can be.

Our life path is a spiritual path, the process of rediscovering our connection to all that is. No matter which direction we choose to take, all paths will eventually lead us home. Every spiritual teaching reminds us of that simple truth. If we resist knowing this truth and pursue a self-centered and purely material way of life, we may encounter more struggle, more difficulties, and more tests than necessary. But even if we do pursue a spiritual path, there are still obstacles and difficulties to be overcome. The difference is that knowing our spiritual essence provides emotional strength and calmness in the face of any stormy life issues, problems and concerns. **Sexual and Spiritual Reawakening** is a simple guide to help you live a more fulfilling, meaningful, and joyful existence.

****

SEXUAL AND SPIRITUAL REAWAKENING

"Use It Or Lose It."

Dr. William Masters and Virginia Johnson

"Love and Sex Go Together."

Dr. Mary Calderone

We are all spiritual and sexual beings. Sexuality teaches. Sexuality heals. Sometimes sexuality hurts. When we allow our heart to feel love and our body to feel pleasure, we are sexual. Being sexual is being alive. Being sexual reawakens us to who we are. As we reawaken, we realize that we are spiritual beings connected energetically to everyone and everything around us. In we explore what it means to be a spiritual and sexual being. We examine our current attitudes, beliefs and behaviors, our personal spiritual and sexual history, and how we can create and sustain our spirituality and sexual aliveness, even if we never attend another church service or never have a sexual partner again.

SEXUAL AND SPIRITUAL REAWAKENING

Becoming One

Take my hand

And join me

On the sacred path to love

Our hands entwined

And hearts engulfed

Our bodies throbbing

Sensing, glowing

Lost in sensual delight

Unaware of self

United

Connected

Belonging

Becoming

Knowing

We are One

Copyright © 3/23/09 Erica Goodstone, Ph.D.

ORDINARY PEOPLE

ORDINARY

YET EXTRAORDINARY

SEX

SEXUAL AND SPIRITUAL REAWAKENING

CHAPTER 1

ORDINARY PEOPLE

ORDINARY YET EXTRAORDINARY SEX

ORDINARY PEOPLE

ORDINARY YET EXTRAORDINARY SEX

She smiles
He strokes her hair
She cries
He comforts her

He talks
She quietly listens
He screams
She calms his fear

*They live together
In separate worlds
Sometimes sharing
Often, all alone*

*And then their bodies meet
The touch feels warm
Familiar
Safe*

*Though years of life
May mar their outer looks
Together they find love
Acceptance, joy*

*No special way
To look or be
Wrapped in arms of love
Their hearts are free*

Copyright © 10/29/99 Erica Goodstone, Ph.D.

Sometimes In An Ordinary Place

Sometimes, when I am in an ordinary place in my everyday life – at the supermarket, buying a newspaper, walking down the street – I glance up at some complete stranger. It could be a man, some man, any man, and I wonder to myself,

Does this man enjoy sex, love women, or fear them both?

Does he know his own masculine beauty and manly strength?

Does he have a sexual problem or a compulsion?

Does he enjoy pleasuring his partner and does he teach his partner how to pleasure him?

I wonder for a while about this man of mind's moment and I walk on. Another man, another moment of thought…. Life's small capsules of universality revealed. All men are lovers. All men are sexual partners, at some time, with someone, if only in their dreams or with themselves.

At other times I notice a woman, some woman, any woman, and I wonder to myself,

Does this woman enjoy sex, love men, or fear them both?

Does she know her own feminine beauty and womanly strength?

Does she have a sexual problem or compulsion?

Does she enjoy pleasuring her partner and does she teach her partner how to pleasure her?

I wonder for a while about this woman of my mind's moment and I walk on. Another woman, another moment of thought…. Life's small capsules of universality revealed. All women are lovers. All women are sexual partners, at some time, with someone, if only in their dreams or with themselves.

On The Street

Next time you walk down a street, any street, pay attention randomly to different men and different women. Imagine what their sexual lives are like or may have been in the past. Imagine what their secrets or private fantasies might be. Observe couples. You may notice the most ordinary looking man or woman, someone you do not find particularly attractive, being hugged and cuddled by someone who obviously cares. You may also notice a very attractive, seemingly successful person being ignored or berated by an unloving partner.

Loving and being loved knows no boundaries. It is not based upon our physical appearance or our financial status. Yes, sometimes we are loved for some false physical or mental i8mage we have created or someone has created for us. But, as we open our hearts to another, pretense and illusion dissolve. Love endures when we are seen and accepted for who we really are.

The Average Man And The Average Woman

The sexy media images have affected all of us. The ordinary man or woman dating another ordinary man or woman, may be unable to appreciate his or her very real partner. Many of us feel deprived, as if we are not getting our fair share of the love, excitement, money and youthful beauty that is out there for the taking.

Many of us also feel insecure about our ability to attract a desirable partner. Women spend thousands of dollars every year to alter hair color, reshape body proportions, and revitalize skin tone and texture. Breast implants, liposuction, face lifts and tummy tucks are quite popular surgeries for women. But even men have become increasingly concerned about physical appearance than ever before. Cosmetic surgeries to add inches to the penis while removing excess fat form the midsection have become big business in the medical profession.

- **Ignore the media messages.**
- **Love the real people in your life.**

Just as we study for our degrees, work hard I our careers, and practice our favorite leisure activities, creating a magnificent relationship with open communication and exciting sex, requires single-minded focus on our chosen partner. With time, patience, concentration, devotion, acceptance and love, you can unleash the hidden passion in even the most reticent partner. You can find the gift of love with your very real and available partners.

Your Sexuality

At this point in your life, your sexuality may be flourishing, suppressed, unsatisfying, or just okay. You may be married or living with a partner in a monogamous, committed relationship. You may be sexually involved with many different partners or may have just lost a beloved partner through a breakup, betrayal, or even death. And perhaps you have never experienced a satisfying intimate relationship.

If you feel your current sex life is satisfying, then sexual reawakening may not be fore you. But if, like so many of us, your sex life has always been or has recently become less than fulfilling, you may decide you want more out of life.

Are you satisfied with your current sexuality, the way you look, the way you feel, and your ability to express yourself intimately with a partner? Is there something you would like to change, improve or experience, perhaps for the very first time?

As you begin the process of sexual reawakening, you gradually uncover and transform your life issues, fears, and intimacy avoidance strategies. According to the Dalai Lama (*The Art of Happiness*, 1998), happiness is the most important goal of life. No matter where you are right now, you truly have the God-given ability to create happiness in all areas of your life, including your most intimate sexuality.

Sex Doesn't Live Here Anymore

Given up on love and sex? Too much trouble…. Too unsettling…. Life is easier, alone, without a partner and without the hassles. If you've been feeling this way, you certainly are not alone. Many of us choose to remain single without a partner or maintain our own separate life within an emotionally unfulfilling marriage or live-in arrangement. We may feel unhappy, but we may also feel safe. Alone in our own world, we know who we are, we feel okay about ourselves, and we are able to go on living. Some of us fill our lives with work, activities, social events, family, friends, and intimate conversations. But we are often starving to be touched, held, and loved, with or without intimate sexuality.

When Viagra, the alleged miracle erection drug, was released in the Spring of 1998, the media revealed that over thirty million men were having erectile problems. What an astounding statistic! And those are the men who had discussed this problem with their medical doctors or therapists. What about men struggling with impotence and other sexual problems who have never told a doctor? What about all the women who suffer silently with their own sense of sexual inadequacy?

Many of us are uncomfortable in our own bodies, feeling overweight, in poor physical condition, or suffering from chronic physical and emotional ailments. When you are physically or emotionally uncomfortable or worried about some aspect of your life, your sexuality becomes less important than overcoming your very real problems. Anxiety and fear are often the antithesis of sexual potency.

Whether you are single, married, cohabiting, widowed, separated or divorced, you may at times feel anxious and uncertain about your sexual

Copyright © 2009, Revised 2023   *Love Me, Touch Me, Heal Me*   DrEricaGoodstone.com

performance or you may sometimes worry about losing your sexual appeal. Frustrated that you cannot find a partner or angry at your current unresponsive and inept partner who does not satisfy your sexual needs, you may be living a life of quiet sexual desperation. You may long to hold on to something you once had, never quite had, or feel you are losing. You may not know where to turn or what to do.

Talking to your doctor about your intimacy concerns is not always helpful. Few physicians, and not very many psychotherapists, are trained to deal effectively with sexual issues. Regardless of the problem, you may be told, "Don't worry about it. At your age, that's normal." Many doctors assume that a man over 40 or 50 or 60 will naturally have a lower sexual drive, lose his erection sometimes and have decreasing pleasurable sensations. Some doctors actually advise women approaching menopause that vaginal pain is something they will just have to live with, that lessened sensation or numbness is normal, and that fewer and less pleasurable orgasms are to be expected.

Not true! There are men and women, who may have felt little sexual arousal when they were younger, that finally begin opening up to their sexuality in their mid-40's, 60's or even 80's. Many couples enjoy their best sexual experiences in their later years when they are no longer burdened by heavy financial, family and emotional responsibilities. In fact, women and men in nursing homes, who are not physically incapacitated, may enjoy sexual intimacy if the facility management is not too restrictive and they are able to find an available partner.

Your level of sexual enjoyment and satisfaction has very little to do with your age, physical attributes, or relationship situation. Regardless of how physically and emotionally intimate you are with another person, your sex life can be flourishing, exciting, a powerful stress reliever or it can become a major source of frustration and misery in your life.

It doesn't matter if you are married or living with a steady partner, engaged to be married, involved with many different partners simultaneously, recently ended a love relationship, lost a beloved partner through rejection or death, or have had a lifelong habit of pursuing non-intimate sex with or without a partner.

Take A Lesson From Mrs. Kalish

A few years ago I received a phone call from a childhood neighbor, an acquaintance of my mother, someone I had not seen for over 20 years. After we caught up on the news from the old neighborhood, she said, "By the way, I have a new boyfriend for the past three years. My previous relationship lasted about 10 years." In my mind I was calculating, "How old can she be?" My mother passed away a few years ago at the age of 76. Maybe Mrs. Kalish was younger. I figured by now she must be about 74 or 75. That's when the clinker hit me.

"I bet you're curious about my age", she said, as if she had read my mind. "I'm 89. and my boyfriend is 93. And I'm having the time of my life. We see each other almost every day. He's a good man - and so much fun. We go to the theater and dancing. This weekend we're going to the beach. My life is pretty happy now. I'm lucky." Before saying goodbye, she asked me if I was lecturing somewhere, saying she would love to come.

Are you really "too old" at 25, 40, 55 or 70 to find love, romance and sexual intimacy? Is it true that "all the good ones are taken?" Do you believe you no longer have the energy for dating at your age? What I learned from Mrs. Kalish is that love and sexuality, romance, happiness and joy, is available to us throughout our lives.

What Do We Know About Sex?

Our sexuality is deeply connected to who we are. If we are having problems in this area of our lives, we may believe there is something wrong with us. Another, more positive and hopeful approach is to view sexual problems as messages about our lives. Our bodies often feel what our minds may refuse to acknowledge. Our bodies remind us to pay attention to ourselves, to listen to our own internal responses.

Researchers Masters and Johnson have claimed that our sexual organs are designed to function naturally, unless interfered with in some way. During normal sleep, healthy males have an erection every 80-90 minutes and healthy females lubricate vaginally every 80-90 minutes. Medication, illness, injuries, surgeries, stress, relationship problems and other emotional upsets can and often do interfere with our normal sexual functioning, even during sleep.

It has been said that men think about sex every 6 to 8 seconds. If this is true, why do so many men nowadays have low sexual desire, inability to maintain an erection, and not so pleasurable feelings during ejaculation? If sex is a natural function, why are so many women lacking in desire and unable to have orgasms? And why are so many couples unable to maintain their desire over the years.

Sex has become a real conflict for many people in our society. Men and women are often angry with each other, angry at themselves, frustrated, and lacking desire. Men are expected to always be ready for sex, to "perform" upon request, to be sexually confident and to know exactly how to pleasure a woman. Women are expected to "be sexy" yet chaste, to show off their bodies, to be easily orgasmic, and to know exactly how to pleasure a man. Both are expected to have high sexual desire and be perpetually turned on, no matter what experiences they have had or not had, no matter what has transpired in their current relationship, no matter how they feel about their partner.

Sexual Response
Is A Barometer of What We Feel

Sexual response is often a barometer of what we feel. If a man dates a new woman, takes her home, feels turned on and then loses his erection, his first reaction usually is: "What's wrong with me?" Perhaps he should ask: "What's right with me?" What is my body telling me? What does she say or do that makes my body tighten up and not want to feel? What memories or fears are being aroused when I'm with her? Do I feel guilty, angry or upset about something? Do I feel safe and secure, manly and significant with this woman?

If a woman does not feel aroused by her lover, her usual response is: "What's wrong with me?" Perhaps she should ask: "What's right with me?" What is my body telling me? What does he say or do that makes my body tighten and not want to feel? What memories or fears are being aroused when I'm with him? Do I feel guilty, angry or upset about something? Do I feel safe and secure, womanly and significant with this man?

Men often complain that there aren't any good women out there. Upon closer observation they may desire a fantasy type woman, one who is totally unavailable. They may fear that women want something from them, so they purposely withhold their love and affection. Unable to get close to a woman, they may eventually feel like giving up, hoping that someday their sex drive and desire will go away.

Women often complain that there aren't any good men out there. They may say that men are domineering, selfish and inconsiderate or nice but not exciting. In looking for excitement, however, they often choose men with psychological problems, addictive or abusive behaviors. Unable to get close to a man, they may eventually they feel like giving up, hoping that someday their sex drive and desire will go away.

When relationships and other people seem difficult or impossible, we need to reevaluate our own lives. We can reawaken something inside of us that will allow us to connect with others in a new way. We can rekindle something in our current relationship or disconnect, grieve our loss, and seek a new, more fulfilling relationship with a more available partner.

Opposites Attract

Mantak Chia, the author of numerous books on The Taoist energetic theories of love and sex, believes: "The flattening of sexual desire between regular partners is due largely to depletion of polarity or sexual-electrical tension." He claims that sexual-electrical tension results from the polarity that exists when two people exhibit opposite and different traits and behaviors. In other words, sexual desire increases when there are differences and conflicts, and diminishes when two people feel too easily compatible, peaceful and calm.

Japanese healing arts describe the universal energy as a balance between two opposing forces, yin, feminine (receptive, cold, dark) and yang (masculine, active, hot, light). Hindus refer to these energies as the balance between Shiva and Shakti. A scientist might analyze the attraction as the meeting of positive and negative poles of a magnet. In magnets, opposites attract, like repels.

Modern psychology offers us the term "codependency" to describe the relationship between two people with opposite yet complementary needs. Neither feels whole without the qualities and behaviors of their codependent partner. In a codependent relationship, the strength of each partner is dependent upon the other person sacrificing a part of themselves, not developing to their fullest potential. But opposites can and do co-exist in full expression in the universe. The energy of shiva and shakti, yin and yang, positive and negative magnetic poles, flow easily back and forth, with a mutual respect for the right of each to exist and self-express.

Without the attraction of opposites, there would be little reason for man and woman to connect, to procreate, and continue the human species. Perhaps, there would also be less emotional pain. But we would be missing the joy, mystery, wonder and excitement that comes from relating to a person with qualities different from our own. How can we know pleasure when we have never known pain? How can a man truly know what it is to be a man without ever knowing a woman? How can a woman truly know what it is to be a woman without ever knowing a man? Deeply knowing an intimate partner involves accepting and honoring our differences, exploring our similarities, and communicating with each other.

Many of us find it difficult or impossible to be turned on by the "right" person, the one who appears to have everything we say we want. In fact, what tends to work best is sex with the "wrong" person, one who doesn't fit our personal relationship criteria. The one who instills passion in us is likely to be the person who does not behave the way we would like, who causes us to feel frustrated, confused, and even angry.

Freud and later researchers concluded that frustration and even hostility often leads to sexual attraction and desire. One explanation may be biological. The limbic system, a set of structures in the interior of the brain believed to be important for sexual behavior, lies very close to the centers of pleasure and aggression.

Close association and easy access, through steady dating, living together, or marriage, can easily dampen our desire. With a new lover, feeling naturally somewhat anxious, and uncertain about the future, we often feel more alert, attentive and turned on.

In this society, we tend to ignore the polarities, sometimes favoring one sex at the expense of the other. We may temporarily lessen the conflicts but will ultimately also lessen the desire, passion and love. Let's bring back the passion, understand and enjoy our differences.

Your Opposite Attractions

Have any of your partners, previous or current, had traits that seemed to be directly opposite of your own?

How did that affect your relationship?

Were you able to accept your differences?

Did one or both of you attempt to change/transform the other?

What happened to the quality of your life together?

Sexual Relating

When I tell people I'm a sex therapist, women often ask: "Why do men always want sex? I want to spend some time so I can get to know him first. Before answering, I usually reflect upon the many men who have asked me, "Why do women always want to get emotionally involved so soon? Why can't I meet a woman who doesn't always pressure me to make a commitment?"

Why do men always want sex? Why do women always want commitment? Let's set the record straight right here and now. To begin with, not all men pressure women to have sex. To many men, sexual intimacy is downright scary. Feeling clumsy, inadequate, unskilled or even dirty, some men totally avoid sexual contact. And many women are freely sexual with a man they desire, following their passion and lust, without love or need for commitment. In fact, a large number of women prefer the challenge of trying to win the heart of an unreliable and self-centered "bad body," someone they can rightfully blame for problems in the relationship, rather than being personally accountable to a steady, reliable partner. A large number of men are truly sensitive, romantic and loyal lovers, showing respect and concern for their partners, while some women are demanding and insensitive. Nowadays, with the threat of AIDS and other debilitating sexually transmitted diseases, both men and women often prefer to know their partners for awhile before becoming sexually involved.

According to sociobiologists, a "normal", "healthy", "unrepressed" male probably does want sex most of the time. Sociobiologists claim that, having evolved from lower animals, human instinctual behavior is not that unique. The survival of most species depends upon the male impregnating as many females as possible in order to carry on the species. In the human male, each ejaculation contains millions of sperm, but most die almost immediately upon entering the female vagina. Among those that survive, only one single sperm cell may survive the long journey up the vaginal canal and actually penetrate the barriers surrounding the female's egg. Just as the individual sperm cells compete with each other, adult males compete with other males to attain the prize, the most beautiful, most fit, and most impregnable woman.

Why is it not in women's best interest, biologically, to have sex with numerous men? According to sociobiologists, women have natural limitations. They are born with a finite number of eggs, 400,000-600,000. Each month from puberty to menopause, usually only one egg matures and is released from the ovary into the fallopian tube, available to become fertilized by one sperm cell from one male. Conception to birth requires approximately nine months of pregnancy, during which time the woman's activities are often naturally restricted. Engaging in sexual activity promiscuously increases a woman's chance of being infected with a sexually transmitted disease which may compromise her fertility later on. It is in the woman's best interest to choose her male partner wisely. For if he does not provide adequate support, she will bear full responsibility of caring for the physical and emotional survival of her children alone.

Why do men tend to want to have sex all the time? They have little to lose and everything to gain by spreading their seed with numerous partners. Why do women usually prefer to wait to get to know a man better? She has everything to lose reproductively.

What Do Men Say They Want?

Women often talk among themselves about what they "think" men want in a woman. Women may believe that men want them to look like a gorgeous model, behave like a properly mannered heiress, and be cool, aloof and disinterested. Yes, among the hundreds of men with whom I've spoken, a small number actually do have very high-line requirements for the eligible women in their lives. Most men say they are looking for something much more simple and attainable. Here's what some men say they want:

"I don't believe I should look for someone to marry. I think I should go out and have good times. When I enjoy being with someone so much that I don't want to be without that person, because we're happy together, then I might decide to get married." Arnie, salesman

"I want a woman who is feminine and soft, not afraid to let a man feel like a man. A man who has pressure and problems at work wants to come home to a woman who will soothe him, massage him and touch him tenderly. I love cuddling and hugging. I think it's a normal need." Roberto, corporate executive

"I might just remain single. I fly planes in my spare time. We have a whole group of guys that take trips to exotic places several times a year. We like adventure, scuba diving, meeting new people from all parts of the world. Some of the guys have gotten married and their wives don't let them come on these trips anymore. I would want my wife to understand my need for adventure and time alone with the guys." Gary, entrepeneur.

"I guess I never really learned to trust a woman, never really wanted to get too close. I'm a pilot, so I'm home for a few days, then off to Boston, Paris, Cairo, Brussels. I have to have a certain kind of understanding in my relationships. Having been independent for so long, I'm 44 years old, I now realize what's important: to get close and to share my inner thoughts with one special person. It's the only way the world can work." Roger, pilot.

"My mother took care of my sister and me since my father died when I was three. I have seen how hard she worked and how much she cared about us. I want a woman who is not afraid to work and to work hard, but I am very willing to share the load and support her. If she's stressed out and upset, I want to be there for her. But I also want her to support me when I need help or comfort or understanding. I want us to share our lives together." William, electrician.

Do these comments sound like men are only looking for stop dead good looks and hot sex?

Ask Men

Ask the men you know, at work, at school, at parties, at the gym, in your neighborhood, at the supermarket, anywhere and everywhere you go, what they want in a woman. Ask the single men what they are looking for. Ask the married men what makes them happy. Their answers might surprise you and actually relieve that insecure anxiety that you just can't measure up to some perfect ideal you've been imagining. Men and women need each other as companions to go through life.

What Do Women Say They Want?

Men often talk among themselves about what they "think" women want in a man. Many believe that women want them to be rich and powerful, handsome, built like a weight lifter, aggressive, and highly sexual. Yes, among the hundreds of women with whom I've spoken, a small number actually do have very high-line requirements for the eligible men in their lives. But the majority of women say they are looking for something much more simple and attainable. Here's what some women say they want:

"I want a man who is focused on me. I don't want to feel uncomfortable when we walk down the street and a pretty girl walks by. I guess I'm insecure, but I want to know he thinks I'm special and isn't that interested in other women." Jane, freelance writer

"I'm tired of these immature men. I want a man who can stand on his own too feet, pay his own bills, and stand up for himself. I don't like bossy, controlling men, but I also don't want to be able to push him around. I want to know I have met my match both socially and intellectually." Alice, corporate vice president

*"Men often expect too much from me. I work hard and need the man in my life to be able to accept that. I want a man who lives a full life, with friends, activities, business, even travel. Our time together is special to me, but I need to

devote a lot of time to my profession. If he's too needy, I want to run the other way, and fast!" Letitia, psychiatric nurse

"I want a man to be the father of my children. If he can afford it, I would like to be an old fashioned housewife. I'd be happy to cook, maybe get some help with the cleaning, and take care of the home and our children. To me, family life is the most important thing. I come from a large family and always dreamed of having lots of children." Jane, administrative assistant

"My husband died a few years ago. Sometimes I feel very lonely. Yes, I enjoy my evenings out with my friends. But I get tired of being only with the ladies. I want to hold hands with a man and feel like a couple again. I really want a companion to share my later years with me." Sonia, retired teacher

Ask Women

Ask the women you know, at work, at school, at parties, at the gym, in your neighborhood, at the supermarket, anywhere and everywhere you go, what they want in a man. Ask the single women what they are looking for. Ask the married women what makes them happy.

Their answers might surprise you and actually relieve that insecure anxiety that you just can't measure up to some perfect ideal you've been imagining. Men and women need each other as companions to go through life. The average man or woman wants the best partner available to share life's ups and downs, to create a family together, to have a sense of belonging, being loved, accepted, connected and not alone.

Marriage And Divorce On The Internet

It was Saturday night. Searching through the mental health chat groups, I discovered "Marriage, Separation and Divorce". My curiosity peaked, I figured I would just check this out, read one or two, and log off. Hours later, I was still reading messages that had been posted over the years.

What a heartwarming experience! Men and women, different ages, nationalities, economic status, life stages, are talking freely, openly, uninhibitedly about their personal marital dilemmas, all presumably from their own homes. Fascinated, I read story after story about the dilemmas and confusions of married life - little or no sex, sexual dysfunctions, money problems, physical abuse, no communication, loss of desire or interest in the mate.

I was touched by the wise, compassionate responses others had given to the "unhappily married" pleas for help and understanding. Never before has there been so much help, comradery and free expression, without the shame, guilt and judgments we fear receiving from our families and friends when we feel most vulnerable.

Your Online Chat

In this exercise, your task is to go online and find out what sites are available to you. However, **if you have a problem, a compulsive need to seek out online sites, then please refrain from doing this exercise**. Instead, recall some of the sites you have visited before. For those of you who have not yet done so, find a chat room, preferably at no cost, with an ongoing discussion about relationships and sexuality. Read the dialogue that has accumulated over time. If you choose to, write in some of your own responses and reactions. Compare what people are saying to the way you currently feel or have felt in the past about your own relationships. If you want, write what you have discovered in your journal. The goal of this exercise is for you to discover what other people are saying and how they are handling situations that may be similar to your own.

Hot Sex On The Web

The internet provides us with a source of comfort, friendship and connection with people we could not meet in any other way. Communicating on the net, we can become anything we choose to be. A person who is generally indecisive, insecure, compulsive, self-serving or insecure in their ordinary life may present an entirely different image with a few carefully chosen words. TV has provided us with many real life scenarios to help us cope better with our own lives. On the web, anything and everything is available. Sensual and sexual fantasy and fulfillment are only a mouse click away. The distinction between reality and fantasy is often blurred. Our real life partners cannot hope to compete with these better than life fantasy relationships.

This is not natural sexuality and certainly not sexual reawakening. Only humans pursue non-contact, non-touching means to satisfy their sexual desires. Although many of us prefer to share ourselves with our intimate partners, a growing number of people have been using the internet and other non-intimate sources (massage parlors, lap dancing, phone sex) to fulfill their sexual needs. Many men and women are partaking of these non-intimate services, sometimes for a lot of money and often at an even greater emotional cost.

We have lost touch with what it means to be human, to connect with another whole human being. Somehow our parents and grandparents knew how to see and accept and love the whole person. As my mother gained weight and grew to a size 16, my father lovingly repeated, "There's more of her to love."

Nowadays, when our partner gains weight or in some other way is not as physically fit, mentally attuned, or financially stable as we expect them to be, we tend to lose our sexual desire. Turning away from the real person in our lives, we may turn to the media or look elsewhere for the unattainable ideal.

Our partner who has gained weight or whose career has hit a downward bump, may actually be at the highest point of their inner awareness. Not being accepted for who they are can lead to resentment, anger and erosion of trust and intimacy. In essence they may feel, "If you won't accept me the way I am, I am no longer willing to accept you the way you are."

It is often easier to avoid facing our own feelings through non-intimate, fantasy sexuality than to share our most intimate thoughts and fantasies with a real human being. There appears to be very little support, in the media or even among our closest friends, for sharing sexual pleasure with our real-life partners. We need to learn how to become close to and love a real person, not in spite of their availability and ordinariness, but because of their availability and ordinariness!

Exploring Internet Sexuality

In this exercise, you are being asked to go exploring through the internet. However, if you have a problem, a need to compulsively go to online sites, then your task is to just recall, without actually logging in and checking any sites.

Look for or recall those explicitly sexual web sites you have either been seeking or avoiding.

Locate a Virtual Community, create your own unique Avatar, and go socializing there.

Examine what you find with a critical eye, without judgment.

Ask yourself very honestly,

Is this what sexuality is all about?

Does virtual sexuality bring me the joy, pleasure, connection and comfort I desire?

What are the benefits or dangers of explicit sexuality online?

What are the benefits or dangers of romantic encounters online?

Good Sex

As a clinical mental health counselor, marital therapist and sex therapist for several decades, I have observed hundreds of men and women as I listened to their stories and sometimes heart wrenching relationship woes. A good sexual relationship is certainly not a "given." Many of us don't place sex as a high priority. We may choose our partners for logical, rather than sensual or emotional reasons. "He's such a good man." "She's kind and nurturing." "He's so handy, he takes care of everything for me." "Sex with her is just okay, but she's a terrific cook and would make a wonderful mother." A good number of us choose a partner with whom we feel safe, someone with whom we may feel a close friendship but very little sexual desire. Many of us are afraid of our own sexual feelings.

Being with someone who does not arouse our sexual passion can give us the false impression that we are not very sexual, that we don't care about sex, need sex, or even like sex. But our bodies will only close down for so long. We may find ourselves dreaming about intimate sexual encounters with strangers and people we barely know. Some of us only become sexually aroused by people who are unavailable and do not appear to need us or love us. In our minds, we may connect love with weakness, vulnerability with inadequacy. We may reject our very real, caring partner in search of some elusive fantasy.

Most of us assume the other person should know how to treat us sexually or should immediately be exactly like or different from our previous lover. We forget how long it may have taken to "get it right" in the past. Or, perhaps, there is no previous lover and we expect this person to make up for all the relationships we never had. Many of us can't even begin to see the other person at first. All we really see is how this person is similar to or different from our past lovers, members of our family, or our closest friends.

We come to our relationships with memories of our past experiences, good and bad, joyful and painful. Although we may verbally express the need and desire for an intimate relationship, we may also have very real fears about getting close to anyone. The barriers to intimacy are often stronger than we realize.

Good Sex for You

Sit quietly, close your eyes, and imagine the most wonderful and perfect sexual experience for you. *Who are you involved with, if anyone? What activities are you participating in? How do you look, feel and express yourself?* Take an imaginary snapshot of your "Good Sex" situation. In the next chapter, we will be exploring all the possible factors that have affected you and may be interfering with your ability to create and have the sexual experiences your desire.

It's The Little Things That Count

What do you focus on in selecting a new lover or a lifetime mate? Many men and women seek a partner who we believe can provide financial security for us, pay our bills, supply us with recreational money, and buy us gifts. Others accept a partner who contributes little or no actual money but provides us with "something" in return for our paying the bills. For some, a dynamite sexual relationship or a very attractive partner that one is proud to be seen with, is enough. For others, a partner who builds and repairs things, a partner who cooks, cleans and takes care of details, is enough for us to choose to stay together.

Usually, some combination of the above, plus more, is what it takes to maintain a relationship. A popular song in the 1950's summed it up in the title: *Little Things Mean A Lot*. The lyrics included the following: *"...say I look nice when I'm not. Touch my hair as you pass my chair, Little Things Mean A Lot. Give me your arm as we cross the street. Call me at six on the dot .... Give me your hand when I've lost the way. Give me your shoulder to cry on. Whether the day is bright or gray, give me your heart to rely on."*

Each of us has those "little things" that mean more, or perhaps are equally as important to us, as money, power, good looks, or passionate sexual intimacy. Identify those "little things" that matter and choose a partner who naturally and easily provides them. Yes, we can train a reluctant partner to do some of those little things we like. But teaching and learning is a slow process, often takes a very long time, requires a great deal of patience, and sometimes results in very little change.

Look inside yourself. *Do you have the patience and perseverance required to teach and persuade your partner to provide those little things for you? Or would you rather switch than fight?* Know yourself and decide. One warning, however: Often, the partner who easily provides us with the little things, does not provide one or more of the "big" things. Conversely, a partner who provides the "big" things, such as money or passionate sex, may not easily provide the little things. The choice is always ours. Choose carefully. Our choice may remain with us for a lifetime!

The Little Things that Count for You

Think about your most passionate and exciting personal sexual experiences. Think about passionate scenes in movies, plays and other people's lives that truly moved you. Think about the types of seemingly unimportant slights, thoughtlessness, and forgetfulness that truly upset you.

In your journal or on a clean piece of paper write the heading, ***"Little Things that Count."*** Now, list as many of these little things that you can remember. Add to this list in the next few days and weeks as more little things that count occur to you.

Ordinary Can Be Extraordinary

Every relationship is a gift. Treat it that way. Let your partner feel like the beautiful Dulcinea or all-powerful Don Quixote in the play *The Man of La Mancha*. If you're currently in a relationship, imagine your partner saying the following words. **If you're not in a relationship, imagine the partner of your dreams saying these words.**

Just for today, be the man or woman of my dreams. Just for today, let me be the man or woman of your dreams. Just for today, give me your undivided love and attention. Just for today, let the miracle of love be ours.

Remember how special I am. I will remember how special you are. Remind me, over and over how much you love me. Look beneath my flaws and blemishes to my beautiful, perfect spirit within.

Treat me like a precious, innocent child, the one you love and adore, the one you shower with gifts. Protect me with your love from the harsh reality of the world. Listen to what I say I want and need. Whisper sweet, loving, kind words into my waiting ears. Tell me, without words, how much you care.

Love me for who I am and everything I want to be. Honor and respect my mind and body. Support me to reach for the highest in myself. Make love to me like you really mean it. Treat my body like a delicate, priceless work of art. Touch me tenderly and lovingly.   Let me feel your magic at play.

Allow me to believe, just for now, that I am the only partner for you. Show you desire me. Hold me. Gaze into my eyes. Kiss my cheeks, my forehead, my eyelashes, my neck, my shoulders. Show me you desire me with your lips, your tongue, your voice, your heart. Massage away my fears, my aches and pains, and my heartfelt longing for love.

Gaze at me from a distance. Ignite my inner fire. Let passion between us build. Dance with me to the rhythm of sweet love. Please don't rush. We have time, lots of time - a lifetime, our lifetime. together.

TEN SIMPLE STEPS

TO

SEXUAL AND SPIRITUAL

REAWAKENING

SEXUAL AND SPIRITUAL REAWAKENING

CHAPTER 2

TEN SIMPLE STEPS TO SEXUAL AND SPIRITUAL REAWAKENING

Come With Me My Love

Come with me my love

Away to the countryside

Where we alone may know

The bliss and joy

And secret passion

Of every man and woman

That ever loved before

And those who may not

Yet have tasted

Life's sweet memories

Once known

Fulfills our sacred soul

With tender dreamy

Thoughtless peace

Tumultuous weary minds

Unwinding

Silent, quiet, still

Humble servants

Bowing their lowly heads

Before the almighty, omnipotent

Power

A single heart

Our heart -- beating as one

Awakened, alive and in love.

Copyright © 8/13/99 Erica Goodstone, Ph.D.

Your Unique Sexual Response Pattern

Each of us has a unique and individual sexual response pattern. This pattern mirrors and reflects the way we are living our lives. What appears to us to be a sexual problem is really a message from our subconscious, manifesting in our sexual response or lack of response.

When we are in our sexual prime and hormones are flooding our bodies, usually our teens to our early twenties, we may be able to easily override our body's subtle messages and willfully continue to "perform" sexually as our mind and ego choose. However, as we age and our hormones are more subdued, we reach a point when we can no longer forcefully override our bodily responses. Yes, we can take stimulants and injections to enhance our arousal, but the stimulating effect will eventually fade if we do not pay attention to the message our body is symbolically giving to us.

Your Body Is Stronger

Than Your Willpower

Even if we are able to override our unique sexual response pattern for a while, our body is stronger than our willpower. A poignant example is the case of a boy who, after a botched circumcision as an infant which left him with a mutilated penis, was reassigned as a female, given a female name, sex reassignment surgery and female hormones to encourage feminine development.

However, no matter how he was encouraged to dress and behave like a girl, his bodily response did not concur. He preferred to urinate standing up facing the toilet. He hated wearing dresses and walking the way he was taught a girl is supposed to walk. Teased mercilessly by his classmates in school for being weird and after spending years on the psychiatrist's couch to accept himself as a girl, when he was finally told the truth about his genetic maleness he was relieved. He knew than that he was not weird. He knew that he was in fact, male, with male traits, male drive, and male desire for females. His body had told him all his life what nobody else had been willing to say -- that he was a male being forced to live as a female. The gender reassignment did not work. Finally, after much reconstruction surgery and two suicide attempts, he emerged as a male and eventually found a woman to marry. (Colapinto, 2000)

Although this is an extreme example, many of us have likewise been attempting to override or suppress our unique sexual response in favor of some image we are attempting to portray. Attempting to hide our sensitive and caring nature, we may feign cool aloof standoffishness. Fearing closeness and intimacy, we may pretend to offer our partners emotional safety as we become increasingly anxious and uncomfortable. Desiring intimacy with a lifetime mate, we may pretend to enjoy one-night stands and non-committed sexual encounters. The list goes on. Our bodies may be quietly and sometimes not so quietly screaming for our attention.

We can continue the pretense for awhile, until our bodily responses finally begin to override our willpower and we are faced with a sexual problem. Without an obvious sexual problem, we might would go on indefinitely behaving in ways that are dramatically opposed to having what we want and are ultimately not satisfying to us. Our sexual problem may be the very catalyst that forces us to stop and examine, not only our sexuality, but the way we are living our lives and relating to others.

As we explore our sexuality, we have the opportunity for change and healing in all areas of our lives. We begin to pay attention to our bodies, what our bodies are telling us to do or stop doing. We listen to our minds, clarifying what we truly need and want. Feeling our emotions, we discover what is true for us. Paying attention to our senses, we feel more connected to the world and all it has to offer in this life.

Your Sexuality Is Not Separate From Your Life

We discover that our sexuality is not separate from the rest of our lives and that our sexuality truly expresses who we are. As we begin to express who we are, life becomes a joyful experience, moment to moment. We feel love and compassion for ourselves and for everyone and everything around us. No longer feeling separate and alone, the world becomes a safe and pleasant place to be. Regardless of our age or physical condition, people are naturally drawn to our warm smile and pleasing demeanor. Love is all around us, everywhere we turn. Sexual Reawakening is the process that brings us back to ourselves, allowing us to open our hearts, give love to, and receive love from, our chosen partners.

Ten Simple Steps To Sexual And Spiritual Reawakening

The following exercises will assist you to reawaken your sexuality, no matter where you are in your life at this very moment. If at all possible, please set aside a block of uninterrupted time before you begin. You can always do these exercises on different days, but the effect will be most powerful if you complete the entire process in one session. Have your journal or some plain white paper and a pen or pencil ready before you begin.

Factors That Have Influenced Your Sexuality

You are about to review your own sexual history. This exercise may stir up feelings and memories you didn't even know you had. Have tissues nearby if you begin to cry. Have a pillow nearby to punch if you feel angry. In your journal or on a sheet of paper, write your answers to the questions.

After completing each section, close your eyes and reflect upon that aspect of your sexual history.

The first, and probably most significant step along the path toward sexual reawakening, is to examine your current life, the way it is right now, not the way you wish it was, not the way you hope it will become, but the way it truly is right now. For some of us this is the most difficult step. If your style is to make excuses, blame others for your problems or deny that you have any problems at all, this first step may be hard for you to comprehend. However, with persistence and the willingness on your part to tell the truth, the whole truth, and nothing but the truth -- at least to yourself at first -- you may be surprised to discover how quickly your life begins to change.

STEP 1

Where Are You Right Now?

Your Current Relationship Status

And Your Sexual Lifestyle

Close your eyes. Take a few slow, deep, easy, and quiet breaths. As you inhale, allow your breath to fill your body cells and relax your muscles. As you exhale, allow the tensions of your body and the concerns of your mind to dissolve.

Your Current Lifestyle

What is your current living situation: married, separated, divorced, widowed, single, living with an intimate partner, living with your parents or other relatives, living in a room in your parent's home with a private entrance, living with a non-intimate roommate, living alone?

Are you financially independent, sharing expenses, or relying on someone else's income to support you?

Where do you live (city, suburbs, country)?

What are your current home and work environments like for you?

What is your current financial situation?

What is your daily activity and stress level?

What is your typical daily diet?

How much and what kind of exercise do you regularly do?

What types of drugs (prescription or recreational), vitamins or herbs do you regularly take and how have these affected you?

Do you have any unhealthy or compulsive habits: smoking cigarettes, drinking alcohol, overeating, dieting, overspending, gambling, sexual compulsions?

How have the above factors affected your life and your sexuality?

Have any aspects of your lifestyle changed? How? When? What caused the change? How does your current lifestyle affect your life and your sexuality?

Close your eyes and reflect upon your responses.

Your Gender Identity and Gender Roles

Are you satisfied with being male or female?

Do you ever wish you could be the other sex?

What do you believe males should do or be?

What do you believe females should do or be?

Do you fit your own idea of the way men or women should be and what they should do?

Do you fit what you believe is the way men or women should be in this society?

Has your satisfaction with being male or female changed? How? When? What caused the change?

Have your beliefs about male or female roles and behaviors changed? How? When? What caused the change?

How have your satisfaction with your gender and gender roles affected your life and your sexuality?

Close your eyes and reflect upon your responses.

Your Health: Physical, Emotional, Sexual And Spiritual

Think about any illnesses, operations, injuries, aches and pains, or other physical problems you are currently having or have had in the distant past or in the recent past.

Has your physical health changed? How? When? What caused the change?

How has your physical health affected your life and your sexuality?

Have you had any emotional upsets, traumas, or problems causing you distress, causing you to seek help or to take medication in the past? Recently? In the past?

Has your emotional health changed? How? When? What caused the change?

How has your emotional health affected your life and your sexuality?

Close your eyes and reflect upon your responses.

Your Age, Physical Appearance, and Body Image

How old are you?

How do you feel about being your current age?

Are you comfortable or uncomfortable with your body as it is?

Has your physical appearance and comfort with your body image changed? How? When? What caused the change?

How has the physical appearance of your body and your body image affected your life, your sexuality and your spirituality?

What effect does your current age have upon your life and your sexuality?

Close your eyes and reflect upon your responses.

Your Partner Availability

How easy or difficult is it for you to find or connect with an available sexual partner?

Has your partner availability changed? How? When? What caused the change?

How has your partner availability or lack of availability affected your sexuality?

Close your eyes and reflect upon your responses.

Copyright © 2009, Revised 2023   *Love Me, Touch Me, Heal Me*   DrEricaGoodstone.com

Step Two

Where Did You Come From Originally?

Your Conception, Birth

And Earliest Years

The second step is to review your origins: your birth, early parenting, and how your earliest beginnings have affected your current life. For some of us, this second step is even more difficult that Step 1. However, if you've already practiced being totally honest with yourself, you may find your answers flowing easily. As you examine your origins, notice any judgements you may have, good and bad, about yourself, your parents or other caretakers, the way life has been for you, the way you believe life should be, what you feel you deserve or don't deserve, and the way life is.

You are about to go on an imaginary journey back to the moment of your own conception. Allow your mind to participate fully. Do not censor any thoughts that arise.

Allow your imagination to run free, recalling times you can only know intuitively.

Imagine that special date, 20, 30, 40, 50, 60, 70, or 80+ years ago, the moment when your mother and father performed the sexual act that created you.

Your Conception

How do you imagine your parents felt about each other before, during and after the moment when you were conceived?

Were either of your parents experiencing stress, physical or mental illness, under the influence of alcohol or drugs (prescription or recreational) while you were being conceived?

Close your eyes and reflect upon your responses.

Your Mother's Pregnancy Carrying You

How did your mother describe her pregnancy when she was carrying you?

Were there any complications?

How did she say she felt physically and emotionally?

How did she describe her sleep, exercise and rest?

Were your parents thrilled, conflicted or disturbed about your impending birth?

Did either of your parents want you to be the other sex?

Did your parents lose any children before you were born?

What effect did your mother's pregnancy have upon your life and your sexuality?

Close your eyes and reflect upon your responses.

Your Mother's Labor and Birthing of You

How did your mother describe her experience of labor when she was giving birth to you? How long did it last?

Was your father present in the delivery room and did he participate?

Who else was present in the delivery room?

Did you willingly and easily emerge or was there some dfifficulty?

Were you in a twisted or breech birth position?

Was the umbilical cord tangled around your neck?

Did you resist being born and find yourself pulled out with forceps?

Were you born through your mother's vaginal canal or cut out of her abdominal cavity by a caesarian section?

Were you born prematurely and were you placed in an incubator?

Was anything physically wrong with you when you were born?

What effect did your birthing process have upon your life and your sexuality?

Close your eyes and reflect upon your responses.

After Your Birth

How was your mother's physical and emotional health after your birth?

Were you breastfed and until what age?

Were you held and nurtured and by whom?

Did you sleep in the same bed or room with one or both parents or caretakers?

Were you left alone, neglected, or abused for any period of time?

What effect did your early infancy have upon your life and your sexuality?

Close your eyes and reflect upon your responses.

Step 3

What Happened Along the Way?

Your Sexual and Relationship History

Your Sexual Education

How was sexuality talked about and treated in your family of origin?

Who did you live with in your earliest years: mother, father, both parents, relatives, adoptive parents, foster parents, siblings, or someone else?

Were your parents or early caretakers physically affectionate toward each other.

Were your parents or early caretakers physically affectionate toward you?

Did you ever observe your parents or someone else in the sex act? How did you respond?

Where and from whom did you learn about sexuality? At what ages?

Has your sexual education changed? How? When? What caused the change?

How has your sexual education affected your life and your sexuality?

Close your eyes and reflect upon your responses.

Your Earliest Sexual Relationships

Recall and describe your earliest sexual experiences, as an infant, young child, adolescent and teenager, as much as your memory will allow. For each stage of life, answer these same questions:

With whom were you involved? What happened? Who initiated?

Did you want to be involved or were you pressured, seduced, coerced or forced into submission against your will?

What emotions did you feel and were your feelings reciprocated by the other person?

How were you treated and how did you treat others?

What effect did those early experiences have upon your current sexuality?

Close your eyes and reflect upon your responses.

Your Adult Sexual Relationships

Recall and describe your most significant sexual relationships during each decade of your adult life (twenties, thirties, forties, fifties …eighties….)

Describe your sexuality, how you felt about your body, your appearance, and your overall feeling about life.

Recall your hopes and dreams for your future.

Who loved and nurtured you and who neglected, abandoned or abused you?

Who did you love and nurture and who did you neglect, abandon or abuse? Did your sexuality change? When? How? What caused the change?

How have your sexual relationships as an adult affected your life and your sexuality?

Close your eyes and reflect upon your responses.

Copyright © 2009, Revised 2023   *Love Me, Touch Me, Heal Me*   DrEricaGoodstone.com

The Significance of Your Sexual History

What events, situations, and people are significant in your sexual history?

How has your sexual history affected your life and your sexuality?

How has your sexual history, or what you know about it changed? Why?

Close your eyes and reflect upon your responses.

Step Four

Your Sexual Identity

And Partner Preferences

The Kinsey Heterosexual/Homosexual Continuum

Many of us are confused about our sexual identity or sexual partner or object preferences. The Kinsey Continuum has been a useful source to help define for ourselves where they fit. In massive sexual surveys of the 1940's and 1950's, Alfred Kinsey and his colleagues discovered that most people exhibited degrees of homosexuality and heterosexuality, with bisexuality representing a midpoint. They created a seven-point heterosexual-homosexual continuum. People fit on the continuum according to two criteria: homosexual or heterosexual behavior and attraction to same sex or opposite sex. People in category "0," exclusively heterosexual, claimed no attraction, desire, or sexual activity, ever, with the same sex. People in category "6," exclusively homosexual, claimed no attraction, desire, or sexual activity, ever, with the opposite sex.

In Kinsey's studies, about 4 percent of men and 1-3 percent of women were categorized as exclusively homosexual, "6". A larger percentage were considered predominantly homosexual, "4" or "5", or predominantly heterosexual, "1" or "2". The largest percentage of people were classified as exclusively heterosexual, 50 - 92%. Thirty-seven percent of men and 13 percent of women claimed to have reached orgasm through homosexual activity at some time after puberty.

A 1970 nationwide survey conducted by the Kinsey Institute, a 1988 survey, and a 1993 Louis Harris poll, had results similar to the earlier Kinsey studies. Studies indicate that a large number of men and a smaller but still significant number of women have engaged in homosexual experience during their lives, and a very small percentage, 1-4%, within the last year to five years.

Where Do You Fit on the Kinsey Heterosexual/Homosexual Continuum?

Look at the Kinsey Heterosexual/Homosexual Continuum below. Circle the number that most accurately describes your experiences throughout your life.

0...... exclusively heterosexual, having had no homosexual experiences at any time in your life

1...... almost exclusively heterosexual with one or more homosexual experiences

2...... mostly heterosexual with some homosexual experiences

3...... bisexual, indicating you have had sexual experiences with the same or opposite sex to about the same degree

4...... mostly homosexual with some heterosexual experiences

5...... almost exclusively homosexual with one or more heterosexual experiences

6...... exclusively homosexual, having had no heteresexual experiences at any time in your life

Copyright © 2009, Revised 2023   *Love Me, Touch Me, Heal Me*   DrEricaGoodstone.com

THE KINSEY CONTINUUM

| 0 | 1 | 2 | 3 | 4 | 5 | 6 |

Heterosexual　　　　　**Bisexual**　　　　　**Homosexual**

(*Human Sexuality in a World of Diversity*, 1995)

Your Sexual Identity and Partner Preferences

Where do you fit on the Kinsey Continuum?

Do you define yourself as heterosexual, bisexual, homosexual?

How do you feel about your sexual identity?

Have your sexual identity and partner preferences changed? How? When? Why?

How have your sexual identity and partner preferences affected your life and your sexuality?

Close your eyes and reflect upon your responses.

Step Five

Why Do You Want Sex?

What Do You Hope to Gain, Become or Experience?

Each of us has different reasons for choosing to have sexual relations with another person. At different times in our lives, we may have sex to feel pleasurable sensations, to play like children, to relieve tension, to alleviate pain, to avoid facing our problems, to feel comforted and touched, to express our emotions, to create a family, to explore our spirituality, or to discover our own true nature,.

Why Do You Want to Have Sex?

What is your reason for having sex or for currently not having sex?

What do you hope to learn, give, receive, become, or have through sexual contact?

What do you desire, fantasize and dream about?

How do you feel about having children or becoming a parent?

Do you want to have children with your current partner or with someone else?

Copyright © 2009, Revised 2023   *Love Me, Touch Me, Heal Me*   DrEricaGoodstone.com

How is sex better than touching, hugging, giving or receiving a massage?

Is there any other way for you to achieve the same sensations, feelings and goals?

How has your reason for wanting sex affected your life and your sexuality?

Close your eyes and reflect upon your responses.

Importance Of Sexuality In Your Life

How important is sexuality in your life?

Has the importance of sexuality in your life changed? How? When?

What caused the change?

How has the importance you have placed on sexuality affected your life and your sexuality?

Have you ever been celibate? For how long?

What effect did being celibate have, if any, upon your life and your sexuality?

Close your eyes and reflect upon your responses.

Your Current Sexuality

Are you currently being sexual with a partner: your spouse, live-in partner, casual date, steady partner, person other than your live-in partner, other?

How does your body feel before, during and after sexual relations with your current partner?

Are you currently celibate? For how long? For what reason?

How often do you stimulate yourself sexually and in what preferred ways?

Do you reach orgasm easily or with difficulty?

How do you feel before, during and after you stimulate yourself?

How does your current sexuality compare to each decade of your previous life?

What has remained the same? What has changed? When and how did it change?

When were you most happy, most fulfilled?

When were you least happy, least fulfilled?

What have you done in the past to improve your condition?

What are you doing now to improve your condition?

How is your current sexuality affecting your life?

Close your eyes and reflect upon your responses.

Copyright © 2009, Revised 2023   *Love Me, Touch Me, Heal Me*   DrEricaGoodstone.com

Your Sexual Function and Dysfunction

Are you satisfied or upset with your sexual functioning at this point in your life?

Are you currently experiencing any sexual problems?

* Desire problems

* Arousal problems

* Orgasmic problems

Have your problems been recent or lifelong?

Have these problems happened only in certain situations or in most circumstances?

Has your sexual functioning changed? How? When? What caused the change?

How have your sexual dysfunctions, if any, affected your life and your sexuality?

Close your eyes and reflect upon your responses.

So You Think You Have a Sexual Problem

When our bodies do not respond the way we think they "should," we are receiving a powerful message. Maybe we have been trying to force our bodies to do something we don't really want to do. Our brain sends the message to our

Copyright © 2009, Revised 2023   *Love Me, Touch Me, Heal Me*   DrEricaGoodstone.com

pituitary, the master gland, signaling our ovaries or testes and other glands to secrete the hormones needed for us to become aroused. If our brain fails to send the proper signals, our glands will not secrete the needed hormones. We will either not become aroused, lose our arousal, or be unable to experience the pleasurable release of orgasm. We cannot ignore our body's messages and function with precision. We are not mere physical machines. We have a mind, emotions, five basic senses, a neuromuscular system, an autonomic nervous system, organs, tissues and glands -- and all of them affect each other.

Just as we cannot turn on a car ignition with the wrong key, insufficient gas or oil, a cracked starter, or worn spark plugs, we cannot "turn on" our sexual apparatus without the proper human fuel. That proper fuel is unique to each one of us and often different for the same person at different times. If we don't know what thoughts, feelings, visual images, words and sounds, physical sensations and moral principles ignite our private parts, then we may interpret our body's message as a sign that we have a problem, are not performing well, and are somehow inadequate. Perhaps that "problem" that won't go away is merely our body's way of saying: "Pay attention to me."

Your Ideal Sexual Life

Close your eyes and imagine your sexual life being exactly the way you want it to be.

Where are you? Who is with you? What are you doing? How are you feeling?

Close your eyes and reflect upon your responses.

Step 6

What Is Your Sexual Style?

Sexual Pleasure, Variety

and Risk Taking Behavior

Many of us assume our friends have the same sexual desires and preferences that we have. Many of us believe that we can generalize and say that "men like...." and "women want...." Yet every one of us is a totally unique individual with our own fingerprint and specific DNA code. We have our own preferences and style in everything we do, from the way we eat, dress, work, play and talk to the types of friends and lovers we choose. Each of us has our own unique sexual style, needs, desires, interests and preferences. Why not allow our unique sexuality to emerge?

Through our intimate connections with others, we can resolve long held conflicts about our deepest sexual selves. Keeping our true sexual desires hidden from fear of being rejected, embarrassed or abandoned, we may be hurting ourselves or hurting someone else.

Sharing our sexuality in all its fullness offers our partners the opportunity to expand their own sexual expression.

Your Sexual Desire Level

What do you believe is your level of sexual desire: hyperactive (overactive), hypoactive (underactive), or moderate?

Has your desire level changed? How? When? What caused the change?

How has your sexual desire level affected your life and your sexuality?

Close your eyes and reflect upon your responses.

Your Sexual Arousal Style

How do you become aroused?

What type of stimulation or techniques do you require?

How long does it take?

Has your sexual arousal style changed? How? When? What caused the change?

How has your sexual arousal style affected your life and your sexuality?

Close your eyes and reflect upon your responses.

Your Sexual Orgasmic Style

How easily do you orgasm and how long does it take?

Do you have difficulty attaining orgasm?

Are you able to control the timing of your orgasm?

Does it take longer than you would like for you to have an orgasm? Why?

Does your orgasm happen sooner than you would like? Why?

Are your orgasms satisfying?

Has your orgasmic style or level of sensation changed? How? When?

What caused the change?

Copyright © 2009, Revised 2023   *Love Me, Touch Me, Heal Me*   DrEricaGoodstone.com

How has your orgasmic style affected your life and your sexuality?

Close your eyes and reflect upon your responses.

Your Sexual Resolution Style

How do you feel and behave after you have had an orgasm?

Are you affectionate, cold, indifferent, bored, restless, feeling guilty and ashamed?

Do you fall asleep, get out of bed, leave?

How do you feel waking up in the morning next to your partner?

Has your sexual resolution style changed? How? When?

What caused the change?

How has your sexual resolution style affected your life and your sexuality?

Close your eyes and reflect upon your responses.

Your Preferred Sources of Sexual Stimulation

What is your preferred source of stimulation: visual images, auditory messages, kinesthetic, touch sensations?

Copyright © 2009, Revised 2023   *Love Me, Touch Me, Heal Me*   DrEricaGoodstone.com

Do you prefer to be the *recipient, victim, aggressor, perpetrator, or mutual partner?*

Which visual images, auditory messages, or kinesthetic sensations do you prefer: live person, intimate partner, strangers in the street, topless bars, call girls, prostitutes, massage parlors, videos, movies, internet sites, chat rooms, phone sex, magazines, photographs, self-pleasuring, other?

Have your preferred sources of stimulation change? How? When? Why?

How have your visual, auditory and kinesthetic preferences affected your sexuality and your life?

Close your eyes and reflect upon your responses.

Your Preferred Sexual Locations

At home: on a couch, in a bath or shower, in another room - explain, on a terrace, porch or outdoor area, hotel or motel room, automobile, public place with the danger of being caught, on a beach, in a hot tub, other

Which of the above sexual locations do you prefer? Which do you engage in frequently? Which have you seldom or never experienced?

In which locations have you been forced to have sex against your will?

In which locations would you like to have sex?

In which locations are you afraid to have sex?

Have your sexual location preferences changed? How? When?

What caused the change?

How have your sexual location preferences affected your life and your sexuality?

Close your eyes and reflect upon your responses.

Your Sexual Activity Preferences

Kissing on the lips, French or deep tongue kissing, sexual intercourse, cunnilingus, fellatio, anal Intercourse, analingus, fisting, sado-masochism, bondage, toys, role play, self-pleasuring alone, self-pleasuring with a partner present, ménage-a-trois, group sex, other

Which of the above sexual activities do you prefer?

Which do you engage in frequently?

Which activities have you seldom or never experienced?

Which activities have you been forced to do against your will?

Which sexual activities would you like to do?

Which sexual activities are you afraid to do?

Which sexual activities do you find disgusting or revolting?

Have your sexual activity preferences changed? How? When?

What caused the change?

How have your sexual activity preferences affected your life and your sexuality?

Close your eyes and reflect upon your responses.

Your Preferred Sexual Positions

Missionary Position -- man on top, woman on top, doggie style, spoon style -- woman's back to man, sideways -- facing each other, other specific positions, experiment with different positions

Which of the above sexual positions do you prefer?

Which sexual positions do you engage in frequently?

Which sexual positions have you seldom or never experienced?

Which sexual positions have you been forced to do against your will?

Which sexual positions would you like to do?

Which sexual positions are you afraid to do?

Have your preferred sexual positions changed? How? When? What caused the change? How have your preferred sexual positions affected your life and your sexuality?

Close your eyes and reflect upon your responses.

Your Sexual Performance Style

What is your sexual performance style: aggressive, passive, combination?

Is your sexual style narrowly focused and repetitive or multi-faceted and changing?

Is your style quick and fast or long and slow?

Has your sexual performance style changed? How? When? What caused the change? How has your sexual performance style affected your sexuality and your life?

Close your eyes and reflect upon your responses.

Your Sexual Pleasuring Style

Do you prefer pleasuring your partner?

Do you prefer being pleasured by your partner?

Do you prefer mutual giving and receiving of pleasure?

How has your preferred interaction style affected your sexuality, your life?

Has your sexual pleasuring style changed? How? When? Why?

Close your eyes and reflect upon your responses?

Copyright © 2009, Revised 2023   *Love Me, Touch Me, Heal Me*   DrEricaGoodstone.com

Your Sexual Communication Style

How easily do you communicate your needs to your partner?

How easily can your partner communicate his or her needs to you?

Has your sexual communication style changed? How? When? What caused the change? How has your sexual communication style affected your sexuality and your life?

Close your eyes and reflect upon your responses.

Your Sexual Commitment Style

Are you monogamous, choosing to stay with one partner for life?

Are you a serial monogamist, choosing to stay with one partner at a time, until the relationship ends?

Are you promiscuous, preferring to play the field sexually, with many different partners?

Has your sexual commitment style changed? How? When? Why?

How has your sexual commitment style affected your sexuality and your life?

Close your eyes and reflect upon your responses.

Step 7

What's Blocking Or Stopping You From Creating Joyful Intimate Sexual Relationships?

Sex Does Not Begin In The Bedroom

A man and woman enter the bedroom, tear off their clothes and jump into bed. A married couple undress into their pajamas and meet each other under the covers.

Two people get into bed, turn their backs to each other, and turn out the light.

What happens next in bed is often the culmination of hours, days, weeks, months, even years, of courtship, loving interactions, or hostile exchanges, indifference, frustration, or even boredom. Sex does not begin in the bedroom. It starts with the way we look, act and interact with each other and by what we feel inside - all day long.

What interferes with our personal enjoyment of our own sexuality depends upon our unique experiences, our bodily and emotional memories of those events, and our current beliefs about love, sexuality and intimate relating. Our own personal programming determines our sexual responses. When we feel threatened by closeness, even the most gentle and tender touch by a loving partner may be perceived by us as pressure, demand, aggression, even violence. If we have been programmed to always please others, if we feel in any way inferior to our own idea of the way we should be, our sexual responsiveness may suffer. If we believe we are sexually inadequate in some way, we may fear that we will have to change. Change is always frightening because it involves the unknown.

The first step in reawakening our sexuality is to discover what is currently blocking or interfering with our ability to feel and enjoy pleasure. Some of us can only allow our sexual feelings to emerge when we are in the privacy of our own home, alone by ourselves. Some of us avoid physical contact even with our own body.

How Do You Look and Feel?

Stand in front of a mirror and observe yourself (with or without clothing).

Observe the way you are standing? Are you standing tall and proud, slouching, forcefully holding your body erect in a state of tension, or comfortably relaxed in your own presence?

Observe your breathing? Is it full and rhythmical or shallow and even held?

Observe your facial features, the quality of your skin, the expression on your face?

Are you looking your best or do you appear to be tired, older than your years, stressed out or relaxed and content?

Observe the rest of your body?

Are you satisfied with your physical appearance, your weight, your shape, your fitness level, your muscle tone?

Now go internally.

Are you satisfied with your personality and the way you present yourself to the world?

Are you satisfied with your life right now or is there something that you want to change?

What have your emotions been telling you about the way you are living your life?

Copyright © 2009, Revised 2023   *Love Me, Touch Me, Heal Me*   DrEricaGoodstone.com

Are you satisfied with your education, work, career, and finances or is there something you would like to change?

Are you satisfied with your family, your home life, and the quality of your intimate and non-intimate relationships?

Are you satisfied with the amount and quality of touching, loving, and sexual expressiveness in your personal life and most intimate relationships?

Taking a long, honest look at ourselves, our current lives, and what we truly desire, can be difficult, but well worth the time and effort. If we want a passionate sexual relationship, sometimes we need to change behaviors that are keeping people away. We may have to give more than we thought was necessary or not as much as we naturally give. We may have to ask ourselves questions to discover what we really want. We may also have to find out what our potential partners want. We don't have to have all the answers and solutions. Others can help. Why waste any more time struggling, suffering and remaining unhappy? Relief may be just a phone call, workshop, self-help book, or therapy session away.

We need to learn how to ask and how to receive the answers we get. We need to be able to truly listen and to hear what our partners say they want, not what we think they should want.

Step 8

How Can You Overcome Your Blocks And Create Joyful Intimate Sexual Relationships?

Sexual Healing

As we begin to heal the disconnection between our body, mind and spirit, we can no longer tolerate verbal abuse, tiny humiliations, control, manipulation and lack of acknowledgement from others. Whether we are in a loving relationship, an unhappy situation, or have been alone for years, as we reclaim ourselves, our desire for sexual contact is sometimes temporarily diminished. We often need to turn our focus inward, pay attention to our own self first, before going back out into the world to connect with another. Many religions practice celibacy to help us let go of physical connection to the outside world, returning our focus back to the self, back to spirit, source, creator, God.

Our sexual organs can be powerful allies, if we let them. Listen and they will tell us all we need to know about love and our relationships. Ignore the messages or control our bodies with our mind or our willpower, and our sexual organs will seem to betray us with their exasperating honesty.

What do we want our sexual organs to do? Perform for us? Perform for someone else? Or assist us to open our hearts, feel the love inside, and bring pleasurable sensation to ourselves and others? It's that simple. Performing brings us into our mind, away from our bodily feelings. Feelings bring us into our body. Once we connect within, it is easy to connect with others.

Your Sexual Healing

How do you want sex to be in your life?

What needs healing in your body, your mind, your emotions or your spirit?

What steps have you taken to heal your body, your mind, your emotions and your spirit?

Copyright © 2009, Revised 2023   *Love Me, Touch Me, Heal Me*   DrEricaGoodstone.com

Being Celibate For A Month, Six Months, A Year or Longer

If you are truly serious about reawakening your sensuality and sexuality, you may choose to remain celibate for awhile, examining your life, your thoughts, and your emotions. You can use this private time to determine what you really want in a partner, a lover, a steady companion, or a lifetime mate. When you are ready, you can return to the world of sexual activity and sexual connection. After a brief hiatus, you will then be able to approach your love life with insight, wisdom and the power of knowing "I can do without it and still be okay."

What would it be like to forego sexual connection for an entire month, 30 or 31 days? What would it be like to abstain for 6 months, for one year or for longer than that? How would your lifestyle, health, energy level and emotions be affected? Some of us have already been sexually abstinent for months, years, or even decades. Some of us have never actually had any sexual experiences with others. And some of us have been seeking sexual contact for so long, with such intensity, that we often approach potential partners like a panting animal in heat. Many of us jump in and out of relationships quickly, rarely taking time between relationships to be alone, to be celibate, and to contemplate what we really want in our life.

For those of us who have rarely gone without sexual contact for even brief periods of time, **what would it be like for you to totally refrain from sexual contact for a month or longer?** Without an outlet for the accumulation of emotional and physical tensions, you might find yourself feeling agitated, nervous or depressed and lethargic. You might feel lonely, isolated, insecure about your sociability, closed off, and less interested in the world around you. You may have difficulty sleeping, your mind racing and reviewing the day, flooded with thoughts, evaluating your actions, obsessing over minor details. Without your usual and expected dose of sexual activity, you might even feel as if you are going crazy. You might find yourself obsessing about how you would compare to their current lovers. You may become overwhelmed with your fantasies, desires, longing, craving and neediness. Or, if sexual relationships have been problematic for you, you may actually find yourself sleeping better, having more energy for work, for pursuing creative projects, or for spending time with friends. You may even rediscover a forgotten interest in some hobby or other leisure activity.

You can choose to fill your time with activity, traveling, gambling, shopping, exercising, or even working. You can temporarily satisfy your sexual desires with online social networking,. You can suppress your feelings with conversation and food. Or you can suppress your feelings with mind-altering chemicals, drugs, cigarettes, or alcohol. Being celibate for awhile offers you a rare opportunity to look inside, examine your true feelings, notice the many ways you attempt to use and suppress your sexual energy. You can then focus on your dreams without the emotional complication of sexual intimacy with another person.

In a difficult relationship, sex can be the last avenue for getting close. The fear is, if you take time off from the one area of closeness between you, all sorts of bad things will happen. Actually, stopping that last link to pleasure and intimacy, you may be able to see your relationship more clearly for the first time. You may observe your partner's attributes, both favorable and unfavorable, without being swayed by your own physical desires and needs. Brief periods of refraining from sexual contact can help you to discover your own inner longing and reflect upon your own unmet needs. Then, you can begin to heal your relationship with yourself first, and then with your intimate partner/s.

Many of us can only delve so far into our own nature. To understand yourself and your relationships more fully, you have many choices. You can pursue private psychotherapy, relationship, couples and sex therapy, workshops, body therapy, and body psychotherapy, and even personal coaching.

Step 9

Making A Commitment to Your Own

Sexual And Spiritual Reawakening

A Healing Journey Inward

Have you felt your heart patter lately?

Do you sense your organs smiling?

Is there a glint in your eyes and a lilt in your voice?

Does your body feel free and alive?

Do you move confidently and gracefully with strength and purpose?

If not, then maybe you are ready for a new experience.

Sexual Reawakening is the return of your body/mind system to a sensual state it once knew or may have never known. It is not measured by the frequency of sexual contact, the intensity or number of orgasms, the amount of sexual desire or the number of intimate relationships. It does not even require having a partner.

What appears to be a sexual problem in your life may not be a problem at all. The obvious symptom, unreliable erection, lack of pleasurable sensations, or inability to reach orgasm, may be used by your conscious mind as a smoke screen, a mask, a clever device to cloud and confuse the real issue. Freud and other psychotherapists have written volumes about our unconscious, neurotic and psychotic defenses. All of us are masters at hiding the truth from ourselves. But how many of us are brave enough to tackle our deception, delve into the turmoil in our minds, and strive to reach for a level of authenticity, truth and joy in our lives?

Once we journey inside to our own core, the healing process has already begun. This is what Reawakening is all about. We reconnect to those lost parts of ourselves, those parts that hold us back from good feelings, from connection, from love. Aren't we all attracted to and in awe of a person who seems self-confident and secure? Wouldn't you like to approach life, love and romance on a sure footing? Let's begin to celebrate the joy of life and the wonder of our own precious relationships.

Your Commitment to Your Own Sexual Reawakening

In your journal or on a clean sheet of paper, write the heading

"My Commitment To My Own Sexual Reawakening."

Copyright © 2009, Revised 2023   *Love Me, Touch Me, Heal Me*   DrEricaGoodstone.com

Close your eyes and imagine your sexual reawakening as a fête a complis, a completed event. Imagine how you look and feel and express yourself. Imagine the people or non-human animals, plants, or elements of nature that are sharing your good feelings with you. Slowly open your eyes, pick up your pen and write freely.

Do not censor your thoughts. Write whatever thoughts come to you. Read your commitment every day. Add to it and alter it as your feelings change. But remember, it is your commitment, your slow steady focused progress toward your final goal that will result in transformation of your life.

Your Commitment to Your Own Spiritual Reawakening

In your journal or on a clean sheet of paper, write the heading **"My Commitment To My Own Spiritual Reawakening."**

Close your eyes and imagine your sexual reawakening as a fête a complis, a completed event. Imagine how you look and feel and express yourself. Imagine the people or non-human animals, plants, or elements of nature that are sharing your good feelings with you. Slowly open your eyes, pick up your pen and write freely.

Do not censor your thoughts. Write whatever thoughts come to you. Read your commitment every day. Add to it and alter it as your feelings change. But remember, it is your commitment, your slow steady focused progress toward your final goal that will result in transformation of your life.

Step 10

Sexual And Spiritual Reawakening

At Last!

Finding a love partner in life is a blessing, a gift from God. Many of us have intense attractions toward others. Many of us have shared a romantic whirlwind of love and intimate feelings, with someone, for awhile. Then reality hits us in the face. Just those qualities that most attracted us at first are the very qualities we find irritating, agitating, boring, or even hateful, in our partners as we spend time together.

I believe we choose our partners to heal those parts of ourself that need healing. The partner who attracts us probably has certain strengths or abilities that complement the areas in which we feel we are lacking. As we get to know each other, our weaknesses, compulsive behaviors, or flaws become glaringly obvious to both of us. That's when we have the opportunity to either heal or run away.

If we stay for awhile and face our vulnerabilities and inadequacies, we have an opportunity to gain our own inner strength from our partner's outer strength. We can heal even the most deep-seated traumatic memories through loving connection with another human being. In intimate relationships we exchange energy and we feed each other with touch and love and our sexual being. In intimate relationships we have the most powerful opportunity to heal our lives.

It is also possible to solve our inner problems when we are not involved in a relationship, when we are living in an emotional hiatus between relationships. After a period of intense self-exploration, a point may come when we are ready to reconnect in a new relationship. That's when our relationships truly become a celebration of joyful connection without the fear of losing our identity.

If each of us does the inner work, self-examination and life review, the joy in our lives will be immeasurable. We will then become an inspiration to others, sharing our light and love, peace and joy with everyone who meets us.

As discussed earlier in this book, people who have gone through near death experiences, in reviewing their lives, claim they were not asked, "How much money did you make? How beautiful or sexy or intelligent were you? How many times did you have sex? How great a lover were you in bed?"

No. The only question asked was, "How did you love?" Lifetime experiences were evaluated in terms of how much love you felt and shared with others. In the end, nothing else seems to matter at all.

Sexuality is God's gift to us, teaching us how we love or don't love, through bodily experiences of exquisitely pleasurable sensations. Many of us have forgotten the true purpose of sexuality in our lives.   Enhancing your senses and then gaining control over them brings you closer to your own self and to the divine. Suppressing and denying your natural senses, behaving in emotionally, physically, or sexually destructive ways, feeling uncontrolled desire, compulsively seeking thrills and promiscuous sexual adventures, usually indicates that you are disconnected from your own core. When you value non-intimate activity more than contact and intimacy, we are you are probably experiencing a split or disconnection between your mind, your body and your true spiritual self.

When you feel your connection to your own inner core, you can't help but treat all life including animals, plants, ourselves and other humans with love, respect, and compassion. You know how to love and be loved. You face each day with humility, grace and thankfulness for the gift of our very lives.

- **Are you ready to find your true love in yourself and with another?**

- **Are you willing to share your own beautiful light with the world around you?**

SEXUAL AND SPIRITUAL REAWAKENING AT LAST!

SEXUAL AND SPIRITUAL REAWAKENING

CHAPTER 3

SEXUAL AND SPIRITUAL REAWAKENING ... AT LAST!

Now The Time Has Come

Now the time has come

I've spoken to my hungry heart

Unveiled its secret longing

As I carve away

The ragged edges

Of my lonely life

Senses sparkling

In the light of day

Penetrate the darkness

As its wings enfold me

Wisdom flowing outward

Cells alive, ablaze

With love

Armor dangling

By a single thread

I await the subtle signals

Of your enduring love

Transparent eyes reveal

The story of your private heart

I hear your silent words

Rumbling

In the center of my core

What are you telling me

My love?

Has your body ached

To reconnect

With something, someone

Greater than this earth

This life

This place?

Then take my hand

And let me lead you

Down the path

That we will make

Together

Copyright © 2009, Revised 2023   *Love Me, Touch Me, Heal Me*   DrEricaGoodstone.com

The time has come

My love

Let's play like children

Romping in the sun

Our hands entwined

Our hearts engulfed

Our bodies throbbing

Sensing, flowing

With delight

In love

In pleasure

Now

Sensually alive

Sexual and Spiritual

Reawakening

At Last!

Copyright © 8/14/99 Erica Goodstone, Ph.D.

Sexual And Spiritual Reawakening Will Transform Your Life

Spiritual and Sexual Reawakening are total life-transforming events. It is not just the culmination of required rituals, disciplined practice, hard work, or specific exercises. It does not require having a partner. Spiritual and sexual reawakening is expanding and controlling all of your senses, coming face to face with your own inner being, your soul, your God essence. No place to hide. Nothing to do but let go and feel the love that has always been there. Spiritual and sexual reawakening is being reborn into life, living every day like a bright eyed, innocent child -- with awe and wonder, excitement and joy, and total aliveness.

Spiritual and Sexual Reawakening are about returning to your true self, regaining your integrity, reclaiming what is truly yours. It is about removing self-imposed boundaries and restrictions. You re-discover that love and beauty surround you - everywhere. Spiritual and sexual reawakening brings you back to nature. You open your eyes and see the forests, smell the flowers, taste the fruit, hear the wind, and touch the earth. With all of your senses, you feel your connection to everyone and everything that exists.

Spiritual and Sexual Reawakening is a life experience. It occurs when you are in a place of total presence, aliveness and connection, to yourself, to life, and to others. It is about listening to your body, your mind, and all of your senses, observing and tempering your automatic responses.

Sexual Reawakening Is About Freedom

Sexual reawakening is about freedom - freedom to love, freedom to touch, and freedom to feel; freedom to say "yes" and freedom to say "no." It is the freedom to explore your own and your partner's bodily sensations, without shame, guilt, or embarrassment. As you gradually increase your sensual awareness, tensions in your body lessen, allowing you to tune in to your sensations and freely express your emotions. Your capacity for intimacy and creative expression naturally flourishes.

Spiritual Reawakening

Is About Freedom

Spiritual reawakening is also about freedom – freedom from the prison of automatic emotional responses, both positive and negative, freedom from your own preconceived ideas about the way life should be, freedom from your own circular mental thought patterns that keep you stuck and unable to move on, and freedom to be fully alive in every moment. As you gradually increase your spiritual awareness, your mind becomes more naturally at ease. You find yourself not holding on so much, not needing so much, not even wanting so much. Negative situations and less spiritually minded people seem to drop away from your every day experiences. Your capacity for acceptance, fulfillment, appreciation, gratitude and joy naturally flourishes.

Sexual Reawakening Is About Soul Connection

Sexual reawakening is not about keeping your eyes open and staring at your partner during sex. That's okay, but it is not essential. If it was, then all people with visual impairments would have less than adequate sexual experienceds. Even with severe visual problems, we can and many of us do, have exquisitely intimate sensual and sexual experiences.

Sexual reawakening is not about the words we communicate. If it was, then all people with speech and hearing impairments would have less than adequate sexual experiences. Even with severe speech and hearing problems, we can and many of us do, have exquisitely intimate sensual and sexual experiences.

Sexual reawakening is about soul connection. Physically challenged, mentally disturbed, and chronically ill people always retain the capacity to connect to their own soul and to their partner's soul. As long as you are conscious, as long as you are alive within your physical body, through simple touch with any or all of your senses and through intimate sexual contact, you can easily have access to your own and your partner's soul.

Spiritual Reawakening
Is About Acceptance

Spiritual reawakening is about acceptance, learning to accept and even honor each other, for all the ways we are the same and for all the ways we differ and can learn from each other. Spiritual reawakening is knowing that every person is unique with a particular family background, relationship history, lifestyle and perception of the way love is. You discover that each of us has special gifts and talents as well as inadequacies and blind spots. You learn that what is easy and natural for one person may be difficult for another.

Sexual Reawakening Is About Exploring Your Own Unique Love Style

Sexual reawakening is uncovering and exploring your own unique love style and sexual response pattern. You learn to teach your partner/s what you want them to learn. You carefully pay attention to what your partners are teaching you about yourself, about their self, and about the world. You realize that everybody is teachable, everybody must be taught, and that YOU may have to be the example first. You understand that learning is slow and it happens step by step, day by day, experience by experience, through repetition and practice. As you continue to expand your spiritual awareness, you discover that most of us learn best when treated with compassion, kindness and patient acceptance.

Sexual reawakening is about developing the sensitivity, awareness, and patience to give and receive love with all people in your life, especially your most intimate partner/s. You discover that love is all there is. You recognize that love often brings up anything unlike itself for the purpose of release and healing. You learn to look beyond the immediate moment to unleash the unlimited potential within yourself and your chosen partner/s.

The Process Of Sexual Reawakening

Now, you are ready to begin the process of Sexual Reawakening. In the last chapter, you examined your history, your sexual desires and sexual preferences, your overall health and lifestyle, your relationship and commitment style, and what has been preventing you from creating the sexual and love relationships you have now desire. At this point, you understand what you need to do, or to stop doing, to create more fulfilling love in your life. Now you are ready to take that step into the unknown, to truly face yourself and to continue your own personal transformation that has has already begun.

Discover Every Man And Woman

In Your Partner's Eyes

Look deeply into your partner's yes and observe this precious being in front of you. If you don't currently have a partner, look in the mirror at yourown self. Stay fully present.

Discover every woman in this one woman. Discover every man in this one man.

Make love a priority. Teach each other. Love each other.

Trust that both of you can and will learn to love.

Allow love to prevail every moment of every day, every time you are together, fully clothed or fully unclothed.

Play at being lovers. Love with all your senses.

Reconnect to the joy and pleasure our sexuality was meant to be.

Once you allow this deep and loving connection to solidify, your very real partners will begin to offer the sweet ambrosia of your dreams. Every man will become the man of steel, hard as a rock, who can go all night, or at least feel as if he can -- because he won't have to perform for you, prove himself to you, try to be better for you. There'll be nothing for him to prove to anyone. Every woman will become the goddess she was born to be, regardless of her natural endowments, age or physical appearance. Watch the masks and layers of defense peel away as you peer into each other's souls. **Most of all, play and have fun!**

Your Ideal Man/Your Ideal Woman

In your journal, describe your own ideal man and your own ideal woman.

How does your current partner compare to your ideal man or woman?

If you do not currently have a partner, choose someone from the past or someone with whom you would like to become intimately involved.

How do you compare to your ideal man or woman?

How would your ideal man or woman respond to your current partner? How would your ideal man or woman respond to you?

Reflect upon your responses.

Your Sexual Experiences

Sit quietly and take a few slow, deep, easy, and rhythmical breaths. Allow your body to relax. Begin to reminisce about a recent sexual experience. If you have not had a partner for a long time, reminisce about an experience with a previous partner or reminisce about an experience of self-stimulation.

What did you feel in your body?

What were you thinking and believing about yourself, your body, your partner, your partner's body, your responses, your partner's responses?

What did you do with your partner?

What did you say to each other?

What did you feel in your body before you started, during physical contact, and after the sexual contact ended?

Take a moment now to write your answers to the above questions in your journal or on a clean piece of paper.

Your Partner's Sexual Style

Have your partner stand and face you directly. If you do not currently have a partner or your partner is unwilling to participate in this exercise, look at a photograph of your current partner, a previous partner, or someone you would like as a partner.

As an observer, what do you notice?

Describe to your partner what you see -- physical appearance (weight, posture, shape, skin, hair, eyes), attitude and general mood (confident, insecure, worrier, angry, agitated, nervous), clothing and style.

How do you feel about your ideal partner's sexual style?

What sensations do you feel in your body?

In your journal, describe your ideal partner's sexual style and its effect upon you. Describe your ideal partner's physical appearance, attitude, approach toward you, words and sounds, behaviors and body movements, smell and taste, thoughts and feelings, style of touching and responsiveness to being touched. Describe the way your body responds.

Your Sexual Style

Stand directly facing a mirror, preferably a full length mirror in which you can see your entire body. If all you have is a small mirror, then observe your face and move the mirror around to glance at the rest of your body. Take a long slow, easy, and deep breath.

Imagine stepping outside yourself and becoming a distant observer of you, the woman or man, today, right in this moment.

As an observer, what do you notice?

Describe to yourself what you see -- physical appearance (weight, posture, shape, skin, hair, eyes), attitude and general mood (confident, insecure, worrier, angry, agitated, nervous), clothing and style.

In your journal, describe your own sexual style and its effect upon your partner. Describe your own physical appearance, attitude, approach toward your partner, words and sounds, behaviors and body movements, smell and taste, thoughts and feelings, style of touching and responsiveness to being touched. How do you feel about your own sexual style? Pay attention to your bodily reactions. Describe them now.

Your Sexuality

Our sexuality is a wonderful gift. We get to experience pleasurable and exquisite sensations. We become intimately connected with ourself and with others. But for so many of us, our sexuality is hardly pleasurable. Attempting to deny our sexual feelings, we hide behind a disinterested persona. Expressing our sexuality may cause us to feel anxious and insecure. The mere thought of sexual contact and physical intimacy may bring back painful memories and send us into a state of panic.

Sexual and sensual exploration, alone or with a loving partner, feels wonderful. Sharing yourself with another makes you feel accepted and connected. Openly sharing your deepest feelings with another helps you to know your own self, what you like and dislike, what you feel, what you want and who you are. When you allow yourself to let go and fully experience your sexual aliveness, you may have a sense that you are more than your physical body, that you are actually a powerful spiritual being.

Sexuality is the mystery of life itself. Sexuality is not only for the very sexy, the very beautiful, the sleek and slender, the very brilliant, or the very skilled man or woman. Sexuality is not only for young adults or blossoming adolescents. Even if we are hard of hearing, unable to see, barely able to talk, walking with a cane, or totally paralyzed with very little physical sensation, every one of us has sensual desires, needs and feelings.

Why then are so many of us afraid of this naturally wonderful part of life? At first glance, it may appear that our current age, our current state of health, our current partner, previous lovers, or our earliest sexual experiences are the reasons we are not enjoying our sexuality now. However, when we touch and are touched by another and when we feel sexually aroused, bodily memories fill our senses. Our bodies may recall what our minds have long forgotten: the way we were touched in our earliest moments on earth and the stimuli we received while still in our mother's womb. Reconnecting us to preverbal memories and unexpressed emotions, our sexuality, with or without a partner, becomes a direct link to the deepest part of our knowing, our inner soul.

What Is This Marvelous Thing Called Sex?

Afraid of failing, of not performing, of not appearing to be a stud or seductive vixen, many of us are turning to drugs to enhance our lagging desire and sexual arousal. Bypassing our bodily sensations, emotional needs and unique sexual response pattern, we attempt to conquer our fears and overcome our natural body responses. Here is a typical scenario of the modern quick fix style of sexual contact with our most intimate partner.

A man and woman decide to have sex one evening. Shortly after dinner, each takes a pill to enhance their own sexual arousal. Sitting and facing each other silently, they wait…. In about 45 minutes, a flush begins to cover their partner's face. That's the signal that they are both ready to have sex. They proceed to the bedroom to complete the act.

Is this what sexuality is all about? If you are a couple wanting to produce a baby, maybe taking an arousal enhancement pill can remove the fear of not being able to perform and can assist you to have sexual intercourse at the exact moment of ovulation. However, regularly relying upon a pill to become sexually intimate with a partner, is attempting to bypass and ignore your natural bodily erotic signals. Relying on a potency pill does not teach a man or woman about the nuances of what it takes to satisfy their own or their partner's sexual needs. A pill does not eliminate your sexual fears, remove your sexual inhibitions, or eradicate memories of trauma or sexual abuse.

Your Sexual Concerns

If your sexual responsivity is less than what you want it to be, it would be beneficial for you to do some self-exploration. Ask yourself the following questions:

* *What am I afraid of?*
* *Why do I need to "perform" and who am I performing for?*
* *How do I feel about my sexual partner?*

How do I feel about my own body, about enjoying sexual contact and orgasmic pleasure?

What are my senses, my mind, and my intuition telling me about my partner, my sexuality, and my current lifestyle?

If you attempt to bypass your anxious feelings by taking a pill, you may miss the opportunity to face your deepest fears and create lasting love and happiness in your life.

Fears and insecurities about your sexuality often prevent you from trusting your inner knowing. The answers to most of your conflicts and confusion lie in your very own body. When you pay attention to y body signals and accept the messages you receive, sexual reawakening has begun.

When you pay attention to your bodily signals, you want to communicate your needs to your partner/s. In a loving sexual relationship, there is a natural balance between attempting to please a partner and asking for what you want. But sex is not just about following instructions, like directing traffic. Many of us have been turned off to having sexual relations because our partner told us what to do, what not to do, how to feel, how not to feel. In short, someone else determined for us what our sexual behavior and emotional responses should be. Perhaps, we have been the person directing the show. In an attempt to please us, our partner's natural passion may have been suppressed. Here are some examples of words, requests and demands that may interfere with your natural sexual expression.

"Please don't. I don't want to. No, no, no…!"

"Ouch, you're hurting me!"

"Stop, I don't like when you do that!" "No, that's irritating me!"

"Touch me here. Yeah, right here. Ooh!"

"A little softer. Press here. That's right. Ahh!"

Don't move. Hold it. Stay still if you don't want me to come!"

"Is this the way you like it? Tell me what to do!"

"How was that for you? Did you have an orgasm?"

Do your most intimate sexual experiences often sound like this? Is this what sexuality is all about? Is that all there is? Do you feel as though you are always trying to please your partner or always expecting your partner to please you? Do you feel as though you or your partner can never quite get it right?

Copyright © 2009, Revised 2023   *Love Me, Touch Me, Heal Me*   DrEricaGoodstone.com

Your Senses and Your Sexuality

All of our senses are intimate. We hide our heads in shame after a wrongdoing. We do not look directly into another's eyes when we are avoiding the truth. Children hide behind mommy's skirt when they do not want to be seen. Many of us are afraid to sing or voice our own opinion in front of people. We use deodorants and colognes to avoid letting another smell us "au naturel." We wear make up to hide our blemishes and enhance our appearance.

Animals, totally accepting their own bodies and bodily functions, often delight in sniffing and licking each other's most intimate body parts – in public with no shame. Taste is one sense we usually share only with our most intimate lovers. Some of us choose not to share the intimacy of taste at all. Many of us abhor deep kissing and refuse to engage in oral-genital contact. Most of us are repelled by fluids that emanate from the nose or ears or anus, even our own. In some cultures, all the natural body fluids and sounds are seen as natural life expressions.

In some Asian cultures, belching and releasing gas through farting are encouraged as natural releases, as natural as sneezing and coughing. In these same cultures, drinking one's own urine, known as Urine Therapy, may be encouraged to increase one's natural immunity. Yogis, who have a deep connection to their own bodily functions, regularly practice numerous kriyas or cleansing techniques. To cleanse the nasal passages, they may insert a long piece of gauze into one nostril and retrieve it through the other nostril. To cleanse the throat or intestines, they often insert a long piece of gauze deep down into the throat and then slowly pull it out. Some men have practiced inserting a piece of gauze into the tip of the penis and then slowly retrieving it. More familiar to western cultures is the use of enemas and internal juice cleanses.

Your Senses and Your Sexuality

Close your eyes. Take a few slow, easy, rhythmical breaths. Allow your body to relax.

Imagine yourself being sexually intimate with your partner.

Notice what it is like for you to connect with your partner with each of your senses.

Do you enjoy the contact or do you feel uneasy, frightened, insecure, agitated, terrified, bored, or some other emotional response?

Observe how you feel and then write your responses in your journal.

* Gaze into your partner's eyes and maintain eye contact for 3 minutes

* Give and receive gentle touch, deep pressure touch, sensual touch, and sexually intimate touch

* Speak with graphic words to describe your partner's body and the way your partner's body feels to you.

* Allow natural sounds to emerge from your body and throat

* Listen to the words and sounds expressed by your partner

* Sing to your partner and listen as your partner sings to you

* Breathe deeply, slowly, and in rhythmic synchronicity with your partner's breathing

Seeing, Your Partner and Sex

How does your partner look to you?

Is he or she attractive, appealing, and sexy in your eyes?

Does he or she fit your pictures of feminine or masculine beauty?

Does anything annoy, bother, disturb you or turn you off about their looks?

Hearing, Your Partner and Sex

What does your partner say to you?

How do their words feel in your body?

Do their words please, tease, titillate, excite you or turn you on?

Do their words upset, irritate, annoy, or hurt you?

How do you feel about the sound and tone of your partner's voice?

Does your partner's body or throat release sounds? How do those sounds affect you?

Tasting, Your Partner and Sex

How does your partner taste to you - sour, sweet, bitter, pungent, salty...?

Do you like the taste of your partner's skin, mouth, breath?

Do you enjoy giving oral sex to your partner?

Does your partner enjoy receiving oral sex from you?

Does your partner enjoy giving oral sex to you?

Do you enjoy giving oral stimulation to your partner's anal area?

Does your partner enjoy giving oral stimulation to your anal area?

Is there any other place you enjoy or do not enjoy tasting on your partner's body?

Is there any other place your partner enjoys or does not enjoy tasting on your body?

Copyright © 2009, Revised 2023   *Love Me, Touch Me, Heal Me*   DrEricaGoodstone.com

Smelling, Your Partner and Sex

How does your partner's smell or scent affect you?

Do you find his or her natural scent pleasing, pleasant, offensive, or unpleasant?

Do you like or dislike his or her unique scent?

Does your partner wear perfume or cologne and do you like the fragrance?

How does your natural body scent affect your partner?

Does your partner like the perfume or cologne you wear, if you do?

Touching, Your Partner and Sex

How does your partner's touch feel to you: gentle, soothing, rough, too light, ticklish, too hard, aggressive, too tentative, just right...?

How do you touch your partner?

Do you enjoy being touched by your partner?

Does your partner's touch arouse you on sexually?

Do you enjoy touching your partner?

Does your touch arouse your partner sexually?

Do you have a similar desire or need for a certain frequency and amount of touch?

Copyright © 2009, Revised 2023   *Love Me, Touch Me, Heal Me*   DrEricaGoodstone.com

Does your partner touch you only as a prelude to sex?

Do you touch your partner only as a prelude to sex?

Are you comfortable touching your partner in public?

Is your partner comfortable touching you in public?

Talking, Your Partner and Sex

What do you say to your partner during sex, during dinner, during activities, in light conversation, in heavy conversation?

Who talks more, louder, more assertively or more aggressively?

What tone of voice do you tend to use with each other?

Do either of you scream, insult, verbally abuse, humiliate and shame the other?

In what circumstances --in private, in public, with close friends, with relatives?

Can you freely say what you feel and talk about the things that matter to you?

Does your partner listen willingly and do you feel heard and understood?

Can your partner freely say what he or she feels and talk about the things that matter? Do you listen willingly and does your partner feel heard and understood?

Your Bodily Sensations

Your Partner and Sex

What sensations are you aware of feeling in your body when you are with your partner -- in non sexual situations and during intimate sexual encounters? What body parts feel relaxed, tense, open, closed, accepted or rejected?

Your Mind, Your Partner, Love and Sex

Mind Mapping

You are about to create a map of the way your mind thinks.

Take out four clean sheets of paper or write in your journal. On four separate pages draw a large circle in the center of the page. On each circle, draw ten separate lines at the outside of the circle extending outward away from the circle.

On the first page, in the center of the circle write your own name.

Without censoring or hesitating, on each line extending outward away from the circle write a word that you associate with yourself. Whatever words come into your head, write them on one of the vertical lines pointing outward from the circle. For example, when you see your own name, you might respond with such words as: sexy, powerful, strong, inconsiderate or such words as: lazy, shy, ugly, poor, insecure. Add more lines to add more words if you need them. Now, like branches of a tree, draw additional lines extending outward from the lines you have already created, adding new words that occur to you upon observing the word already written. For example, if you have written "sexy," additional words that may occur to you are: long legs, silky hair, confidence, charming, aloof. Continue to allow the words to flow. Add additional branches as new words occur to you. You may begin with a word like ugly and branch off into poor complexion, too short, unappealing and then find words like sensitive, caring, compassionate, giving. Allow your mind to continue to make connections. Keep writing words until you feel your have exhausted your thinking process for now.

On the second page, in the center of the circle write your partner's name or, if you do not currently have a partner, write the name of a previous partner or someone you currently desire to know better.

Without censoring or hesitating, on each line extending outward away from the circle write a word that you associate with yourself. Whatever words come into your head, write them on one of the vertical lines pointing outward from the circle. Add more lines to add more words if you need them. Now, like branches of a tree, draw additional lines extending outward from the lines you have already created, adding new words that occur to you upon observing the word already written. .

Copyright © 2009, Revised 2023   *Love Me, Touch Me, Heal Me*   DrEricaGoodstone.com

Allow your mind to continue to make connections. Keep writing words until you feel your have exhausted your thinking process for now.

On the third page, in the center of the circle write the word "Love."

Repeat the above process allowing your mind to expand upon ten different branching thoughts about love.

On a fourth page, in the center of the circle write the word "Sexuality."

Repeat the above process allowing your mind to expand upon all your branching thoughts about love.

When you have finished, place all four circles in front of you and compare the words listed in each.

Notice the words you use to describe yourself, your partner, love and sex.

Reflect upon your responses.

Are there any words that you used in all four mind maps?

What have you discovered about your thoughts, ideas and beliefs about yourself, your partner, love and sexuality.

Your Spiritual Reawakening

Mind Mapping

Open to a new page in your journal. **In the center write your name followed by the words "Spiritual Reawakening,"**

for example, "Erica's Spiritual Reawakening."

Without censoring or hesitating, on each line extending outward away from the circle write a word that you associate with yourself as your awaken to your own spirituality.. Whatever words come into your head, write them on one of the vertical lines pointing outward from the circle. Add more lines to add more words if you need them. Now, like branches of a tree, draw additional lines extending outward from the lines you have already created, adding new words that occur to you upon observing the word already written. . Allow your mind to continue to make connections. Keep writing words until you feel your have exhausted your thinking process for now.

Take a moment to compare your spiritual reawakening words to the words you used to describe yourself, your partner, love and sexuality.

Find those words that you repeated in more than one category.

Find those words in your spiritual reawakening mind map that are missing in the other mind maps.

Reflect upon what all this might mean about what your have been focusing on, what you have been thinking you need, and what you truly value.

Letting Your Senses Speak To Your Partner

Sit facing your partner. If you do not have a partner, face your own self in a mirror.

Actually, the only partner we ever really need is our own self and our connection to God. Now, gaze into your partner's eyes or your own eyes.

Breathe slowly and deeply together with the person in front of you.

Hold hands with your partner or with yourself.

Allowing Your Lips to Speak

Kiss your partner or yourself respectfully, gently, butterfly kisses on the face, eyelids, and ears.

Kiss the front, back and side of the neck, moving the hair out of the way.

Seduce your partner through your lips.

Allow your lips to speak, to sing, to tell their story, to express how much you love.

Kiss to awaken your partner's or your own soul.

Allowing Your Eyes To Speak

Kiss, caress, love and seduce your partner or yourself with your eyes.

Look with soft eyes, sensual eyes, bedroom eyes.

Feel the energy rising within you and between you, expressed through your eyes.

Define the outline of your partner's body or your own body with your eyes.

See beneath the outer appearance to the beautiful soul inside.

Breathing Your Love

Breathe deeply, slowly, and in sync with your partner's breathing.

Pant, breathe heavily, and exaggerate the motions and the sounds of your own breathing. Expand and extend your breathing.

Hold and release your breath.

Feel your breath spreading throughout your body, connecting you more fully to your partner and to your own self.

Sounding Your Love

Allow soft sounds to emerge from your throat.

Let the sounds become louder and louder.

Begin with a gentle "Ah." Say it with soft eyes and slow deep breathing.

Expand and intensify the sound of "ah."

Spread the sound of "ah" all over your partner's or your own face and body.

Make the sounds "Ay" – "Hay" – "Say"

Feel the sensation spreading through your body.

Make the sounds "Oh" - "Woh" - "Soh – "Noh."

Allow the energy to build as you say "No - o -o "

Make the sounds "Oo" and "Woo" and "Soo."

Explore your partner's and your own face and body with "ooh."

Make the sounds "Eee" - "Whee" - "See."

Observe the feelings and sensations.

Make the sounds "You -oo" - "Mou-oo " - "Wou-oo."

Feel the sensations of all the sounds opening the channels in your energy systems.

Speaking Your Sensual Love

Speak to your partner's or your own body parts, using sensual, alluring and seductive words.

I love your womanly wonderful round curves.

I love your potent powerful male body.

Say what you believe your partner's or your own body wants to hear.

Your vagina is wet and moist and open to me.

It wants to hear me talk.

Your penis is your manhood.

Let it show me how powerful you are.

Speak in a language that is not your native tongue. Exaggerate the accent.

Je t'aime mon amour.

Amore.

Let the words of passionate love open your throat. Speak from deep in your throat.

I love your strong and sexy body, my man of powerful means

I love your beautiful female body, my woman of my dreams

Practice speaking sensually to your partner as if rehearsing for a Broadway play.

Be convincing! Find the words and sounds that open your own heart and throat and loins.

Copyright © 2009, Revised 2023 *Love Me, Touch Me, Heal Me* DrEricaGoodstone.com

Discover the words and sounds that make your partner's loins and heart long for you.

Strengthening Your Internal Sexual Muscles

Inhale, squeeze your PC muscles, the muscles that allow you to refrain from urinating.

Exhale, release your PC muscles.

Inhale, squeeze your PC muscles, touch your partner or yourself gently.

Speak those sensual, loving words you have been practicing. Allow the words to flow from your heart.

I love your sweet sensuous smile and the soothing curves of your womanly body.

I love your masculine muscles that bulge from your hard firm frame of a man.

Exhale, release your PC muscle, continue speaking softly as you touch your partner or yourself.

Let me linger in the softness of your cheeks and sweet smelling hair.

Let me linger in your broad strong shoulders and your thick manly hair.

Kissing, Touching, Sounds and Words

Kiss your partner or yourself gently, firmly on the eyelids, cheeks, jaws, neck, throat, or behind the ears.

Caress your partner's or your own shoulders as you gently kiss the neck and chest.

Do not approach the intimate sexual body parts.

Do not blow in the ear.

Do not kiss the lips.

Do not use your tongue.

Remember - less is more!

Tease your partner's or your own body with gentle words and kisses and touches.

Touch and kiss and repeat those sensual words you have practiced for awhile.

Then be quiet, sit back, breathe together, and gaze into each other's eyes.

Moving Your Body

Put on an imaginary silk body stocking while your partner watches or your watch yourself in the mirror.

Brush your own hair as you allow your head to gently move in circles.

Copyright © 2009, Revised 2023   *Love Me, Touch Me, Heal Me*   DrEricaGoodstone.com

Bend your knees, keeping your feet together, knees together, and hands firmly on your thighs.

Circling your Knees

Inhale, squeeze your PC muscle and circle your knees to the right five times.

Exhale, release your PC muscle and circle your knees to the left five times.

Chopping Wood

Lift both your arms, gently arch back and imagine chopping wood.

As you bend forward, repeat the sounds as strongly as you can: Ah, Oh, Oo, Ee, Ay, Eh.

Circling Your Hips

Inhale, squeeze your PC muscle and circle your hips to the right five times.

Exhale, release your PC muscle and circle your hips to the left five times.

Move your hips in a figure 8, five times to the right and five times to the left.

Circling Your Torso

Inhale, move your torso, your upper body in a circle five times to the right.

Exhale, move your torso, your upper body in a circle five times to the left.

Rocking Your Pelvis

Inhale, move your hips forward and back five times in a pelvic rock.

Exhale, move your hips backward and forward five times in a pelvic rock.

Letting Your Partner Guide Your Body

Take turns being the mover and the person being moved. If you don't have a partner, stand in front of a mirror and imagine doing these exercises with a partner.

Put an imaginary body stocking on your partner, slowly and carefully.

Remove an imaginary sweater from your partner, caressing your partner's body.

Brush your partner's hair, sensually and lovingly.

Move your partner's knees in a circle five times to right and five times to left.

Move your partner's hips in a circle five times to right and five times to left.

Move your partner's torso in a circle, five times to right and five times to left.

Move your partner's hips in a figure 8, five times to the right and five times to the left.

Move your partner's hips five times forward and backward and five times backward and forward, in the pelvic rock.

Moving Together

Put an imaginary body stocking on both of you, slowly and carefully.

Remove an imaginary sweater from both of you, caressing your partner's body.

Brush each other's hair, sensually and lovingly.

Move your partner's hips together in a circle five times to right and five times to left.

Move your partner's torso together in a circle five times to right and five times to left.

Move your partner's hips in a figure 8, five times to the right and five times to the left.

Move your partner's hips five times forward and backward and five times backward and forward, in a pelvic rock

Female partner turn your back to the male partner, sit in his lap as both hold her knees and circle five times to the right and five times to the left.

You Are Handsome/Beautiful

Sexy And Powerful

Sit and face each other, inhale and squeeze your PC muscles, exhale, release your PC muscles and say the following words:

Woman says: *John (Say your partner's name), You are a sexy, handsome, powerful man.*

Man answers: *Yes, I am a sexy, handsome, powerful man.*

Man says: *Liz (Say your partner's name), You are a sexy, beautiful, powerful woman.*

Woman answers: *Yes, I am a sexy, beautiful, powerful woman.*

Touching and

Gazing Into Each Other's Eyes

Very, very slowly, barely moving, approach each other's faces.

If you do not have a partner, approach your own face in the mirror.

Place gentle kisses on each other's throats and necks and chest and shoulders.

With your hands, gently feel your partner's hair and head and forehead.

Copyright © 2009, Revised 2023   Love Me, Touch Me, Heal Me   DrEricaGoodstone.com

Now reach for your partner's lips with your lips.

Kiss the lips as if to discover every sound and every movement, every corner, every sensation, every meaning, every word.

Allow your tongue to get excited. Let your tongue begin to wonder what it would be like to explore your partner's throat.

Now gently take turns letting one person's tongue slowly, softly, gently, and fully. Explore your partner's throat and teeth and inner cheeks. Move your tongue in and out. Circle your tongue to the right, to the left, in figure 8's, and up and down.

With your tongue say,

> *Hello, I love you.*

> *I'm here with you. You're safe. I'm curious and excited.*

> *I desire you. I'm thrilled to be with you.*

Taste your partner's essence with your tongue.

Gently and lightly nibble and caress your partner's lips.

With your lips and tongue and fingers say, "I love you."

Hugging Your Partner

Breathe deeply, slowly and in rhythm with your partner as you hug a full body hug.

If you do not have a partner, hug and caress your own body as fully and sensually as you possibly can.

With your partner or yourself maintain contact with as many body parts as you both can. Allow your toes and knees and thighs and pelvis touch.

Allow your hips and bellies to touch.

Let your chest and ribs and shoulders touch.

Gaze into each other's eyes and gently rub each other's cheeks and nose.

Allow your foreheads and chins to gently connect.

Press your lips together in a firm and open, gentle kiss.

Allow your hands to gently and firmly explore your partner's or your own body.

Take time to sense and feel the texture, shape and warmth of every body part you touch. Begin by caressing the neck and shoulders, arms and elbows, wrists and hands and fingers.

Move to the upper back and chest.

Allow your fingers to explore and caress the face, gently touching the eyelids, lashes, eyebrows, and cheeks.

Trace the contour of the lips.

Move your hands to the lower back and hold the belly firmly in your grasp.

Caress the hips and thighs, explore the knees and calves, ankles and feet.

Play with the toes.

Yes, it's wonderful to have a live, full-bodied partner. But, even without a partner, now you know you can always enjoy your own sensuality and sexuality. You may choose to be with another person, but you no longer need a partner to enjoy your own sensual and sexual aliveness. You can feel sensual, sexual, and happy, all alone, by yourself, at any time.

Following Your Own Senses

My toes tingle as I spread them on the floor. Outstretched arms reaching for the sky, I breathe in the morning sunlight. My yawning lips part into a beaming smile. Peering through the shutters, my waking eyes glimpse the beauty of this brand new day. Listening intently, my ears awaken to the sounds of the morning -- birds chirping, horns honking, dogs barking, people talking. The sweet fragrant scent of freshly brewing coffee boosts my morale as I quicken to ready myself. Splashing cool water on my face, I glance briefly at the image in my bathroom mirror. Stepping into the steaming shower, my voice begins to hum and sing a favorite tune. Lathering up my hands, I spread the soft aromatic soap all over my gradually awakening body. My cells filled with life, my body stretched and warmed, my pores open and receptive, I step from the shower onto the fluffy bathroom mat. Briskly drying my body with the velvety crinkly towel, I run my fingers along the soft clean fabrics soon to be embracing and enveloping my body. Dressed and ready to go, I take one final appreciative look at my own image in the full length mirror. All my morning senses satisfied, I sit down to eat a healthy balanced breakfast. My day has begun.

Sexual And Spiritual Reawakening At Last!

Sexual Reawakening begins when you take your first breath in this world and ends with your final breath. Between those two momentous events, sensual and sexual reawakening occurs anew every moment of your life, if you pay attention and allow the sensations to build. You can choose to experience all of your senses or you can limit your sensual exposure, lessen your sensual pleasure, and prevent your sexual reawakening. We are multi-dimensional sensual and sexual beings. How sensual and sexual do you want to be? The choice is always yours, limited only by your personal beliefs, values and actions.

Yes, you can share it with a partner. Yes, you can focus on your sexual organs. And yes, all of your senses can come alive, with or without a partner, with and without sexual arousal - awakening, acknowledging, accepting, and loving your own God-given self.

By now you have discovered that it is truly a sensational world. Your senses keep you connected to the world around, your environment and the people closest to you. Your body, your mind and your imagination allow you to feel the most exquisite physical sensations and the most joyful emotions. Your senses also bring you awareness of danger and painful sensations of physical injury. Your mind can help you to withstand the pain, overcome the pain and often not even feel the pain when focused elsewhere. Your mind can also intensify the pain beyond what your senses actually cause you to feel.

Your brain is probably your most powerful sexual organ. Through your brain, you allow the flood of hormones to fill your body and arouse your senses. Your mind is even more powerful. Your mind is actually the true creator of your life. Think about it, focus on it, dwell on it, obsess about it, and you will probably bring it into being.

Nothing has ever been created without somebody first thinking about it in their mind. Do you want to create love? Then begin to focus on love in your mind, your heart, your dreams, your fantasies, your interactions, and your whole being. Do you want to create healing in your life? Then begin to focus all your attention on healing whatever you need to heal. Use your mind to imagine you are already completely well. In the future present state of mind all healing occurs, all manifestation occurs, all things are created.

What then is **Spiritual Reawakening**? You are not your body with all its moveable parts, internal organs, systems, physical sensations, pains and pleasures that you feel. You are not your calculating, intelligent brain and all its interrelated functions. You are not your emotional states.

Then who and what are you? Whether you choose to believe it or not, whether you like the idea or not, you are, always have been, and always will be, a spiritual being inhabiting a physical body. When your heart stops and your brain stops functioning, your body no longer performs its routine functions. Not one part of your body can move without your thought – even internal organs that you may never have considered having the potential to respond to your thoughts. Some of your thoughts are conscious, but much of your thinking is beyond your conscious awareness - unless you diligently practice mindful awareness.

Spiritual leaders will tell you. People who practice meditation and mindfulness will tell you. People who have had intense religious, out of body, paranormal or some type of unexplainable spiritual experiences, will all agree that we are spiritual beings. We are not just brains and bodies, interacting with others, performing our life roles, and passing from this earth. We are more than many of us choose to realize.

Knowing that you are truly a spiritual and energetic being, you realize that you are energetically connected to everyone and everything in this world and beyond. Your energy affects others. Even your thoughts, like radio waves, spread out way beyond your own brain.

Check it out. Enter a place where some negative energy is accumulating – hostility, rage, or danger. Notice how your body feels in that environment. Observe your thoughts, your energy, and your focus. Then find a place where loving, healing, positive energy is building – love, touch, kind words, compassion, and sensitivity. Notice how your body feels in that environment. Observe your thoughts, your energy, and your focus.

This book has introduced you to some concepts, beliefs and ideas that may be new to you. Maybe you have had a sense that perhaps you really are more than your body, yet you have not really explored this possibility beyond that passing thought. Maybe you are more advanced and have studied spiritual wisdom from one or many sources over a span of many years. Wherever you currently are, you can find like minded people to help you expand to a higher, more consistently fulfilling state of mind. We are all on the path to sexual and spiritual reawakening. This is a lifelong path. Enjoy the journey now.

FOOTNOTES

Chapter 1

1. Lama, Dalai, Cutler, Howard C. (1998). The Art of Happiness: A Handbook for Living. NY: Riverhead Hardcover, Penguin Books.

Chapter 2

1. Colapinto, John. (2000). As Nature Made Him: The Body Who Was Raised As A Girl. NY: Harper Collins.

2. Nevid, Jeffrey S., Rathus, Spencer A. Human Sexuality in a World of Diversity (2nd Ed.) (1995). NY: Allyn & Bacon, pp. 274-276.

CONGRATULATIONS!

By finishing *SEXUAL AND SPIRITUAL REAWAKENING,* **Part IV in the** *LOVE ME*, *TOUCH ME, HEAL ME* **Complete Book,** *y*ou now may realize that we are all sexual beings and that feeling your sexual aliveness reawakens you to who we are. By allowing full sexual expression into your life, you cannot help but discover your true spiritual nature. You are a spiritual being. Connecting to your spiritual nature and spiritual potential enables you to have a greater acceptance and appreciation of life. The path of discovering your spiritual connection can be difficult, painful and may reveal to us our deepest, darkest, most unloving personal attributes. Your life path is a spiritual path, the process of rediscovering your connection to all that is. No matter which direction you choose to take, all paths will eventually lead you home. Every spiritual teaching reminds us of that simple truth.

My goal in writing this book was to act as a guide and a mentor along the path of self discovery. If you resist knowing and living this truth and you decide to pursue a self-centered, ego-gratifying, and purely material way of life, you may encounter more struggle, more difficulties, and more tests than necessary. But rest assured, no matter which path you follow, you are already on your way home. My wish is for you to have a speedy, fulfilling, life affirming and joyful return home to love through physical, emotional, sexual and spiritual reawakening.

Have any of the words or exercises in this book touched a sensitive place in your thoughts, emotions or beliefs?

Are you ready to Lose

- **Your fears?**
- **Your doubts?**

Are you ready to Create

- **Love and healing?**

It's NOT Too Late!

NOW IS THE TIME TO CREATE HEALING AND LOVE IN <u>YOUR</u> LIFE!

LoveNow.life/HealingThroughLoveSession

ALSO BY DR. ERICA GOODSTONE

KINDLE BOOKS

Beautiful Bare Feet: Fetish or Fantasy
Be Who You Are: The Greatest Gift of All
The Delicate Dance of Love
Your Body Believes You
It's a Sensational World
Touching Matters - The Profound Effects of Body Therapy
Let All Your Senses Speak – As You Heal
Touching Stories
Ordinary People, Ordinary Yet Extraordinary Sex
Sexual Reawakening: 10 Simple Steps
Sexual and Spiritual Reawakening – At Last!
The Science Of Being Well - Wallace D. Wattles author,
   Annotated and Illustrated by Dr. Erica Goodstone
The Science Of Getting Rich - Wallace D. Wattles author,
   Annotated and Illustrated by Dr. Erica Goodstone

Books and EBooks are available at
Amazon.com, Smashwords.com and Lulu.com

DIGITAL PROGRAMS

Love Touch Heal Video Series
Healing Through Love Audio Series
Love Lessons For Your Soul
Love Touch Heal Relationship Program

VIRTUAL SUMMITS

Men and Love Series
Women and Love Summit
Sexual Reawakening Summit
Love Me Touch Me Heal Me Summit
Healing Recovery Retreat
Miraculous Healing Master Class Summit
Science And Poetry of Love Summit
The Science of Being Well Docuseries

Programs, courses and summits available at
https://DrEricaGoodstone.com

AMAZON REVIEWS

If you have enjoyed reading this book, please consider leaving an Amazon review. The author will be most grateful because this enables her to reach more people who want to create more love in their lives.

www.ingramcontent.com/pod-product-compliance
Lightning Source LLC
Chambersburg PA
CBHW080933300426

44115CB00017B/2796